Same-Sex Marriage

Fierce and often ugly battles are being waged, especially in the United States, over who is allowed to marry, what marriage signifies and where marriage is headed. Kathleen Hull examines these debates, and data from interviews with over seventy people in same-sex relationships, to explore the cultural practices surrounding same-sex marriage and the legal battle for recognition. Arguing that the cultural and legal dimensions of marriage are closely intertwined, she shows how same-sex couples use marriage-related cultural practices, such as public commitment rituals, to assert the reality of their commitments despite lack of legal recognition. Though many same-sex couples see the law of the state to hold a unique cultural power to legitimate their relationships and identities, Hull finds that their opponents equally look to the law to re-establish a social normalcy that excludes same-sex relationships. This is a timely look at a contentious issue.

KATHLEEN E. HULL is an Assistant Professor of Sociology at the University of Minnesota.

Same-Sex Marriage

The Cultural Politics of Love and Law

Kathleen E. Hull

CAMBRIDGE
UNIVERSITY PRESS

CAMBRIDGE UNIVERSITY PRESS
Cambridge, New York, Melbourne, Madrid, Cape Town, Singapore, São Paulo

Cambridge University Press
The Edinburgh Building, Cambridge CB2 2RU, UK

Published in the United States of America by Cambridge University Press,
New York

www.cambridge.org
Information on this title: www.cambridge.org/9780521672511

First published 2006

Printed in the United Kingdom at the University Press, Cambridge

A catalogue record for this book is available from the British Library

ISBN-13 978-0-52185654 – 6 hardback
ISBN-10 0-521-85654 – x hardback
ISBN-13 978-0-52167251 - 1 paperback
ISBN-10 0-52167251 - 1 paperback

For my parents, Frank and Katherine Hull
And for Kate

Contents

Tables

Preface

On May 17, 2004, Massachusetts launched a new era in the legal treatment of American gays and lesbians by becoming the first state to issue marriage licenses to same-sex couples. In less than two decades, the country had moved from the US Supreme Court ruling in *Bowers v. Hardwick*, which ridiculed the idea that homosexual behavior deserved protection under the Constitution, to Massachusetts' *Goodridge v. Department of Public Health*, which bestowed equal legal recognition for same-sex couples in at least one US state. The developments in Massachusetts sparked a fresh wave of activism, debate and controversy around same-sex marriage. Before the *Goodridge* ruling even took effect, local officials around the country began issuing marriage licenses to same-sex couples in a show of support, drawing media attention and the outrage of social conservatives. Politicians and activists opposed to same-sex marriage moved quickly to prevent another ruling like *Goodridge* elsewhere in the United States. An amendment to the US Constitution to block same-sex marriage nationwide gained the backing of President George W. Bush but foundered in Congress. By the end of 2004, one-third of the states had written bans on same-sex marriage into their constitutions. Although the same-sex marriage issue did not dominate the 2004 presidential election, some political analysts believe it played a critical role in galvanizing social conservatives to cast votes for President Bush.

Most of the research for this book was completed before the arrival of same-sex marriage in Massachusetts, but the results of this research are highly relevant to the current political and legal climate. What the United States will have for the foreseeable future is a patchwork system of rights and recognition for same-sex relationships. Gay and lesbian couples in a few areas of the country will have access to some or most of the legal rights of marriage. (Even the Massachusetts marriages are not recognized by the federal government, meaning that same-sex couples do not enjoy full marriage rights anywhere in the United States today.) In most of the country, same-sex couples will continue to lack access to legal recognition, even as they avail themselves of the chance to enact marriage culturally through various practices, and the legal and political struggles over relationship rights will persist. In this turbulent national climate, insight into the perspectives of ordinary same-sex couples is more valuable than ever.

This study provides a window onto the motivations, experiences and frustrations of same-sex couples in an environment of continuing ambiguity and ambivalence. Couples can adopt marriage as a cultural model for their intimate commitments, and in some cases can obtain religious recognition for their unions, but they cannot secure full and unambiguous legal recognition of these unions as marriages. Some states and localities offer other forms of legal recognition, such as domestic partnerships or civil unions, but the legal meaning of such statuses outside their originating jurisdiction is often unclear. Ambivalence also persists among some gays and lesbians about the suitability of marriage as a cultural model of commitment and a legal goal. As the legal, political and cultural climate continues to shift and evolve, the insights and experiences of the couples profiled in this study offer an opportunity to consider what these changes and conflicts might mean from the perspective of those American citizens who are most directly affected by the issue of same-sex marriage.

Writing this book presented many stimulating challenges, not the least of which was staying on top of such a fast-evolving research topic. I could not have seen this project through to publication without the help of many fine people and supportive institutions. My greatest debt is to the participants in the study, who so generously shared their experiences and insights with me. I learned from every person I interviewed, and I found these conversations immensely interesting. I hope the study participants will share my satisfaction in finally seeing their stories in print. I also wish to acknowledge the members of the Same-Sex Marriage List, an excellent listserv devoted to the topic of legal same-sex marriage (http://lists.qrd.org/mailman/listinfo/marriage). The work of the list's moderators and contributors helped me stay abreast of new developments related to the legal recognition of same-sex couples in the United States and abroad.

This book started as my dissertation at Northwestern University and benefited from the thoughtful guidance and cogent critiques of my thesis committee members: Wendy Griswold, Robert Nelson, Wendy Espeland and Ellen Lewin. Orville Lee also gave valuable feedback in the early stages of the project. Many graduate school colleagues lent support in various ways, but special thanks go to Lisa Amoroso, Brian Donovan, Brian Gran and David Stevens.

I have benefited from the support of many wonderful colleagues in the sociology department at the University of Minnesota. I am especially grateful to Penny Edgell, Doug Hartmann and Erin Kelly for reading chapter drafts and responding with detailed, constructive comments. Ron Aminzade has been an enthusiastic supporter of my work and gave me great advice on the ins and outs of academic book publishing. Other department colleagues who have been especially supportive include Liz Boyle, Joe Gerteis, Ann Hironaka, Ross Macmillan, Ann Meier, Jeylan Mortimer, Joachim Savelsberg, Evan Schofer, Rachel Schurman, Robin Stryker, Teresa Swartz and Chris Uggen. I also wish to thank scholars from other institutions who have shared ideas on my work and expressed enthusiasm for the project at various stages, including Scott Barclay, Baptiste Coulmont, Jon Goldberg-Hiller, Beth Hoffman, Anna-Maria Marshall, Sally Merry, Laura Beth Nielsen and Verta Taylor.

I am grateful to many good friends and supporters who gave moral support and practical advice as the book developed. My special thanks go to Deborah Smith, David Krewinghaus, John Fiedler, the Saturday morning womyn, Corinne Kawecki, Maureen Sweeney, Greg Brewer, Stephen Welcome, Carol Wichers and Sue Wolfe.

My research profited from the opportunity to present work in progress in various forums. I wish to thank the discussants and audience members who responded to talks based on this project at the annual meetings of the American Sociological Association and the Law and Society Association. I also appreciated the chance to present my work in Northwestern University's Culture and Society Workshop and in the sociology departments of Northeastern Illinois University and the University of Pennsylvania. At the University of Minnesota, I received useful feedback at presentations to the Sociology Department Workshop, the Engendering Politics Workshop and the Feminist Studies Colloquium.

The junior academic's most precious resource is writing time, and such time was provided to me through the generous support of my universities. My project was supported with a Dissertation Year Fellowship from the Graduate School at Northwestern University, a Faculty Summer Research Fellowship from the Graduate School of the University of Minnesota and a Single Semester Leave from the College of Liberal Arts at the University of Minnesota. I also received a small grant for research assistance from the Life Course Center in the Department of Sociology at Minnesota.

At Cambridge University Press, I was fortunate to have two editors, Sarah Caro and John Haslam, shepherd my manuscript to publication; I thank Sarah for taking an interest in the project and John for seeing it through. I also thank copy-editor Monica Kendall and production editor Jackie Warren for their expert assistance. Parts of Chapter 4 appeared in "The Cultural Power of Law and the Cultural Enactment of Legality: The Case of Same-Sex Marriage," *Law and Social Inquiry* 28: 629–657 (copyright 2003 by the American Bar Foundation). Parts of Chapter 5 appeared in "The Political Limits of the Rights Frame: The Case of Same-Sex Marriage in Hawaii," *Sociological Perspectives* 44: 207–232 (copyright 2001 by the Pacific Sociological Association). I thank the University of Chicago Press and the University of California Press respectively for permission to reprint this material.

In the end, this is a book about recognizing families, so it is fitting that I close by recognizing my own. My brother Ron and his partner, Mark White, have been a reliable source of encouragement throughout the development of this project; I thank them for their interest in my work and occasional comic relief. My parents, Kitty and Frank Hull, could not be more wonderful. From my youngest years to the present, they have fostered in me a love of reading and learning, taken pride in my accomplishments and pushed me to go the distance ("Write on!"). I could not have written this book without their unstinting support. And finally, I thank my partner Kathryn Hansen, who has been a calming and loving presence through so many highs and lows. Kate, thanks for believing in me and helping me remember what really matters in life. I know there's plenty of lightness and laughter still ahead for us.

Same-sex marriage timeline

1971   *Baker v. Nelson*: Minnesota Supreme Court rejects a claim to marriage rights by a same-sex couple, the first such reported case in the United States. An appeal to the US Supreme Court is dismissed the following year, and other state rulings unfavorable to same-sex marriage follow, including *Jones v. Hallahan* (Kentucky Court of Appeals, 1973) and *Singer v. O'Hara* (Washington Court of Appeals, 1974).

1993   *Baehr v. Lewin*: Hawaii Supreme Court rules that denial of marriage licenses to same-sex couples appears to violate state constitution's equal rights amendment. Court remands case for trial, asking the government to show a compelling interest in limiting marriage to opposite-sex couples.

1996   Defense of Marriage Act: Anticipating possible legal recognition of same-sex marriage in Hawaii, US Congress passes and President Clinton signs the Defense of Marriage Act, which establishes a federal definition of marriage as a legal union between one man and one woman and declares that states will not be required to recognize same-sex marriages performed in other states. Dozens of individual states pass similar laws stating that they will not recognize same-sex marriages performed elsewhere.

       Hawaii ruling: Circuit Court Judge Kevin Chang rules that the State of Hawaii has failed at trial to demonstrate a compelling interest in denying marriage licenses to same-sex couples, and orders the state to begin issuing licenses to same-sex couples. The ruling is stayed pending appeal.

1998   State constitutional amendments: Voters in Hawaii and Alaska pass the first state constitutional amendments prohibiting state recognition of same-sex marriage. These amendments fore-close further court challenges to state marriage laws. Nebraska and Nevada later pass similar amendments.

1999   *Baker v. State of Vermont*: Vermont Supreme Court rules that the denial of marriage licenses to same-sex couples violates the Common Benefits Clause of the state constitution. The court orders the legislature to revise marriage statutes to include same-sex couples or create an alternative legal vehicle for delivering the rights and benefits of marriage to these couples.

2000   Civil unions: Vermont Legislature creates civil unions for same-sex couples, a new legal status that delivers all the state-level rights and benefits of marriage to same-sex couples. Non-residents are allowed to enter civil unions but the unions are not recognized by other states or the federal government.

2001   Netherlands: The Netherlands becomes the first country to legally recognize same-sex marriage.

2003   Belgium: Belgium is the second country to grant legal recognition to same-sex marriages.

        Lawrence v. Texas: US Supreme Court overturns state anti-sodomy laws, making homosexual conduct legal nationwide. In his dissent, Justice Antonin Scalia warns that the ruling paves the way for legal same-sex marriage.

        Canada: The province of Ontario grants legal recognition to same-sex marriage in June 2003, soon followed by the provinces of British Columbia (July 2003) and Quebec (March 2004). The Canadian federal government announces plans for legislation to make same-sex marriage legal nationwide.

        Goodridge v. Department of Public Health: Massachusetts Supreme Judicial Court rules on November 18 that the denial of marriage licenses to same-sex couples violates the state constitution and orders the state to begin issuing licenses in 180 days.

2004   Civil disobedience: San Francisco Mayor Gavin Newsom begins issuing marriage licenses to same-sex couples on

February 12 despite state law limiting marriage to opposite-sex couples. Local officials in New Mexico, Oregon, New Jersey and New York follow suit by issuing licenses or performing civil marriage ceremonies for same-sex couples. These local actions are eventually halted by court orders, and the supreme courts of California and Oregon later rule the licenses in their states invalid.

Federal amendment: President George W. Bush announces his support for amending the US Constitution to block same-sex marriage, citing the *Goodridge* decision in Massachusetts and the issuance of marriage licenses to same-sex couples in San Francisco and New Mexico.

Massachusetts marriages: On May 17, Massachusetts becomes the first state in the country to recognize same-sex marriages.

State constitutional amendments: Between August and November, thirteen more states pass constitutional amendments banning same-sex marriage. Some amendments are broadly worded to prohibit not only legal marriage but other forms of legal recognition such as domestic partnership or civil unions.

2005   California domestic partnership: California's expanded domestic partnership statute takes effect January 1, providing virtually all of the state-level benefits and protections of marriage to registered couples.

Civil unions redux: Connecticut becomes the second state in the country to recognize same-sex civil unions granting state-level benefits of legal marriage, and the first state to enact civil unions through voluntary legislation rather than in response to a court order.

More amendment action: Kansas becomes the eighteenth state to pass a constitutional amendment blocking same-sex marriage; activists in other states push for similar amendments.

International developments: Spain and Canada become the third and fourth countries to recognize same-sex marriages; laws creating civil partnerships and civil unions take effect in Great Britain and New Zealand respectively.

1 Marriage, culture and law

Marriage: Personal commitment. Pillar of civilization. Spiritual covenant. Legal bond. Political football. Source of social status. Site of gender
inequality. Tool of sexual regulation. Dying institution. Partnership for
reproduction and childrearing. Path to material gain. Reflection of
divine love. Legalized prostitution.

One of the most central institutions in modern social life, marriage is
currently a site of contestation rather than consensus. In contemporary
American society, the meaning and boundaries of the marriage institution are up for grabs, in both cultural and legal terms. Fierce and
sometimes ugly battles are being waged over who is allowed to marry,
what marriage signifies and where marriage is headed. Marriage has
never been a static institution, but it is hardly an exaggeration to assert
that at the start of the twenty-first century, marriage potentially faces one
of its most significant transformations in history. In the United States
and around the world, the demands of gay and lesbian couples for social
and legal recognition of their relationships represent a dramatic challenge to the marriage status quo. In their families, their friendships, their
churches and synagogues, and in courts of law, many same-sex couples
are pursuing inclusion in the institution of marriage by defining and
celebrating their relationships as marriages and asking friends, families,
religious authorities and the state to do the same. And many people
who oppose the idea of expanding marriage to include these couples
regard same-sex marriage as a profound threat to the institution of
marriage and the stability and well-being of society in general.

This book examines the phenomenon of same-sex marriage in the
contemporary US context. Recent legal developments have brought
increased attention to the question of same-sex marriage and greater
visibility for same-sex relationships. But in the raging public debates
over same-sex marriage, the voices of ordinary same-sex couples are
sometimes difficult to hear. Despite extensive media coverage of the
same-sex marriage issue, we know relatively little about what marriage
means to ordinary gays and lesbians in the United States. Why do some

gay and lesbian couples aspire to marriage as a way of organizing their intimate life? What can be learned from their efforts to construct an identity as "married" for themselves through cultural practices such as public commitment rituals? Why do other gay and lesbian couples reject marriage as a model for their own intimate life? Why do same-sex couples want legal recognition for their relationships, and how important is legal marriage to these couples? The perspectives of ordinary same-sex couples are the primary focus of this book, but I also explore recent public debates over legal same-sex marriage and compare the terms of these debates to the perspectives of same-sex couples.[1]

A theme that runs throughout this book is the mutual implication of law and culture in the institution of marriage. The legal and cultural dimensions of marriage can be teased apart for analytic purposes, but they are often closely connected in how gay and straight people alike think and talk about marriage. Same-sex marriage provides a unique vantage point for considering the relationship between the legal and cultural aspects of marriage. Marriage is increasingly available to American gay and lesbian couples in *cultural* terms, but remains mostly inaccessible in *legal* terms. Same-sex couples can use a range of cultural practices to define their relationships as marriages: public or private commitment rituals (which sometimes include the participation of religious officials), exchange of rings, use of marriage-related terminology to refer to their partners and their relationships. But same-sex couples are much more limited in their ability to access the legal dimension of marriage. Massachusetts is the only US state that currently issues marriage licenses to same-sex couples, and most other states explicitly refuse to honor same-sex marriages performed in other states or countries. My in-depth interviewing of committed same-sex couples reveals that the cultural and legal dimensions of marriage are deeply intertwined in the lives of gay and lesbian couples, and my analysis of public debates over same-sex marriage demonstrates that many non-gay Americans conflate the legal and cultural dimensions of marriage in their thinking about same-sex marriage.

This book makes two broad arguments about the relationship between the legal and the cultural dimensions of same-sex marriage. First, close examination of same-sex couples' cultural practices of marriage suggests that marriage is an extremely powerful cultural model of relationship, one that often attracts couples even in the absence of legal rights and benefits. Many (but not all) same-sex couples embrace marriage as a cultural form even when they cannot obtain it as a legal status. Lack of access to the legal dimension of marriage does not cause all same-sex couples to reject marriage. Instead, many use cultural practices to celebrate their relationships as marriages outside the law of the state, in a sense creating an alternative or parallel legality for their commitments outside the framework of official (state) law. And the meanings that such couples attach to their cultural enactment of marriage are partly colored by the denial of state recognition. In this sense, the meaning of some same-sex couples choosing to embrace the cultural dimension of marriage must be interpreted in relation to the denial of legal marriage to these couples. I argue that this cultural enactment of marriage outside of official law represents a form of political action, even though the couples usually do not describe their actions in political terms. It is a form of politics that targets cultural values and beliefs rather than the policies of the state. Important symbolic resources are at stake in this kind of cultural politics: recognition, identity, inclusion and social support.

The second main argument of the book concerns the cultural power of law. In the case of marriage, the law of the state has a unique cultural force that paradoxically both transcends and connects with the specific rights, benefits and protections afforded by legal marriage. The cultural power of law is evident in the way many members of same-sex couples describe and explain their desire for legal recognition of their relationships. Almost all of the gays and lesbians interviewed in this study expressed an interest in accessing the practical rights and benefits of marriage, things like tax benefits, access to health insurance, and having one's partner designated as next of kin in emergency situations. But many also spoke of the social legitimacy that legal marriage would bring to same-sex relationships, the sense that legal recognition would render same-sex couples socially normal and culturally equal to heterosexual married people. This legitimacy is part of law's perceived cultural power. It is more abstract than the specific tangible legal benefits of marriage but also rooted in those more tangible provisions. By treating all relationships equally in legal terms, the law has the perceived power to render all relationships culturally similar. The desire to capture the cultural power of law is most transparent among those gays and lesbians who insist that nothing short of marriage itself is acceptable; they assume that receiving the specific rights and benefits of marriage under another name would not have the same cultural impact.

The cultural power of law is also reflected in the words of a very different set of actors, the opponents of legal same-sex marriage. Many of the most impassioned objections to state recognition of same-sex marriage either assume or articulate the tremendous cultural influence of law. In public debates over same-sex marriage, opponents frequently offer moral and religious arguments for reserving the institution of marriage to opposite-sex couples, revealing the close interconnection of the legal and the cultural in the way that many people think about marriage. Many opponents of same-sex marriage also ground their objections to same-sex marriage in the broader cultural messages that legal recognition might send, that is, that homosexuality is normal or at least acceptable, and that committed same-sex relationships deserve the same treatment as heterosexual marriages. In other words, some of the objections to legal recognition of same-sex marriage are based less on a desire to withhold the specific legal benefits of marriage from same-sex couples than on a concern with the broader cultural significance of treating same-sex relationships as the legal equivalents of heterosexual marriages.

The cultural politics of marriage, family and sexuality

The current conflicts over same-sex marriage both reflect and contribute to broader cultural anxiety about the meaning and future of marriage. The changes in marriage and family in the United States over the past several decades have been remarkable in their scope and speed. Increases in divorce, cohabitation, single parenting and female labor-force participation, along with declines in the marriage rate, have challenged assumptions and beliefs about "normal" families and relationships in a way that is disturbing to some and liberating to others.

The divorce rate accelerated sharply starting in the mid-1960s and more than doubled over a twenty-year period (DaVanzo and Rahman 1993). Although the divorce rate stabilized during the 1980s and 1990s, recent estimates suggest that roughly half of all marriages forming today will eventually dissolve (Cherlin 1992). Meanwhile, the marriage rate has been falling since the early 1970s as a result of increases in cohabitation, people marrying later and possible increases in permanent singlehood. Unmarried cohabitation is an increasingly common practice and has lost much of its social stigma. Only one in ten marriages was preceded by cohabitation in the late 1960s and early 1970s, but now the majority of marriages start as cohabitations (Smock 2000), and about one in twenty American households are now headed by cohabitors (US Census Bureau 2001, Table 49). The number of households headed by single parents has risen substantially in recent years, the combined result of the high divorce rate and increasing numbers of births to single mothers. Today one-third of all births are to unmarried mothers and almost one-quarter of all family households are headed by single parents (US Census Bureau 2001, Tables 50 and 74). Changes in gender roles within families have paralleled the changes in family forms. Mothers are now more likely than ever to be employed in the paid labor market, and the increase has been especially dramatic among mothers of young children; more than half of all married women with children under age 6 now work full time, year round (Cohen and Bianchi 1999). In response to these trends, more families are making arrangements for child care outside the home and more parents are squeezed by what sociologist Arlie Hochschild (1997) calls a "time bind" as they attempt to combine work and family roles.

A variety of alternative family forms are taking shape as a result of these recent trends. Households headed by single parents are now a commonplace and expected feature of American life. Divorce and remarriage have produced a variety of "blended" families that integrate stepparents, stepchildren and stepsiblings to form new family units. And gay and lesbian couples increasingly seek to form viable family units of their own, either by acting as co-parents to children from previous marriages or by becoming parents together through artificial insemination, surrogacy, adoption or foster parenting.

These relatively swift and highly visible changes in family forms and roles have sparked debate over both the causes and the consequences of change, making family structure and "family values" central concerns in American cultural politics. The alleged problem of fatherlessness in American families has become a major rallying cry of religious and cultural conservatives (Blankenhorn 1995; Popenoe 1996; cf. Stacey 1996). A self-proclaimed "marriage movement" has emerged to declare a marriage crisis and promote efforts to replace the existing "divorce culture" with a renewed "marriage culture" (CMFCE, IAV and RCFP 2000). These marriage advocates support a range of policy proposals intended to combat the erosion of marital stability. Specific proposals, some already being implemented in parts of the United States, include mandatory marriage education for high-school students, mandatory marriage counseling for couples seeking a divorce, and reform of state divorce laws to reintroduce fault-based divorce. A few states have passed laws that require marrying couples to choose between a standard marriage and a more restrictive "covenant marriage" designed to reduce divorce.

New beliefs about sexuality have accompanied the rapid changes in family forms. The linkages between sex, reproduction and marriage that were once taken for granted have loosened as a result of changing attitudes, trends toward greater gender equality and rapid technological developments. Improvements in contraceptive technology, especially the advent of the birth-control pill, facilitated the separation of sex and reproduction, thereby reducing the risks associated with "casual" or non-marital sex. The sexual liberation movement that emerged in the 1960s gradually eroded the social stigma attached to premarital sex and cohabitation, and recent developments in reproductive technologies and practices – such as in vitro fertilization, artificial insemination, surrogate pregnancies and the prospect of human cloning – have weakened the association between heterosexual sex acts and biological reproduction.

Partly inspired by the sexual revolution and the women's movement, a visible and vocal gay liberation movement burst onto the national scene in the late 1960s and early 1970s. While the birth of the modern gay and lesbian movement is often pegged to the Stonewall riots in New York City in 1969, homophile organizations such as the Mattachine Society and the Daughters of Bilitis laid the groundwork for the movement in earlier decades by forging gay and lesbian social networks in urban areas and advocating for greater social acceptance of sexual minorities (Adam 1987; D'Emilio 1983). After the Stonewall riots, in which patrons of New York gay bars took to the streets to protest police raids on gay establishments, the gay and lesbian movement blossomed into a larger, more visible and more confrontational force. The various gay liberation-ist groups that dominated the movement at the start of the 1970s eschewed the cautious conformism of earlier homophile groups and favored more radical goals and tactics. However, more reform-oriented groups that focused on accomplishing change through existing political channels soon emerged alongside the liberationist groups and evolved into today's mainstream gay and lesbian rights movement. Many commentators on American gay and lesbian politics have noted the ongoing tensions between those espousing a more radical and confrontational approach (liberationists and queers) and those preferring more moderate, assimilationist, rights-oriented goals and tactics, that is, the mainstream gay rights movement (Bernstein 2001; Gamson 1995; Rimmerman 2002; Seidman 2002; Vaid 1995; Warner 1999). As I discuss in Chapter 3, this tension emerged quite prominently in debates within gay and lesbian communities and movements over the issue of same-sex marriage.

The gay and lesbian rights movement has achieved considerable success over the past several decades, in areas ranging from family law to workplace protections to hate-crimes prevention. The movement faces a large and well-organized opposition, mainly led by Christian conservatives (Herman 1997), but a recent study of gay rights battles from the early 1970s to the early 1990s found that the policy successes of gay rights supporters far outnumbered those of gay rights opponents, and the relative success of gay rights advocates has increased over time (Werum and Winders 2001). Particularly dramatic successes came in 1996 and 2003, with two momentous decisions by the US Supreme

Court. In the 1996 decision, *Romer v. Evans*, the Court ruled unconstitutional a Colorado amendment that repealed existing gay rights laws and prohibited the future passage of such laws in the state. The 2003 decision in *Lawrence v. Texas* repealed the anti-sodomy laws that remained on the books in thirteen US states, making homosexual sex legal throughout the country for the first time in history. Many observers viewed the *Lawrence* decision as especially significant, because it undermined the legal basis for the differential treatment of gays and lesbians; after *Lawrence*, discriminatory laws and practices can no longer be justified by arguing that the behavior that defines the class of people receiving different treatment is criminal. The *Lawrence* ruling also represented an important symbolic victory for gay rights advocates because it overturned the Supreme Court's own 1986 ruling in *Bowers v. Hardwick*, in which the majority opinion had dismissed as "facetious" the idea that the Constitution might afford protection for homosexual conduct. Only seventeen years later, finding in favor of two men challenging their conviction under the Texas anti-sodomy law, the majority in *Lawrence* stated that the "petitioners are entitled to respect for their private lives" and complained that the *Bowers* ruling "demean[ed] the lives of homosexual persons."

The mounting policy successes of the gay rights movement have been paralleled by a veritable explosion in the cultural visibility of gays and lesbians. From television sitcoms to the silver screen, from daytime talk shows to the covers of news magazines, gay and lesbian lives, real and fictional, had become ubiquitous in American culture by the close of the twentieth century (Gamson 1998; Walters 2001a). Large corporate advertisers are more often willing to risk alienating some potential customers to include gay images and themes in their marketing, in order to target a newly discovered and supposedly wealthy gay niche market (Chasin 2000; Gluckman and Reed 1997). These trends toward greater cultural openness have likely made it easier than ever for gays and lesbians to come out.

But some are skeptical about the meaning and extent of this new cultural acceptance of gays and lesbians. Prominent gay rights activist Urvashi Vaid (1995) warns that the political and cultural mainstreaming of gays delivers only "virtual equality": without deeper cultural transformations, recent trends toward cultural visibility and political inclusion fall short of making gays and lesbians fully equal citizens and participants in American life. Likewise, Steven Seidman (2002) argues that gays and lesbians are increasingly free to live "beyond the closet," but this freedom is exercised within a world of continuing heterosexual dominance, in which sexual minorities are tolerated but denied full equality in key social institutions such as the family and the workplace. Despite high-profile policy victories and trends toward cultural assimilation, gays and lesbians continue to face significant religious and social disapproval and ongoing legal disadvantage. In short, the cultural and political status of gays and lesbians remains a site of struggle in the American culture wars.

Mainstream society's continuing ambivalence toward sexual minorities is perhaps nowhere more evident than in the controversies raging around the recognition of same-sex relationships. These controversies make the most sense when viewed in the context of a climate of heightened awareness and anxiety about the meaning and consequences of transformations in family forms as well as sexual identities and practices. Conservative rhetoric links changes in the meaning and stability of marriage relationships, the range of what are considered "normal" family structures, and the legitimacy of various sexual identities and practices to social problems such as crime and poverty and to a more general concern about the threat of social breakdown. The specific issue of recognizing same-sex relationships has now emerged as a major battleground, and it is a battle that is being waged on several fronts. From religion to popular culture to workplaces to the law, same-sex marriage and related forms of recognition are testing the limits of mainstream society's tolerance and acceptance of gays and lesbians.

Major religious denominations are struggling with the question of whether and how to recognize same-sex commitments without abandoning centuries of religious tradition. Some major denominations – including Roman Catholicism, the Southern Baptist Convention, Orthodox Judaism and the Church of Jesus Christ of Latter-Day Saints (Mormons) – have been unwavering in their official opposition to blessing or recognizing same-sex unions. The Catholic Church has been perhaps the most vociferous opponent, extending its opposition beyond the realm of religious practice to address civil acknowledgement of same-sex relationships. In 2003, the Vatican released a pronouncement urging Catholic bishops and politicians to fight any attempts to grant legal recognition to gay relationships, calling same-sex marriage the "legalization of evil" (Congregation for the Doctrine of the Faith 2003). Several mainline Protestant denominations are mired in ongoing debates on the question of blessing or recognizing same-sex couples, finding it difficult to reach a resolution that will satisfy a broad majority of their adherents. In 1996 the United Methodist Church instituted a rule prohibiting its clergy from performing same-sex union ceremonies, a position that was reaffirmed at its General Conference in 2000 despite a well-organized campaign to overturn it. In other Protestant denominations, debates over same-sex union ceremonies rage on, but clergy have the option to decide whether to perform the rituals. Only a few major religious denominations have given their full support to same-sex union ceremonies, including the Unitarian Universalist Association, the United Church of Christ, Reconstructionist Judaism and Reform Judaism. Debates over recognizing same-sex relationships will persist in the religious sphere for years to come.[2]

The growing visibility of gays, lesbians and their relationships in popular culture and in the workplace has sometimes stirred controversy and provoked backlash. To cite just a few prominent examples from recent years: protests greeted the 1994 episode of the television sitcom *Roseanne* in which the title character engages in a same-sex kiss. Three years later, the coming-out of Ellen DeGeneres – both as herself and as the lead character in her eponymous sitcom – mushroomed into a major media event. The Rev. Jerry Falwell called the comedian "Ellen Degenerate" and the network affiliate in Birmingham, Alabama refused to broadcast the coming-out episode of the show. (ABC cancelled the sitcom the following year, prompting DeGeneres to accuse the network of homophobia.) In 1996, the Southern Baptist Convention launched a high-profile boycott against the Disney Corporation to protest its extension of domestic partner benefits to its gay and lesbian employees. In 2005, the Public Broadcasting Service cancelled an epi- • sode of a popular children's show because it featured a Vermont family headed by a female couple. (In one of her first public pronouncements, the newly appointed Secretary of Education had expressed concerns about the episode.) Religious conservatives have even mounted campaigns to protest non-human fictional characters they perceive as gay or gay-friendly, such as Tinky-Winky the Teletubby and cartoon character SpongeBob SquarePants. For some cultural conservatives, apparently no battles over positive representations of sexual difference are too trivial to fight.

In summary, rapid changes in marriage, family structure, sexual identities and sexual practices characterized the final decades of twentieth-century American life. These changes prompted the emergence of heated cultural battles over family values, the future of marriage and the propriety of various forms of sexual identity and sexual practice. In the case of homosexuality, the focus of the culture wars has largely shifted from the question of the treatment of gays and lesbians as individuals to recognition of same-sex relationships. The halting movement toward legal same-sex marriage, sketched in the next section, takes place in this broader context of conflict and concern about changes in marriage, family and sexuality.

Legal same-sex marriage in the United States and abroad

The 2003 decision by the Massachusetts Supreme Judicial Court in *Goodridge v. Department of Public Health*, finding a right to marriage for same-sex couples in the Massachusetts constitution, is the most recent and dramatic development toward legal recognition of same-sex marriage in the United States. Massachusetts' high court ruled that "[l]imiting the protections, benefits, and obligations of civil marriage to opposite-sex couples violates the basic premises of individual liberty and equality under law protected by the Massachusetts Constitution." The state had attempted to defend its refusal to grant marriage licenses to same-sex couples based on three rationales: creating a favorable setting for procreation, fostering optimal conditions for childrearing and preserving scarce resources. The court ruled that none of these goals constituted a rational basis for excluding same-sex couples from marriage. "The marriage ban works a deep and scarring hardship on a very real segment of the community for no rational reason," the court concluded, ordering the state to begin issuing marriage licenses to same-sex couples on May 17, 2004.

The *Goodridge* decision brought a flood of renewed attention to the issue of same-sex marriage in the media and the political sphere. President George W. Bush announced his support for a federal constitutional amendment to block same-sex marriage nationwide. The Massachusetts legislature began the process of amending the state constitution to overturn the decision, although the earliest such an amendment could take effect would be November 2006. The *Goodridge* ruling and the backlash against it also inspired a new form of civil disobedience among local officials around the country, spearheaded by San Francisco Mayor Gavin Newsom's decision to issue marriage licenses to same-sex couples in early 2004. Newsom's action prompted similar actions in other local jurisdictions around the country, including Multnomah County, Oregon, which includes the city of Portland. (The California Supreme Court and the Oregon Supreme Court later ruled that the licenses issued in their respective states were invalid.)

Efforts to establish recognition for same-sex relationships actually date back to the 1970s, but only attracted widespread attention starting in the 1990s, when developments in the state of Hawaii made legal same-sex marriage in the United States a serious possibility (see p. xiii for a timeline of same-sex marriage developments). A lawsuit brought by three same-sex couples seeking the right to marry garnered a favorable initial ruling from the Hawaii Supreme Court. The state high court had found that denial of marriage licenses to same-sex couples appeared to violate the state constitution's equal rights amendment barring gender discrimination. When the case was sent back to the district court for trial and the district court ruled in favor of the couples, recognizing their right to marry under state law, opponents successfully organized to block same-sex marriage by amending the state's constitution to limit marriage to opposite-sex couples. The developments in Hawaii provoked legislative activity to block same-sex marriage throughout the United States, resulting in the passage of the federal Defense of Marriage Act in 1996 and similar laws in most individual states.

The Hawaii case and the ensuing legislative backlash represented a serious setback for proponents of legal same-sex marriage, but the high court in another liberal state, Vermont, revived the hopes of same-sex marriage advocates with its 1999 ruling in *Baker v. State*. In response to a suit brought by three same-sex couples, the Vermont high court overturned a trial court decision and found that denial of the benefits and protections of marriage to same-sex couples violated the Vermont state constitution.[3] The court's ruling imposed a duty on the state legislature to remedy the situation by either revising the marriage statutes to allow same-sex couples to marry or passing legislation to set up a parallel, alternative legal vehicle for providing the state-level benefits and protections of marriage to same-sex couples. The legislature chose the latter option. After months of sometimes rancorous debate, the Vermont legislature passed a law establishing "civil unions" as an alternative legal structure that offers same-sex couples all the benefits and protections provided by marriage under Vermont law. The full provisions of the act took effect in July 2000, and by the end of 2003 over 6,000 couples had registered civil unions with the state.

Several states continue to battle over the issue of legal recognition for same-sex relationships, and the US Congress is considering an amendment to the US Constitution to prohibit same-sex marriage. States continue to pass or consider "defense of marriage" acts (DOMAs) intended to block same-sex marriage at the state level (only eleven states now lack a DOMA). Some states have passed what same-sex marriage activists call "super-DOMAs," laws that block recognition not only of same-sex marriage but of civil unions or domestic partnerships as well. At both the state and national level, opponents of same-sex marriage are now focusing on constitutional amendments to block legal same-sex marriage. The proposed Marriage Protection Amendment would amend the US Constitution to define marriage as the union of one man and one woman and prohibit courts from finding a right to marriage for same-sex couples in state or federal constitutions. (The federal amendment would also prevent courts from finding a right to the "legal incidents" of marriage for same-sex couples, even if delivered under another name such as civil unions.) In the 2004 election cycle, thirteen states amended their constitutions to prohibit same-sex marriage (and in some cases other forms of relationship recognition as well). At this writing, a total of eighteen states have amended their constitutions to block same-sex marriage, and several other states are actively considering constitutional amendments. But elsewhere gay rights supporters are pursuing relationship recognition through the courts and the legislatures. Court cases seeking the right to marry are pending in a number of states. Advocates in several states have proposed legislation to implement legal recognition for same-sex couples. Besides the creation of civil unions in Vermont, the greatest legislative successes to date have come in California, where an expanded domestic partnership law took effect in January 2005, and in Connecticut, where a civil unions law went into effect in October 2005. The California and Connecticut laws grant same-sex couples who register as domestic partners or enter civil unions virtually all of the state-level rights, privileges and responsibilities of married couples.[4]

The United States has been much slower to grant legal recognition to same-sex relationships than many other Western countries, in which a rapid trend toward heightened recognition has been evident over the past fifteen years (Merin 2002). At this writing, four countries recognize legal same-sex marriage: the Netherlands became the first country to grant same-sex couples marriage rights in 2001, followed by Belgium in 2003 and Spain and Canada in 2005.[5] Denmark, Norway, Sweden, Iceland and Finland have granted relationship rights through registered partnerships, which provide almost all of the benefits of marriage to same-sex couples. Civil unions giving same-sex couples the same rights as married couples took effect in New Zealand and the United Kingdom (they are called "civil partnerships" in the UK). The French civil solidarity pact law makes a more limited set of rights available to both same-sex and opposite-sex couples, and the German life partnership act extends a similar set of rights to same-sex couples only. Hungary and Portugal include same-sex couples under their laws regulating common law marriage. Partial legal recognition exists for same-sex relationships in several other developed countries, including Australia, Argentina and Brazil. In 2003, the European Parliament issued a report urging member states of the European Union to extend marriage and adoption rights to gays and lesbians. But with the possible exception of the developments in Canada, these international moves toward same-sex relationship rights so far appear to have had little impact on the US dialogue on relationship rights for same-sex couples.

Understanding same-sex marriage: theoretical frameworks

Throughout this book, I use several broad concepts to frame my discussion of same-sex marriage. In particular, the concepts of culture, politics, law and legality are central to the arguments I make and the interpretations I offer. Here I will briefly sketch these core concepts and their relation to broader theoretical conversations that I engage throughout the book.

Culture and politics

The concept of culture generally refers to the symbolic or expressive dimension of social life, the way people use symbols – language, rituals, imagery – to make and share meaning. In this study I conceive of culture as a kind of social structure (or set of structures), a force that often guides people's behavior in certain directions but also furnishes people with tools and resources that make meaningful individual actions and choices possible. By querying the meaning of cultural practices related to same-sex marriage, I join a broader conversation in the social sciences about the role of culture in social life and the relationship of social structure and individual behavior.

Social scientists have not converged on a single, unified conception of culture, but it is at least possible to identify dominant strands of thought. Historian William Sewell, Jr. (1999) argues that two competing visions of culture have emerged in academic discussions over the past few decades. One view, elaborated in the influential work of anthropologists Clifford Geertz (1973, 1983) and David Schneider (1976), treats culture as a system of symbols and meanings. This conception emphasizes the systemic qualities of culture, the orderly and enduring patterns of relationship among cultural symbols, as well as culture's relative autonomy from other dimensions of social life. In the system view, culture hangs together in a coherent way and is not merely a by-product of other social forces. The second view of culture, which emerged largely in reaction to the system view, sees culture as "a sphere of practical activity shot through by willful action, power relations, struggle, contradiction, and change" (Sewell 1999, 44). This view of culture as practical activity rejects the notion of culture as a stable, coherent, orderly meaning system, preferring to emphasize that culture is a constantly shifting terrain of power, conflict, strategy and resistance. The practice view of culture has been articulated by influential scholars such as Pierre Bourdieu (1977), Ann Swidler (1986) and Sherry Ortner (1984).

While practice theorists have been quite dismissive of the meaning-system perspective, Sewell makes a convincing argument that it is a mistake to regard these two competing visions of culture as incompatible or mutually exclusive. Cultural practices are powerful and effective only because they occur in the context of relatively stable systems of shared meanings. (For example, the effectiveness of burning the flag as a symbolic form of protest depends on everyone recognizing the meaning of the flag as a national symbol.) And cultural meaning systems endure or change because of the concrete actions taken by cultural actors, actions which reinforce existing meanings or shape them to serve new ends. (The flag could not persist as an effective national symbol if citizens did not routinely venerate it and display it.) Thus, "the important question is not whether culture should be conceptualized as practice or as a system of symbols and meanings, but how to conceptualize the articulation of system and practice" (Sewell 1999, 47). In short, Sewell maintains that culture is *both* meaning systems and practical activity, and cultural analysis should explore the relationship between these two dimensions of culture: how cultural meaning systems constrain or facilitate cultural practices, and how cultural practices transform or reproduce meaning systems. Sewell argues that cultural practice derives its power from "the ability of actors to play on the multiple meanings of symbols – thereby redefining situations in ways that they believe will favor their purposes. Creative cultural action commonly entails the purposeful or spontaneous importation of meanings from one social location or context to another" (1999, 51).

This notion of the interdependence of cultural practice and meaning systems proves useful for thinking about same-sex marriage as a cultural phenomenon. In some ways the cultural enactment of same-sex marriage through rituals and other practices clearly reflects and reproduces existing cultural meaning systems, particularly beliefs and ideas about marriage and commitment. But these cultural practices of same-sex commitment also have the potential to reshape existing meanings and symbols. Same-sex couples who use cultural practices to frame their relationships as marriages draw from dominant cultural meanings about marriage, family, love and maturity. Both the choices they make and the way they talk about their cultural practices borrow heavily from existing cultural models of marriage and family. Many of these couples also invoke dominant cultural discourses of love and commitment to explain their own cultural practices, and some reinforce cultural understandings of marriage as an important life-course marker, interpreting their own participation in marriage as a transition to a new life stage. Yet same-sex couples also make creative use of marriage as a cultural form. Ann

Swidler's (1986) metaphor of "culture as a 'tool kit' of symbols, stories, rituals, and world-views, which people may use in varying configurations to solve different kinds of problems" (273) seems apt for the case of same-sex commitment rituals. Specifically, many same-sex couples use these rituals to address the problems of stigmatization, invisibility and uncertainty confronting them both as individuals and especially as couples, and this cultural practice can be read as a protest against gay and lesbian oppression that challenges the dominant beliefs and practices around marriage. At the same time, despite the potential of these cultural practices to transform prevailing cultural understandings of marriage, these couples do not describe their own actions as attempts at large-scale structural change. They do not frame their participation in public commitment rituals as political, as an effort to redefine the institution of marriage or to influence public policies related to same-sex relationships.

Should same-sex couples' use of marriage-related cultural practices be read as a kind of political action, even though the couples themselves usually do not think of their choices in this way? The traditional academic conception of the political equated politics with "the realm of institutionalized politics and the behaviors of formally recognized political actors" (McAdam 1988, 60), but a growing interest in the influence of social movements, and the feminist movement's insight that "the personal is political," have led many scholars and activists to think about politics more broadly, for example by taking seriously the political impact of marginalized social actors and reconceiving formerly "private" and "personal" behaviors and troubles as political matters. With the rise of the so-called new social movements such as feminism, environmentalism and gay rights in the latter half of the twentieth century, some observers detected a shift toward a new kind of politics that focuses on issues of lifestyle, identity and values more than economic distribution. These new social movements are more likely to work outside traditional political channels to achieve their goals, by influencing people's daily lifestyle choices and by challenging dominant cultural meanings and perceptions.[6] And the emergence of fiery culture wars over issues like abortion and homosexuality has further demonstrated the politicization of values and meaning.

Same-sex marriage provides a fascinating case study for exploring how and when the cultural becomes political. One aspect of same-sex marriage clearly fits the traditional definition of the political: same-sex couples, with the support of the organized gay and lesbian movement, are using formal political channels (courts and legislatures) to petition the state for legal recognition of their relationships. A broad range of rights, benefits and responsibilities would accompany this legal recognition. Well-organized counter-movements have emerged to block these moves for legal same-sex marriage. This represents traditional politics in the sense that opposing groups seek to influence the state and secure a particular policy outcome. But what about the cultural manifestations of same-sex marriage, including the celebration of same-sex commitments in public ceremonies and the use of marriage terminology to refer to same-sex relationships? Does it also make sense to think of these cultural practices as political acts? Does it matter whether same-sex couples themselves describe their own cultural practices in political terms? Is the refusal of some same-sex couples to engage in cultural practices associated with marriage itself a kind of political choice? I will argue that same-sex couples' decisions around the cultural enactment of commitment are in fact political choices, despite the fact that the members of same-sex couples – especially those who embrace the marriage model of commitment – often do not consciously frame these choices in political terms. In other words, the cultural politics of same-sex marriage extends beyond public contests over state recognition of same-sex relationships and includes the appropriation of the cultural practices and symbols of marriage by same-sex couples.

Law and legality

My interest in the relationship between the cultural and legal dimensions of same-sex marriage is largely inspired by the recent turn toward cultural approaches in the study of law and society. Scholars developing a cultural approach to law have examined the operations of law in everyday life, including outside of traditional legal arenas, to appreciate the impact of law as a cultural force (see Sarat and Kearns 1993; Sarat and Simon 2003; Marshall and Barclay 2003). Two important concepts emerging from this cultural turn in the study of law and society are legal consciousness and legality. I use these concepts to frame my investigation of same-sex marriage as a legal issue and to explore the relationship between the cultural and legal dimensions of same-sex marriage.

Legal consciousness has been defined as "all the ideas about the nature, function, and operation of law held by anyone in society at a given time" (Trubek 1984, 592), or more simply as "the ways people understand and use law" (Merry 1990, 5). Recent work on legal consciousness applies interpretive methods to individual narratives in an effort to describe how various social actors experience and understand the law. Important studies explore the legal consciousness of average citizens (Ewick and Silbey 1998; Yngvesson 1988; Feeley 1979; Engel

1984; Nielsen 2000, 2004), working-class Americans (Merry 1990; Ewick and Silbey 1992), the poor (Sarat 1990), people with disabilities (Engel and Munger 2003), victims of racial and gender discrimination (Bumiller 1988), social activists (McCann 1994), and lawyers and their clients (Sarat and Felstiner 1989). In *The Common Place of Law*, Ewick and Silbey (1998) elaborate the concept of legality, which they define as those meanings, sources of authority and cultural practices which are in some sense legal although not necessarily approved or acknowledged by official law (the law of the state). In light of this broad definition of legality, Ewick and Silbey expand the concept of legal consciousness to encompass a range of social practices that both reflect and construct legality. "In this theoretical framing of legal consciousness as participation in the construction of legality," they state, "consciousness is not an exclusively ideational, abstract, or decontextualized set of attitudes toward and about the law. Consciousness is not merely a state of mind. Legal consciousness is produced and revealed in what people *do* as well as what they *say*" (1998, 46).

This approach to legal consciousness as the enactment of legality advances theorizing about the role of law in everyday life in two senses. First, it invites researchers to examine the impact of law in broader terms. While traditional approaches to legal consciousness were primarily interested in how people use and understand official law (the "law on the books"), Ewick and Silbey's approach expands legal consciousness to include ideas and actions that in some sense implicate legality, even in the absence of official law. Second, this new approach emphasizes the *enacted* quality of consciousness, meaning that legal consciousness is readable from people's behaviors as well as their words and ideas. In both of these senses, Ewick and Silbey's approach to legal consciousness argues for a more expansive inquiry into the role of law in everyday social life.

In this book I elaborate a view of law as an influential cultural structure.[7] The power of official law, the law created and enforced by the state, has important cultural and symbolic dimensions. And law, broadly defined, is itself a cultural construction and a cultural resource. The words and practices of people in committed same-sex couples reveal both the cultural power of official law and the cultural enactment of legality where official law is absent. Some same-sex couples use rituals to fulfill some of the functions normally performed by official legal recognition; in this sense, same-sex commitment ceremonies can be interpreted as enactments of legality outside official law. People can enact legality through cultural practice even when they are not consciously aware of a specifically legal meaning attaching to their action. At the same time, many members of same-sex couples, regardless of whether they have participated in commitment rituals, perceive the law of the state as a unique cultural resource, one with the power to render identities and relationships culturally similar by declaring them legally identical. Thus the case of same-sex marriage calls attention to law's distinctive cultural power, above and beyond its capacity to deliver specific rights, benefits and protections to individual citizens.

Description of the study

This study uses in-depth interviewing, participant observation and content analysis to examine the meaning and practice of same-sex marriage from the perspective of ordinary same-sex couples and the terms of public debates over legal recognition of same-sex marriage. This mix of research methods allows a comprehensive analysis of same-sex marriage, attending to both its legal and cultural dimensions and incorporating the viewpoints of a range of key social actors, including a variety of same-sex couples, officiants at same-sex ceremonies, the general public, and social movement actors on both sides of the battles over legal recognition.

I examine debates over legal recognition in the states of Hawaii and Vermont to analyze public dialogue on same-sex marriage, performing content analyses of letters to the editor (Hawaii) and public testimony (Vermont). The content analysis is supplemented with background information from media accounts of the contests over same-sex marriage in these two states. I describe the details of the content analysis method in Chapter 5.

My primary empirical focus is the meanings and practices of same-sex marriage from the perspective of everyday gay and lesbian couples. Because my main interest was understanding how these couples think about marriage in relation to their own intimate commitments and how some choose to enact marriage culturally, in-depth interviewing was the most appropriate method for this part of the study. These interviews constitute the empirical core of my research. To better analyze the ritual practices of some couples, I supplemented the interview findings with participant observation at four commitment rituals and review of various artifacts from the rituals of other participants, including videotape and audiotape recordings of rituals, texts of rituals, photographs, programs and invitations.

I conducted interviews with 71 study participants from same-sex couples, representing 38 different same-sex couples. In most cases (54 participants), both members of the couple were interviewed together.

In a minority of cases (12 participants), both partners of the couple were interviewed separately. I also interviewed 5 study participants whose partners did not participate in the study because of lack of interest or scheduling difficulties. Most interviews took place in study participants' homes, although in a few cases people preferred to be interviewed elsewhere (my home, their workplace or a public place). The interviews were conducted between October 1998 and December 1999, with one follow-up interview conducted in February 2001. Their length ranged from forty-five minutes to three hours, averaging about two hours. All interviews were taped and study participants were guaranteed complete confidentiality. I have assigned pseudonyms to all participants and have sometimes made other changes to their identifying information, such as their occupations, to preserve confidentiality.

My target population for these interviews was "committed" same-sex couples. I mostly relied on potential participants themselves to decide whether they were part of a "committed" couple, and undoubtedly different couples have different definitions of commitment. To ensure some consistency across couples, I defined as minimal criteria for study participation that couples had either 1) participated in a public commitment ritual (an unambiguous effort to signal commitment), or 2) been involved in the current committed relationship for at least two years. I identified potential interview participants through a combination of approaches, including outreach to clergy who perform same-sex commitment ceremonies and to religious organizations catering to gays and lesbians. I also used snowball sampling, asking initial participants to identify other committed same-sex couples who might be interested in participating in the study. And I made limited use of my personal networks in the Chicago area gay and lesbian communities to recruit some participants, especially from underrepresented categories including racial/ethnic minorities and working-class people. I deliberately recruited roughly twice as many people who had held a commitment ritual as who had not, to facilitate analysis of internal variation in the views and practices of this group. One potential bias resulting from my sampling approach concerns the portion of the sample who had held public rituals. Because I used clergy contacts extensively in recruiting the people who had held a ritual, this part of the sample may be skewed toward couples who have religious affiliations or who used religious officiants in their ceremonies.

The interviews covered a range of topics, from basic background information to issues directly related to same-sex marriage. I began by asking background questions about study participants' personal and family history, past and current socioeconomic status, racial or ethnic identity, sexual identity, and religious and political identifications. I then asked people to tell me their "coming out" story and the history of the committed relationship – how the couple met, how the relationship evolved and how long they had been together. With couples who had held a public commitment ritual, I asked study participants to recount the story of that event: the decision to construct a ritual, the meaning of the event, and personal and social reactions to the event. With couples who had not held a public ritual, I asked study participants about their views on commitment rituals, whether they had attended rituals of other couples and whether they had considered having a ritual themselves, and their reasons for not having one. I asked all study participants about the ongoing arrangements in their current relationship regarding matters such as division of labor, management of finances, legal arrangements to establish protections and mutual understandings, and sexual monogamy. I also asked them to describe the status of their relationship within extended families and friendship networks, that is, how they thought other people in their lives perceived their relationship. I posed a series of questions concerning their views on legal recognition for same-sex relationships, and finished by asking about their relationship to gay and lesbian communities and movements. At the close of the interview, I gave participants an opportunity to ask questions or return to anything that had come up during the interview for further discussion. The interview guides are included in Appendix A.

I also interviewed six clergy who had officiated at same-sex commitment ceremonies to elicit their perspective on the rituals. The clergy's affiliations included the United Fellowship of Metropolitan Community Churches (a Christian denomination with special outreach to gay, lesbian, bisexual and transgender persons; three interviews); the Unitarian Universalist Association (one interview); the United Methodist Church (one interview); and Reform Judaism (one interview). The clergy interviews covered background information on the clergy and his or her congregation, the clergy's experience performing same-sex rituals, and how these rituals compare to one another and to heterosexual wedding ceremonies. The clergy interviews averaged one hour in length. The clergy interview guide is included in Appendix A.

In early 2001, I ran into Brenda Davis, the first person interviewed for the study two and a half years earlier. After a few moments of small talk, Brenda informed me that she was no longer with her partner Kim Pierson, whom I had also interviewed. We did not get into a detailed discussion of their breakup at that time, but a few weeks later I contacted Brenda, who had participated in a commitment ritual with Kim, and asked if she would be willing to be re-interviewed for the study, to provide the perspective of a "divorced" lesbian. She granted me a second interview, and this follow-up interview raised interesting substantive and methodological issues. I discuss these issues in the Epilogue, along with my general views about the kind of knowledge that is produced using the technique of in-depth interviewing.

A brief word about my standpoint as researcher: I am a lesbian who participated in a public commitment ritual more than a decade ago, so my personal concerns and experiences inevitably have influenced this research project. I began this research project with an intellectual curiosity about the choice of some gays and lesbians (including myself) to appropriate some of the cultural elements of marriage in defining and celebrating our own intimate commitments. At the outset of the project, I had mixed feelings about the issue of legal same-sex marriage, seeing it as a clear civil rights issue but also wondering about the impact of fighting for marriage rights on gay and lesbian culture and politics. Over the course of the project some of my personal beliefs have changed, in response to both my own research findings and unfolding developments in the United States and abroad, and I lay out my current thinking on the policy question of same-sex marriage in the concluding chapter. I believe this research benefited in some respects from my status as an "insider" with regard to gay and lesbian culture generally and cultural practices of marriage specifically. Being forthcoming about my sexual identity almost certainly opened a few doors that would otherwise have remained closed, since several potential study participants sought to confirm that I was gay before they agreed to be interviewed. My identity as a lesbian in a committed relationship undoubtedly affected the way I framed this project and interpreted my findings, just as my identity as a sociologist who studies law and culture surely influenced the kinds of questions I asked and the ways I chose to focus my analysis.[8]

Characteristics of study participants

The interview sample of members of same-sex couples includes 41 women and 30 men. Just over two-thirds of the study participants (49) had participated in a public commitment ceremony with their current partner at the time of the interview. This portion of the sample includes 30 women and 19 men. The 22 study participants who had not participated in a ritual are evenly divided by gender. The sample is predominantly white (77 percent), with some representation of Latinos and Latinas, African-Americans, Asians and biracial or multiracial people. The sample is mostly middle class, with nearly even representation of upper-middle-class and working-class people. It is a highly educated sample, with only a quarter of the study participants having less than a bachelor's degree. Nearly two-thirds currently hold some religious affiliation, and the majority described their political views as liberal or Democratic. The sample is nearly evenly divided in terms of residential location, with 40 city residents and 31 suburbanites. The average age of participants at the time of interviewing was 41 years, and the average length of their current relationship was eight years. Appendix B provides more details on sample characteristics, and Appendix C gives a descriptive listing of the individual participants.

The interview sample has some limitations. My research was confined to the Chicago metropolitan area, so the findings may not generalize to same-sex couples living in rural areas, other urban areas or other regions of the United States. The sample is more highly educated and whiter than the population of the Chicago metro area as a whole, and working-class people are somewhat underrepresented. By necessity, extremely closeted gay and lesbian couples are not included in this study – or in other studies of gays and lesbians – because of the difficulty in locating them and securing their participation in research. I chose to focus on gays and lesbians currently in committed relationships, mainly because I assumed their relationship status would lend immediacy to the topic of same-sex marriage. Most same-sex couples today must at least consider whether they want to embrace a marriage model for their relationship and whether legal same-sex marriage is a desirable political goal. The perspectives of gays and lesbians not in committed relationships are not represented in this study, and it is crucial to keep this in mind when considering the results of this research.

The sample also has some clear strengths: it is fairly balanced in terms of gender, urban vs. suburban residence, and study participants' connections to gay and lesbian communities and movements. The gender balance allows me to note gender differences (or the lack thereof) relating to commitment and marriage. The inclusion of a substantial number of suburbanites is useful, because much past research on sexual minorities has focused on urban dwellers (but see Brekhus 2003). And the variation in participants' connections to gay and lesbian communities and cultures adds to the overall richness and diversity of the study. Some participants have social networks that are primarily gay and lesbian, others have mixed straight and gay networks, and still others have predominantly straight social networks. Some participants are deeply immersed in gay cultural and social life through their participation in gay organizations and events, their consumption of gay-related media, or their involvement in the gay rights movement. Others have only very tenuous connections to gay and lesbian cultures and communities, sometimes by choice and other times as a result of various constraints, including socioeconomic status and residential location.

Chapter overview

In the next four chapters I present my empirical findings. Chapter 2 examines how some same-sex couples use a range of cultural practices to define their intimate commitments as marriages. I describe the different ways same-sex couples use cultural practice to enact commitment and marriage. The chapter's main focus is the use of wedding-like public ceremonies to enact commitment. I examine how couples construct these ceremonies and how they describe the purpose and significance of these events. Not surprisingly, many same-sex couples invoke elements of the romantic love ideology that pervades contemporary American culture in explaining their commitment practices. But social context also colors the meaning of public commitment rituals for same-sex couples. The exclusion from legal (and usually religious) marriage, as well as the social stigma that attaches to homosexual relationships, shape couples' understanding of their own commitment practices. The construction of these rituals certainly represents an exercise of agency on the part of marginalized social actors, but the participants themselves frame their practices in personal terms, rather than as political acts.

Chapter 3 shifts to the perspective of same-sex couples who consider their relationships committed but do not use public ritual to express their commitment. I briefly review the intracommunity debate among gay and lesbian elites about the desirability of same-sex marriage as a political goal. Some of the couples in this study cited practical barriers to a public ceremony, but more often these couples expressed a generalized ambivalence or indifference toward marriage as a cultural model of intimacy, and a minority of the people who had not held a commitment ritual voiced explicit critiques of the institution of marriage. Some of these critiques focus on marriage's history as a patriarchal property relationship. Other critiques include questioning the necessity of sexual monogamy within intimate relationships or the viability of a lifetime commitment to one intimate partner. But most of the study participants who had not held a public commitment ritual did not express strong ideological objections to marriage, suggesting that the intracommunity debate over marriage may not be representative of how ordinary gay and lesbian couples think about marriage. I compare my findings to the research on heterosexual cohabitors and their beliefs about marriage. Although heterosexual couples face a different set of options when contemplating marriage, there are some parallels between the motivations of straight cohabitors and those same-sex couples in my study who chose not to enact marriage through public ritual. I also compare the couples in my study who did not hold public commitment rituals with those who did, and find some differences in terms of their general social characteristics but also more similarity than difference in terms of their connection to gay and lesbian communities, cultures and movements.

Chapter 4 explores how members of same-sex couples think about the question of legal marriage. I find virtually unanimous consent among same-sex couples on the need for legal recognition for same-sex couples, and most believe that such recognition should take the form of marriage rather than domestic partnerships or civil unions. Same-sex couples cite three main reasons for wanting legal recognition: the legal and financial benefits, principles of equality and fairness, and the symbolic importance of inclusion in the institution. These perceived benefits of legal recognition often seem to be closely related to one another, as when people state that receiving the concrete financial and legal benefits of marriage would establish their full equality with heterosexuals. Official law represents a powerful cultural resource to many same-sex couples. I argue that in the absence of official law, some same-sex couples are using cultural practices to construct a kind of legality for their relationships outside of official law. Culture is made to do the work that law would otherwise (supposedly) do. Religion, itself an alternative source of "law," often figures prominently in these cultural constructions of legality outside of official law. But the interest of many same-sex couples in the symbolic benefits of legal recognition implies that they attribute to the law of the state a special cultural power, the power to make gays and lesbians socially normal and culturally equal.

Chapter 5 reviews prominent public debates over legal recognition for same-sex relationships and compares the discourses generated in these debates to those of ordinary same-sex couples. Specifically, I analyze textual data from recent debates over same-sex marriage in Hawaii and Vermont. Across time and place, supporters of same-sex marriage consistently emphasize that legal recognition for same-sex couples is a matter of rights and fairness, whereas opponents invoke moral arguments against homosexuality and reject the framing of same-sex marriage as a rights issue. There is a noticeable disjuncture between the two sets of discourses, with supporters eschewing the language of morality and opponents casting marriage primarily as a moral issue. Ironically, same-sex couples' interest in the symbolic benefits of legal recognition is better acknowledged in the public discourses of the opponents than of the supporters of same-sex marriage, who prefer to downplay the social legitimacy conferred by law. And the perspective of same-sex couples who are skeptical about marriage is almost completely absent from these highly visible public debates.

In Chapter 6, I conclude by stepping back to consider what the case of same-sex marriage tells us about marriage generally. I argue that same-sex marriage is a challenging issue for many Americans because it threatens to demystify the institution of marriage. Many people conflate the cultural, religious and legal aspects of marriage. Marriage loses both its naturalness and its perceived sacredness when its cultural, religious and legal components are disaggregated. The chapter closes with reflections on whether legal marriage should be dismantled. I review feminist critiques of legal marriage and juxtapose their concerns with my research findings on the mutual implication of law and culture in modern marriage. I conclude that the specific case of same-sex marriage invites us to think more creatively about the possibilities for using both culture and law to create and sustain important personal relationships of all kinds, including but not limited to intimate sexual commitments.

The primary theoretical contribution of this book is to demonstrate the mutual implication of law and culture in marriage, and the way law and culture interact to invest marriage with meaning for both heterosexuals and homosexuals. The case of same-sex marriage demonstrates both the possibilities of constructing legality beyond or outside the law of the state, and the considerable cultural power of state law. The mutual implication of law and culture is evident in non-gay people's reactions to same-sex marriage as well. In particular, the opponents of legal same-sex marriage often base their arguments on morality, refusing to separate the religious and legal aspects of marriage, and recognize and fear legal marriage's potential to endow same-sex couples with new cultural legitimacy.

In substantive terms, this book expands our understanding of gay and lesbian couples, the way they think about their relationships and the meanings and possibilities of commitment, and their aspirations or ambivalence toward the institution of marriage. The study also enriches our knowledge of how non-gay citizens regard gays and lesbians and the possibilities for and limits to the social and legal inclusion of sexual minorities in American life. Taken together, the theoretical and substantive contributions of this book provide a new perspective on the specific policy question of same-sex marriage as well as on more general debates about the role of the state in recognizing, defining and supporting close human relationships of all kinds.

2   Doing the rite thing: cultural practices of commitment

Is not marriage an open question, when it is alleged, from the beginning of the world, that such as are in the institution wish to get out, and such as are out wish to get in?

– Ralph Waldo Emerson, *Representative Men*

On Valentine's Day 1999, Carol Moore and Judith Klein celebrated their six-year relationship in a commitment ceremony jointly officiated by a rabbi and a personal friend at a downtown Chicago synagogue. The ceremony contained many elements of a traditional Jewish wedding, but the ritual was also crafted to reflect the specific characteristics of the couple being united: same-sex, interfaith and feminist. Near the end of the ceremony, the rabbi invited ceremony guests to sign the couple's ketubah (Jewish wedding contract), which he called "a document which has far greater authority than any legal instrument," and noted that Carol and Judith had taken each other as spouses "not yet in accordance with the laws of this state, but according to a much higher authority, the loving and justice-proclaiming law of the living God." The ketubah listed several promises of mutual love and support and asserted the status of their commitment as a marriage, stating: "We make these promises intending our relationship to be treated as a marriage by ourselves and by all those we meet. This ketubah is evidence of our commitment to one another and should be construed by any government, court or public official as if the laws governing married persons applied to our relationship."

After their ceremony, Carol and Judith followed the lead of millions of newlyweds before them and flew to Hawaii to celebrate their honeymoon. The trip provided new opportunities (or challenges) for asserting their status as a married couple. Carol reported feeling momentary awkwardness at a luau when all newlyweds in attendance were invited to take the dance floor. Judith grabbed her hand and led her to the dance floor, where they joined about thirty heterosexual couples. "I was a little scared," Carol admitted, "but there was no way, if I hadn't done that I

26

would have felt like shit. Because we *are* newlyweds! . . . To have not done that would have been to take a step back. And, you know, there's no way." Then, later in the trip, the couple swung into crisis mode when Judith slipped and injured herself on a hiking expedition and was rushed to the emergency room of a local hospital. Carol described the tension that ensued in her interaction with a hospital staff member. "When I went into the emergency room . . . I went in and said 'my wife [is here],'" Carol recalled. "And she said, 'What do you mean, your partner?' And I said, 'No, my wife!' And I was a little pissed off that she wouldn't accept that. But then, as soon as it was time, I went in there just like anybody else would."

On a sticky midsummer afternoon later that year, friends and family gathered in a small church on the north side of Chicago to witness the wedding of Andrew Minnelli and Tim Daniels. In the entrance area outside the church sanctuary, guests were invited to sign the matte of a large multi-picture photograph frame, which would later be filled in with pictures of the ceremony and reception. Upon entering the sanctuary, guests were greeted by female ushers with elegant lavender programs while a pianist and two flutists played music selected by the couple. The program's cover contained a poetry quotation and the phrase "United in Marriage," followed by Tim and Andrew's names and the date.

Once the roughly seventy-five guests had been seated, a friend of the couple announced that no photography would be allowed during the ceremony except by the couple's professional photographer. The ban on picture-taking, which was reiterated on the back page of the program, was intended to protect the identity of the Roman Catholic priest who was performing the wedding in violation of his denomination's explicit ban on same-sex ceremonies.

The one-hour ceremony included many of the standard components of a Catholic wedding. Andrew and Tim, both in tuxedos, entered from the back of the sanctuary and proceeded to the altar accompanied by their six attendants. The priest greeted the assembled guests and said an opening prayer. Friends of the couple read biblical verses, including an Old Testament passage extolling the virtues of companionship (Ecclesiastes 4: 7–13) and a New Testament reading in which Jesus invites listeners to join him on the path of Christian faith (Matthew 11: 25–30). The exchange of vows and the blessing and exchange of rings followed the priest's homily. Next the congregation joined the priest in saying a blessing over the couple, Tim and Andrew lit a unity candle, and a friend led the reading of the prayer requests. The ceremony concluded with the recitation of the "Prayer of Jesus" (commonly known as the "Lord's Prayer") and a closing prayer and blessing by the priest, and the couple exited to recessional music and guests' enthusiastic applause. Afterwards, guests joined the couple at a downtown Chicago hotel for a formal dinner reception.

Reflecting on the event a couple of months later, Tim described an almost surreal quality to the ceremony. "The service itself I just found to be kind of like a dream," he remarked. "The reception was certainly real! But the service itself was something like a dream. I think I was in a state of shock that we were finally actually there. And this church was just filled with those people who had cared about us, and so many of our friends. It was sort of a magical time."

In this chapter I look at how same-sex couples use cultural practices to celebrate and enact their mutual commitment. Often these cultural enactments of commitment follow the dominant cultural script of weddings and marriage quite closely, despite the fact that same-sex couples face exclusion from the legal institution of marriage. Couples like Carol and Judith and Andrew and Tim draw upon the cultural resources of marriage quite explicitly in their efforts to define their commitments to each other. Other same-sex couples are less insistent on strict adherence to the marriage model, yet many of the cultural forms and assumptions associated with marriage permeate their cultural practices nonetheless.

In contemporary American society, romantic couples use a variety of cultural practices to signify their commitment, and sometimes to define that commitment as a marriage. These cultural practices include everyday behaviors, language choices and public or private events. Everyday practices that may signify commitment range from purely symbolic acts, such as wearing rings or other physical tokens of commitment, to practical activities that have a culturally shared symbolic meaning, such as living together or commingling financial assets. The realm of language offers many options for expressing the nature and degree of commitment. Members of couples must decide on terms for their partners (boyfriend/girlfriend? lover? spouse? husband/wife? significant other?) and their relationship (is it a "relationship," a "marriage," or something else?). And in the workplace or in a variety of social settings, people are confronted with questions about their marital status, and make choices about how to characterize their relationship in response. In addition, many couples use distinct occasions – ranging from private moments that include only the couple to large public events – to mark their commitment through some form of ritual.

Both straight and gay couples rely on these various cultural practices to signal their commitments. In fact, cultural practices are the primary means people use to assess the nature of couples' relationships, even in the case of legally married couples. Married couples do not carry around their marriage certificates as proof of their relationship status; instead, they safely rely on cultural markers such as rings worn on a certain finger and use of terms like "husband" and "wife" to signal that they are married. (Conversely, it is this primary reliance on cultural rather than legal markers of marital status that makes it relatively easy to conceal from others that one is married.) For same-sex couples, cultural practices (including in some cases religious practices) represent the main resources available for defining their relationships as marriages, since legal means are unavailable.

The social context of same-sex relationships inevitably colors the ways that same-sex couples use cultural resources to define their commitments. Part of this social context is the legal unavailability of marriage, and we will see that this lack of access to marriage as a legal status is reflected in the cultural practices of many same-sex couples, especially those who most closely embrace the marriage model for their relationships. For some couples, appropriating the cultural resources of marriage is a way to compensate for the lack of access to the legal resources of marriage. In addition, the lack of legal marriage influences how these couples describe their own cultural practices of commitment, such as the meaning of their public commitment rituals. Another aspect of the social context of same-sex relationships is the generalized social disapproval of homosexuality and homosexual relationships.[1] This disapprobation also influences same-sex couples' cultural practices of commitment, insofar as it sensitizes same-sex couples to issues of acceptance, inclusion, recognition and cultural equality. As a result of prevailing social disapproval of homosexuality and gay and lesbian people's awareness of this disapproval, cultural practices of same-sex commitment occur in contested cultural space: are these relationships deserving of social recognition? Are these commitments deserving of social support and approval? Are these couples in some sense equivalent to heterosexual committed couples? And, in the case of same-sex couples who embrace the marriage model for their commitment, should these relationships be viewed as marriages?

Language, private ritual and everyday commitment practices

Many same-sex couples use language, private rituals and everyday practices to express the depth and nature of their commitment. In terms of language, same-sex couples must make choices about how to refer to their mates and how to describe their relationship. I asked members of couples what terms they used to refer to their mates and their relation-ships. The most common term for mates was partner. Some study participants had other terms that were not drawn from the language of marriage, such as significant other, soulmate, life partner or honey. But the most common choice after "partner" was to use terms associated with marriage: husband, wife or spouse. The use of these marriage-related terms was somewhat more common among couples who had held a public commitment ritual (about half of these couples used such terms at least sometimes), but a significant minority of the couples who had not held a public ritual also made use of marriage-related terms. Likewise, about half of the couples who had held a public ritual and a quarter of the other couples said they would always or usually identify themselves as married if someone asked.

Choice of terminology is often influenced by social context, and sometimes by couples' comfort level with being out as gay or lesbian in various social settings. For example, several couples said they would use the terms husband or wife at home (sometimes in a lighthearted manner), but would present their mates to others as their partner. Dorothy Purnell, a 56-year-old African-American teacher, explained that she would usually call her partner Pam her wife when she was talking with her older lesbian friends, who had come of age in the heyday of butch/femme lesbian culture, but would otherwise refer to Pam with the gender-neutral term partner. A few of the study participants were closeted in their workplaces, and would call their partners their room-mates or housemates, but use more intimate terms in other social contexts. For Christine Pasminski, a 38-year-old white dentist, the separation between work and home language was pronounced; when patients inquired about her marital status she said she was single, but at home she referred to her partner Amanda as her wife. Other study participants described their strategic use of terms related to marriage roles, sometimes using marriage-related terms in a confrontational way. For example, Robbie Caputo, a 26-year-old white accountant, said he usually refers to his mate Alex as his partner, but occasionally uses the term husband when he wants to be clear about Alex's gender or when he wants to "piss people off."

Beyond language choices, study participants identified other cultural practices that symbolized their commitment, including the use of private rituals. Many of the couples who had not held a public ritual described private rituals they had done as a couple to celebrate their mutual commitment. These rituals bore some similarities to public rituals (for example, they often included an exchange of rings and vows), but involved only the couple. Gary Weaver and Jeff Muldoon, for example, purchased wedding rings together several years ago and conducted a brief private ritual for themselves under a tree in their favorite park. Susan Lemus and Bess Hardin also bought rings to exchange and constructed a private ritual to accompany the ring exchange. Their ritual included writing letters to each other describing their thoughts on commitment and going out for an expensive meal at a downtown restaurant. Although their ritual was private, the occasion marked a transition for the couple and the rings a public declaration of commitment. Bess explained:

> The ring part, we had decided that we wanted to wear the same ring, because we like rings and because of the symbol that that brings. And we wanted to wear it on our wedding-ring finger, even though they're not wedding rings, because that seemed important. I guess what I'm saying is that to society, that is an announcement of some kind, that if you wear a ring on that finger you have a relationship, you know? So the ring part was really the big change.

Beyond the private moment of the ritual, wearing the rings was an ongoing public symbol of commitment for Susan and Bess.

Several study participants who had not held public commitment rituals nonetheless viewed their relationships as marriages, and they pointed to other markers of commitment in describing these relationships, such as cohabitation or financial interdependence. Teresa Morton, a 54-year-old white artist, and her partner of seven years, Samantha, do not currently live together. Teresa inherited a lot of money from her parents, allowing her to rent a luxury high-rise apartment in downtown Chicago. Samantha is a school teacher with a relatively low income. This financial disparity has been an ongoing issue in their relationship. Five years ago, Samantha moved into Teresa's apartment, but she hated the building's atmosphere. After two years in the high-rise, Samantha moved out; at that point, Teresa helped her purchase a condominium in an outlying neighborhood and bought a car which Teresa owns but Samantha uses and maintains. Teresa also paid off Samantha's student loans. Although they see each other only on weekends and have not had a public ritual, Teresa considers their relationship a marriage. "I define it as a marriage," she remarked, "just by the nature of the financial commitment."

In a similar way, Dorothy Purnell considers her relationship with her partner Pam Jackson to be a marriage based on the nature of their commitment and interdependent lives. Dorothy and Pam live together in a home that Dorothy owns, and Pam's adult daughter and two children currently live with them. When I asked Dorothy whether she considered her relationship with Pam a marriage, she replied:

Yes, but married in the way that any committed relationship to me . . . married in this metaphorical sense, that when you're in a committed relationship, you've made very similar kinds of commitments that we associate, without the property attachments . . . so marriage just means to me that it's a relationship where people are sharing a life, so in that sense yes.

Dorothy and Pam's relationship constitutes a marriage in Dorothy's eyes, because she believes marriage should be broadly understood to encompass all relationships in which partners are "sharing a life."

In short, same-sex couples find a variety of ways to express and interpret their mutual commitment, including terms for their partners, private rituals, and everyday practices such as commingling finances or more generally "sharing a life." Many of the couples in this study, including couples who had not held wedding-like public commitment rituals, drew on some of the cultural resources of marriage to express their own intimate commitments. These resources include the language of marriage (terms for partners such as husband, wife or spouse, and affirmatively defining the relationship as a marriage), private rituals that incorporate elements of traditional wedding ceremonies (such as an exchange of vows) and everyday practices such as wearing rings. Other couples also use public commitment rituals to draw on the cultural resources of marriage in support of same-sex commitments. The rest of this chapter focuses on these public ceremonies. As highly intentional markers of same-sex commitment drenched in symbolism, these public rituals represent a visible and dramatic embrace of marriage as a cultural model of relationship.

Doing the rite thing: public commitment rituals

A few decades ago, the idea of holding a public commitment ritual might have seemed unusual, if not unthinkable, to the typical same-sex couple in the United States, but today committed gay and lesbian couples can hardly avoid making a decision about whether such an event holds interest for them. Many couples have gay and lesbian friends who have already participated in such rituals and they may have attended such events as guests. About half of the couples in this study who had held a public ritual had previously attended someone else's same-sex ceremony, and in some cases couples reported that these ceremonies had greatly influenced their own desire to have a ceremony and the way they planned their own ritual. Popular culture, especially television and movies, also increasingly depicts same-sex weddings, and in an increasingly positive or at least matter-of-fact way (Lewin 1998, 19–24). The newsworthiness of same-sex marriage as a public policy issue has prompted more news organizations to run human-interest stories on same-sex commitment rituals. Over 200 newspapers around the country now publish same-sex union announcements, and the *New York Times* recently ran a story on same-sex rituals in its style section, in part to speculate on the possible impact of these rituals on heterosexual wedding practices (Brady 2003). A small industry has sprung up to cater to the needs of same-sex couples planning weddings, evident in the rise of wedding fairs, advice books, websites and wedding-specific advertising of goods and services, all targeting would-be same-sex brides and grooms as a distinct market niche. Same-sex couples who consider their relationship committed now must confront the option of a public commitment ritual, even if they ultimately decide against one.

While all committed same-sex couples face the question of whether to have a same-sex ritual, female couples appear to be more interested in public rituals. There are no national data available on the number or type of same-sex couples holding public rituals, but there is considerable evidence suggesting that female couples have a greater likelihood of participating in these rituals than male couples. In my own recruitment of study participants, it was much easier to find female couples who had held a public ritual, and the clergy in this study who had done the largest number of same-sex rituals reported that the couples requesting rituals were mostly female. Some national surveys have found that lesbian couples are about twice as likely as gay male couples to report having had a commitment ceremony (Patterson, Ciabattari and Schwartz 1999, 350–352). Two-thirds of the couples who entered civil unions in Vermont during the first year of their availability were female (Solomon, Rothblum and Balsam 2004, 276).[2] Women were also more likely than men to obtain marriage licenses in San Francisco during the brief period in which the city issued them in early 2004 (Leff 2004). Female couples outnumbered male couples two to one in the first year of legal same-sex marriage in Massachusetts.[3] Taken together, all of this evidence strongly suggests that the majority of couples holding same-sex commitment rituals are female. This gender difference is all the more notable in light of estimates that the population of self-identified gay men is nearly twice the size of the population of self-identified lesbians in the United States (see Laumann et al. 1994, 292–301).

Several different factors likely contribute to this gender difference. Gender socialization may play a role: females are socialized from a young age to aspire to marriage generally and to look forward to the special day of their wedding in particular. (For an exploration of American culture's obsession with weddings, and the gendered nature of that obsession, see Ingraham 1999.) Some female study participants did speak about using their rituals to pursue their lifelong dreams of weddings and marriage, but so did some male participants. Another factor may be parenting status. Lesbian couples are somewhat more likely than gay male couples to have children living with them. According to US Census data, about 34 percent of lesbian couples had minor children in the home in 2000, compared to 22 percent of gay male couples (Simmons and O'Connell 2003, Table 4). This higher rate of parenting could contribute to the apparent gender difference in public commitment rituals if being a parent makes one more interested in publicly defining and celebrating one's partnership, perhaps as a way to create a sense of stability for current or future children, or for the co-parents themselves. A third factor may be cultural differences between the lesbian and gay male communities. Gay men may be less interested in the marriage model because gay male culture does not place a high value on sexual monogamy. Commenting on the gender difference in the Vermont civil unions data, historian John D'Emilio observed: "Marriage implies sexual monogamy. More of the gay male culture is built around sexual adventuring" (Bayles 2004).[4]

Among the couples in this study who had held a public ritual, the idea to have a ritual arose in various ways. Ten of the couples described how they reached the decision to have a ritual through mutual discussion, without one partner being the primary instigator or any formal marriage proposal occurring. Another ten couples reported that one of the partners had made a formal proposal to the other. And in the remaining five couples, there was no formal proposal, but one partner came up with the idea and advocated for the ritual within the relationship. Formal proposals were more common in female couples; almost two-thirds of the female couples reported a formal proposal, compared to only one male couple.

Some partners made their proposals in what could be considered a quite traditional fashion. Kim Pierson, a 37-year-old African-American administrator, made a formal proposal to her partner Brenda Davis several months after she had initially raised the idea of marrying. Wanting the proposal to go smoothly, Kim said she rehearsed it repeatedly with a sympathetic co-worker. Betty Freeman, a 57-year-old African-American bus driver, initially "announced" to her partner Mandy Walker that they would marry, in response to Mandy pushing her for a commitment. Dissatisfied with this approach, Mandy told Betty she required a formal proposal, and she eventually got one. The most elaborate proposal story came from the only male couple to report a formal proposal, Tim Daniels and Andrew Minnelli, whose wedding was described at the start of this chapter. Tim, a 37-year-old white fundraiser, orchestrated the proposal and kept Andrew in the dark until the last possible minute. Giving Andrew a time and place to be ready to be picked up, Tim arranged for a limousine to transport Andrew to a resort hotel where Tim was waiting, engagement ring in hand, in a room full of burning candles.

The timing of the ritual in couples' relationships varied greatly. The couples in this study have been together an average of eight years, ranging from a low of eight months to a high of thirty-six years. Public commitment rituals occurred, on average, about four years into the relationship, although the range was broad. One couple held their public ritual after only a few months together, while another couple used their commitment ritual to celebrate twenty-five years together. For most couples, the ritual occurred fairly early in their relationship; in two-thirds of the cases, the ritual happened within the first three years.

Once couples decide to hold a public commitment ritual, they tackle the planning process. The planning tasks they face do not differ greatly from many of the steps taken by heterosexual couples planning a wedding: finding a location for the ceremony and reception, finding a clergy member to officiate (if the couple so desires), drafting a guest list, making or ordering invitations, deciding on food and decorations, in some cases even registering for gifts. Perhaps the main difference in the planning process for same-sex couples is that they face the possibility of encountering homophobic reactions in their dealings with vendors and potential officiants. But while many study participants said they had worried about such reactions, most were pleased to find that their status as a same-sex couple was not an issue. A few couples mentioned that they hired event planners or relied heavily on friends or relatives to help plan their rituals, but most couples did the planning themselves. With very few exceptions, couples paid virtually all of the costs of the ceremony and reception themselves.

In putting together the details of the ritual itself, almost all couples drew upon written materials and the advice of others rather than trying to create the ritual from scratch. When a clergy member was serving as officiant, couples often used materials provided by the clergy as a starting point for constructing the event. Sometimes these materials were specifically tailored to the needs of a same-sex ceremony, but often they were fairly generic materials that would also be used in planning a heterosexual wedding ceremony.[5] Couples also consulted advice books on same-sex rituals, historical materials, and friends and relatives in putting together their rituals. Anthony Parisi, a 35-year-old white psychologist, held a commitment ceremony with his partner George Brodie after they had been together for two years. Anthony spent time researching the gay history archives in Chicago to find ideas for ceremony readings. Paul Colvin and Dwight Winfrey had been together thirty years when they held a "recommitment" ceremony at their church. (An earlier commitment ceremony, on their twenty-fifth anniversary, had not gone according to their plans, so they decided to try again in a more welcoming church environment.) Paul, a 63-year-old white bookkeeper, had been collecting historical materials on same-sex rituals in various cultures for some time, and drew on this file of historical examples to formulate the vows for their ceremony.

Ethan Levinson and Peter Tyler are white professionals in their 30s who became involved four years ago and had a ritual a year ago, just before relocating to Chicago from the West Coast. Ethan and Peter are not religious and knew they did not want clergy to officiate at their ceremony, so instead they asked friends and family to help them plan their ritual. Ethan had previously attended the ceremony of a female couple, which he described as "essentially a homemade ceremony," and this had made a strong impression on him and had influenced his approach to planning his ritual with Peter. In particular, he admired how this couple had chosen to replace standard wedding practices such as the use of bridesmaids and ushers with "meaningful expressions of support" from people close to the couple. Ethan and Peter's ceremony took place in a friend's backyard with two close friends officiating. The ninety-minute ritual featured instrumental and vocal musical performances, personal remarks by friends, recitations of poetry (including some written specifically for the occasion), comments by the couple (including Ethan's review of same-sex relationships throughout history), the couple's vows pledging lifetime commitment, and an exchange of rings.

A few couples described how they had very consciously set out to create a ritual that did not replicate traditional or straight weddings. Peggy Wong, a 34-year-old Asian nurse, and Anita Lindstrom, a 39-year-old white teacher, had their commitment ceremony at the six-year point in their relationship. Both women have strong religious backgrounds, and a total of five Christian clergy from various denominations officiated at their ceremony. "Church was the focus," Anita commented (perhaps understating the matter). Yet they opted to hold the ceremony in a restaurant rather than a church, and they took great care in planning the service to avoid the appearance that they were imitating a straight wedding. "We knew we didn't want a traditional wedding," Peggy explained, "we didn't want to imitate a wedding." Anita felt that "it ended up being fairly traditional," but noted that the couple "took a lot of care with the language" and the selection of readings to avoid an overly traditional approach. Like Peggy and Anita, Larry Clemens and Brian O'Toole sought to avoid a traditional wedding in constructing their ritual. Larry, a 51-year-old white counselor, and Brian, a 42-year-old white musician, omitted several standard wedding components from their ceremony and chose to call it a holy union rather than a wedding. "We didn't want to be copying a wedding," Larry explained, "and holy union said something different to us." The couple chose not to exchange rings, and avoided other practices they referred to as "stock wedding" material. "There's no pictures of us shoving cake in each other's face," Brian noted. "We didn't do that. I think we were both very intentional about not doing stuff like that."

However, most of the couples in this study did not voice concern about the issue of imitating straight weddings, and in fact incorporated many ritual elements that are clearly recognizable as "standard" wedding practice, at least in the US context. For example, only two couples chose not to use a clergy officiant, only two couples chose not to exchange rings and only one couple omitted a formal exchange of vows. There was a little more variation around other traditional practices, such as choice of setting for the ritual (ten of the couples held their ceremony in a setting other than a church or synagogue), or beginning the ceremony with one or both partners marching down the aisle, or having attendants. But overall, these events were clearly recognizable as wedding-like occasions as a result of their deployment of key ritual elements and symbols.

In fact, some people emphasized that their ceremony *was* indeed a wedding, and they made conscious efforts to reinforce this notion through choice of terminology as well as through the way they constructed the ritual. It was important to Tim Daniels that his ritual with Andrew Minnelli be a "wedding," not a mere "commitment ceremony." "It was very important to Tim, and it became important to me also, that this not be a commitment ceremony, that it be a wedding, a marriage," Andrew explained. In a separate interview, Tim confirmed Andrew's observation:

I'd always wanted to be in a marriage and I wanted to have a wedding. I never dreamed growing up that I wanted to have a union ceremony. I didn't want to have a commitment ceremony, I wanted to have a wedding. . . And Andrew pretty quickly adapted to that and started calling it that too, and interestingly enough, a number of people who before the wedding called it a commitment ceremony now call it a wedding, a marriage.

Sometimes the desire for a traditional wedding caught people by surprise. Brenda Davis is a 44-year-old white professor with a long relationship history. She and her partner Kim Pierson celebrated their commitment in a public ritual after a year and a half together. Brenda had been in college in the early 1970s and had been quite active in the feminist movement. "I was a pretty strong feminist, and I liked to think of myself as a radical lesbian on occasion back then," she noted. She conceded that at earlier periods in her life the idea of a wedding ritual would have seemed unappealing if not silly. But in planning her union ceremony with Kim, she found herself drawn to the traditionalism of weddings and marriage:

It was unclear to me that I wanted a traditional wedding . . . until I started really planning it, then I really wanted a traditional wedding! And the more traditional it got, the more I liked it. And it was just incredible. And there was a part of me left over from the 70s that said I shouldn't like that, but there was enough part of me in the 90s that said, "Fuck it, if I like it, that's what I'm going to do!" So I had that little kind of political discussion with myself at one point, and then it just went away.

Later in the interview, Brenda returned to this idea, commenting: "Toward the end, I was buying fake Lily of the Valley to put all over the place, I mean to that extent! If you had told me twenty years ago that I would do that, I would say you're crazy!"

Whether couples set out to construct a "traditional" wedding or a more innovative ritual, whether the event occurred in a religious or secular setting, and whether or not clergy officiated, many of the rituals shared core components and invoked similar symbols to express the event's purpose and spirit. Spatial arrangements tended to be quite similar, regardless of the kind of space used for the ritual. There was usually a central area toward the front of the space where most of the ritual activity occurred. In formal religious ceremonies this was the area in front of the altar, but even informal or non-religious rituals were characterized by such a spatial arrangement. In many cases the ritual formally began with the entrance of the couple into the ritual space and their procession (often down an aisle through the gathered guests) to this central area in front. Sometimes the couple made this entrance procession together, sometimes each entered individually, and other times each entered accompanied by other significant parties, such as parents, siblings or close friends. If an officiant participated in the ceremony, that individual in some cases entered with the couple but in other instances waited for them at the front of the space. In a minority of cases the ritual included attendants, and these people would also generally participate in the entry procession. Guests were generally seated together facing the central front area of the space. In most cases, the ritual concluded with the couple's exit from the front area, possibly accompanied by the officiant, attendants or other participants in the ritual.

With only a few exceptions, couples incorporated friends or relatives as active participants in the ritual. Most often this participation took the form of readings or musical performances of some kind. Readings might be secular or religious, and in some instances people composed poems or remarks specifically for the occasion. Common themes invoked in the readings included the meaning of love, commitment and covenant. Friends and relatives also participated by leading meditations, conducting specific ritual acts of various kinds, or simply standing in an honored position as witnesses to the event. In one ceremony, the couple involved all of their guests in the ritual by inviting them to come forward individually, light a small candle from candles held by the couple and express their wishes for the couple.

Visual cues attested to the solemn and celebratory spirit of the occasion. Flowers, candles and formal programs were often used to set the tone for the event. One female couple who held their ritual in a party tent set up in their backyard displayed various personal objects that held special meaning for the couple on a table near the front of the space. In many cases, clothing played an important role in signaling the importance of the event. Most couples chose fairly formal attire for themselves. Among female couples, common attire included tuxedos and formal bridal gowns (although veils were usually omitted). Many women chose somewhat less traditional attire, but without sacrificing a sense of formality. For example, several women chose to wear calf-length dresses (often in a shade of white or beige) or tailored pant suits. Male couples generally opted for suits or tuxedos. There was a notable gender difference in the choices couples made about attire: all of the male couples in this study chose to remain within the confines of gender-normative attire for their public rituals, whereas some female couples did not. In about half of the female couples, both partners wore traditionally female or gender-neutral attire, ranging from kimonos to dresses to wedding gowns. But in the rest of the female couples, partners wore attire that hinted at male and female gender roles. In these cases, one partner wore a dress or other traditionally female outfit while the other wore a pant suit or tuxedo. In one case, both members of a female couple wore tuxedos with pink bow ties. A few female participants commented laughingly that nothing, not even their own wedding, would get them into a dress, but in general most couples in which a partner chose gender-atypical or masculine-appearing attire did not seem to consider this choice particularly significant or worthy of discussion.

Taken together, the prevalence of formal marriage proposals and gender-complementary or butch/femme attire among the female couples suggests the presence of gender-role dynamics within some female couples, at least with respect to the cultural practice of constructing a commitment ritual. In fact, in every case in which one female partner chose "masculine" attire and the other chose traditional "feminine" garb, a formal proposal of marriage had occurred and it was the masculine-attired partner who had proposed to the feminine-attired one. There is a long and colorful history of butch/femme roles and images in lesbian cultures in the United States. In the 1940s and 1950s, the emergent lesbian bar culture, dominated by younger and working-class lesbians, virtually required all lesbians to choose a role and enact the corresponding image, regardless of whether this role felt natural or comfortable to them (Faderman 1991; Kennedy and Davis 1993). With the rise of lesbian-feminism in the 1960s and 1970s, butch/femme roles and images came to be viewed as politically incorrect for their seeming reproduction of oppressive gender roles, but butch/femme made something of a comeback in the late 1980s and 1990s, albeit with an ironic distance on the part of some adherents and a conscious recognition of the plasticity of gender and sexual roles rather than an uncritical acceptance of their meaning (Faderman 1991, 263–268; Crawley 2001).

Given this cultural history of butch/femme within lesbian communities and cultures, what should be made of the appearance of masculine and feminine roles in the construction of commitment rituals by some female couples? For some couples, the roles displayed in the construction of these rituals seem to correspond to roles the couple assumes in their daily life together. In the study sample, there are two female couples, both working-class, who appear to have clearly defined "male" and "female" roles within the couple. These couples use the terms "husband" and "wife" and appear to follow traditional gender roles in areas such as household division of labor, with the "wife" or "femme" partner taking on a disproportionate share of household tasks and child-rearing duties (both couples have minor children in their households). But there are other female couples who assumed gendered roles in their rituals but do not seem to have clear gender roles in their daily life. Their deployment of gender roles in the context of their ritual practices is more difficult to interpret. Adoption of gendered practices may sometimes be a self-conscious, ironic move intended to highlight the disjuncture between the traditionalism of weddings and the non-traditionalism of two women marrying, but none of the couples described their choices in this way. Alternatively, some female couples may have felt that wedding tradition suggested or even compelled such gendered practices and images. This interpretation is reinforced by the fact that couples who chose clearly gendered roles or images for themselves in the ceremonies were also more likely to assign gendered roles to other ceremony participants. For example, several of these couples designated friends as "best man" (often actually a female) and "maid of honor" rather than creating more gender-neutral roles for such participants. As anthropologist Ellen Lewin (1998, 247) observes in her study of same-sex rituals, these gendered attire and role choices may reflect the desire to assert the event's authenticity as a wedding. But Lewin's research findings, like my own, suggest that it is only women, not men, who see gender-complementary roles as a resource in creating and asserting authenticity.[6]

Besides readings and music, the most typical components of the commitment rituals included blessings and prayers of various kinds, officiants' remarks or homilies, exchanges of vows and rings, and a statement of community support for the couple. Many couples also included elements such as a wine ceremony or the lighting of a unity candle. Several couples chose to incorporate traditions into their ritual from other religious or ethnic backgrounds. For example, several non-Jewish couples used the Jewish custom of breaking a glass with their feet to signal the end of the ritual. Others used Native American blessings and rituals, Hebrew blessings or Mexican rituals. It is difficult to say whether this sort of ethnic or religious bricolage is more common in same-sex rituals than in heterosexual wedding ceremonies. Commenting on heterosexual weddings, Ronald Grimes notes: "It has become fashionable not only in alternative weddings but also in standard ones to peek at other ways of marrying" (2000, 209). According to Grimes, couples of all kinds are increasingly eager to incorporate ritual elements from other cultures into their ceremonies. But it seems likely, given the lack of civil and often religious recognition for same-sex rituals, that gay and lesbian couples might feel an even greater freedom to roam outside their own ethnic or religious traditions and practices in constructing their ceremonies.[7]

Same-sex rituals as meaning-making activity

A core of consistent themes emerged in study participants' descriptions of the motivations and meanings associated with their public rituals. The rituals represented for many an opportunity to communicate the depth and nature of their commitment both to their partners and to family and friends in attendance. Often participants framed this commitment in the familiar terms of what Swidler (2001) calls the romantic love mythology, a cultural resource for couples of all kinds. But participants also spoke forcefully of their desire to use public ritual to communicate the reality of their relationship and their commitment to others, as well as to assert the fundamental sameness or equality of their relationship with heterosexual marriages. Public rituals also provided some couples with a vehicle for achieving a sense of inclusion in important traditions and continuity in personal life trajectory. Very few participants spoke about the political nature of these events, although some appreciated them as a chance to improvise on received traditions, to create something fresh. And several people found an opportunity for healing and validation in the rituals, viewing them as extensions of their lifelong process of coming out as gay or lesbian.

Romantic love mythology: one true love forever

In her book *Talk of Love* (2001), sociologist Ann Swidler examines how contemporary middle-class Americans talk about love and relationships. Through close examination of interview data, she unearths a seeming contradiction. Most people alternate between two diametrically opposed ways of talking about love. Swidler calls these two forms of love talk the romantic love mythology and prosaic-realism. The prosaic-realist view-point regards love as a gradual, sometimes accidental, process, and the chosen love object as one among many possible loves. Prosaic-realism emphasizes that love is hard work, requiring compromise and flexibility, with no guarantee of long-term success. The romantic love mythology, by contrast, is the stuff of movies: love at first sight, one true love for every person, and love that lasts forever and overcomes all obstacles. Swidler argues that the romantic love mythology retains cultural currency despite its seeming implausibility because it helps people make sense of the powerful institution of marriage. Marriage, after all, asks people to choose a single partner for the rest of their lives, with the confidence that this partner is their destined mate and that their love will last forever. While the prosaic-realist view of love resonates with most people's lived experience of intimate relationships, the romantic love mythology offers a way to conform their understanding of their intimate commitments to the institutional requirements of marriage.

Gays and lesbians are exposed to the same dominant culture as everyone else, and romantic love mythology continues to permeate contemporary American culture, even in the face of high divorce rates, declining marriage rates and the competing discourse of prosaic-realist love (Illouz 1997). Thus it is perhaps unsurprising that many same-sex couples draw heavily on the romantic love mythology when they attempt to explain the significance of their same-sex commitment rituals. In particular, many study participants described their motivations to have a public commitment ritual in terms of their desire to celebrate having found their one true love. In addition, several participants explained that their ritual represented an attempt to both celebrate and enhance the permanence of their intimate partnership.

Reflecting on the meaning of her commitment ritual with her partner Amanda, Christine Pasminski noted that the ceremony affirmed an existing commitment, rather than creating a new one. Christine recalled the mutual attraction and commitment between her and Amanda as sudden and decisive: "Really from the first time we went out there was no question this was the person we would be with for the rest of our lives. We never questioned that, ever. I don't know if that's unusual." Abby Souter, a 43-year-old white office manager, described her immediate attraction to her partner Sarah Robbins, with whom she has had an eleven-year relationship. "It was like, the moment I met her, oh my God!" Abby recalled. Abby explained her desire for a public commitment ritual as part of her larger desire to have one "special person" in her life. "Sarah was that person in my life," Abby remarked, "that I wanted to spend the rest of my life with, and experience all these different things with, so I asked her if she would be a part of my life, my partner, my life partner. And she said yes, eventually!" Because of disappointments in earlier relationships she thought would last "forever," Sarah was initially skeptical about the idea of a public commitment ritual, but after two years together her doubts subsided and they held a ceremony.

Like Sarah, Ken Glascott had begun to question the mythology of "one true love" before he met his current partner William. Ken, a 38-year-old white actor, had been in a series of short and unsatisfying relationships with men prior to meeting William, a 39-year-old white architect. "I was actually to the point in my life that I'd kind of given up on the fantasy of the life partner," Ken admitted, "and . . . I kind of tried to avoid thinking about it a lot, I just kind of put it out of my thoughts, because I'd pretty much resolved to myself that that just wasn't in my life cards to end up that way. So when I met William, it was pretty much, it just kind of went 'boom!' and within a week I think we started talking about a wedding." Ken remembers his new relationship with William wiping out any interest in other men: "It was an instant I'm-not-going-to-date-anyone-else. And it wasn't even verbalized or insisted on in any way, we just spent part of every day with each other . . . every day that we were in the Chicago area, we would see each other in the morning, or the evening, or part of the day, and it involved a commitment on both of our parts . . . We were pretty much inseparable, and it has remained that way." In the same interview, William gave a similar description of his response to meeting Ken. Prior to the current relationship, William had been with a man for seven years, but that relationship had started as a friendship and evolved gradually. In the prior relationship, William said, he "never really had that knowledge . . . that you knew there was a connection, you knew there was someone special, and you're just hit with it and then everything just falls into place automatically. And so that was how I knew that this relationship [with Ken] was correct."

Monique Dillon, a 41-year-old African-American security guard, proposed to her partner Carmen Ruiz after only four months of dating. When I asked Monique what had prompted her to propose to Carmen so early in their relationship, she responded: "It was something that just consumed me . . . I just knew that she, for the first time in my life I just knew that she was actually the one for me, that she was my soulmate, and I had never ever felt that way before in my life." Upon hearing this answer, her partner Carmen chimed in: "I guess there is love at first sight, huh?" Betty Freeman had been involved in many relationships and affairs with women over the years, but until getting together with her partner Mandy, she never felt seriously committed to another woman. When I asked Betty about the decision to hold a public ritual, she replied: "When I made the decision to go that far, I had really made up my mind that this is it, you know, this was really the one that I had been out there looking for all those years." For many couples who decided to hold a public ritual, the event partly represented an opportunity to celebrate having found what they believe to be their destined "soulmates" and life partners.

Another element of the romantic love mythology, the notion of a love that lasts forever, also features prominently in some people's accounts of their public rituals. Sometimes members of couples recall the desire for permanence as a specific motivation behind the decision to hold a public ceremony. Allen Lembas, a 51-year-old white salesman, married his partner Ricky Suarez in a small church service after they had been involved for six months. Allen had been in three short relationships with men since his marriage to his wife ended several years ago, but he was looking for more permanence and stability in his relationship with Ricky. Allen described the meaning of their ceremony in this way: "It just kind of put the frosting on the cake of the relationship, rather than just being so-called lovers or companions, it just gave it a special meaning. Gay couples, straight couples – relationships today just go like revolving doors sometimes. I didn't want it to be another revolving-door type relationship." Other participants echoed this yearning for permanence in their intimate life, and saw public ritual as a way to both celebrate and enhance relationship stability. Natalie Konstantos, a white 50-year-old social worker, refused to live with her partner Becky Rodgers until they had formalized their relationship through a public commitment ritual. With a heterosexual marriage behind her, Natalie looked to the ritual to create permanence in her relationship with Becky, stating: "The meaning of [the ritual] was to openly commit to each other, and make a plan for our lives, to stay together. That was the option, I mean, it was our option because we wanted to do it, because we wanted to make it permanent."

Sarah Robbins, a 41-year-old white graphic artist, was initially ambivalent about her partner Abby's desire for a public commitment ritual. Her relationship history made her fearful of being hurt again, yet she harbored some hope for a more lasting relationship. When I asked Sarah to describe the meaning of the ceremony for her, she explained:

I think some of it was for Abby, she wanted it so much, and I wanted her to know that I do care deeply for her, and that I am willing to make this commitment, so I think that was some of it. I think some of it also was, I needed to feel . . . even though she could walk out at any time, at least this person is giving me their commitment that this is more than just "we're having fun and it'll be as long as it'll be."

For Sarah, the ceremony represented not so much a guarantee of permanence as a signal that Abby shared her interest in relationship stability. Abby had a less cautious interpretation of the meaning of their ritual. "It was really along traditional lines," she explained. "That this was forever . . . as far as I'm concerned, as far as what my commitment was, that this was forever. I was in it for the long haul, for the good and the bad, I was there."

Monique Dillon also emphasized the notion of permanence in describing the significance of her ceremony with Carmen Ruiz:

It meant that I, this is somebody that I know is going to be there for the rest of my life, something I can count on, something I don't have to worry about. People have so many worries and concerns in their life. I don't know, after the wedding, after the ceremony I just felt that this was forever, this is going to be something that will last forever.

This sense of permanence was important to Monique partly because of her relationship history. She had been in several other relationships before getting together with Carmen, but in those prior relationships "something else was always more important to that person, more important than I was."

In fact, a number of participants commented on the significance of the ritual for marking their commitment as more serious and profound than past relationships. Martha Petrillo, a 43-year-old white consultant, had been in a number of relationships with women prior to getting together with her partner Diane Wilson, who had herself been married to a man for thirteen years until his death. Asked to explain the meaning of their ritual, Martha stated: "To me, it was a really huge commitment. I was very nervous. I really felt that even though I had been in a few more relationships than Diane had, with women at least, I really understood this to be very different, and that this was a real, major lifelong commitment for me." This comparing of the current relationship with past relationships suggests a need to assert the permanence of the current commitment in contrast to the instability of past involvements.

Members of couples who were relatively early in their relationship at the time of their ritual were the most likely to stress the idea that the ritual would create permanence in their relationships. All of the participants who described the ritual as a route to relationship permanence had been in their relationships for three or fewer years at the time of the ritual. Couples who have a commitment ritual fairly early in their relationship and who look to the ritual as a source of permanence may be attempting to use the ceremony to resolve what sociologist Anthony Giddens calls the contradictions inherent in the "pure relationship." According to Giddens (1992), the reigning cultural ideal for intimate affiliations is the "pure relationship," which is a relationship "entered into for its own sake, for what can be derived by each person from a sustained association with another; and which is continued only in so far as it is thought by both parties to deliver enough satisfactions for each individual to stay within it" (58). The concept of the pure relationship somewhat parallels Swidler's concept of prosaic-realist love: both are ways of conceiving intimacy that acknowledge contingency and the ongoing possibility of relationship dissolution. The contradiction that rests at the heart of the pure relationship is that commitment is necessary to make the relationship last, but commitment is risky because the relationship might (and should) dissolve if either party becomes dissatisfied with it. Heterosexual couples can turn to legal marriage to relieve their anxiety about the uncertainty inherent in pure relationships (although the real effectiveness of marriage as a bulwark against relationship instability is obviously questionable). Same-sex couples, lacking access to legal marriage and its strictures, turn to commitment rituals in part to try to relieve the same anxiety, and it is the couples with the shortest relationship history as a foundation for their commitment that are most likely to perceive rituals as this kind of cultural resource. Concerns about relationship stability appear less pressing for those couples who have been together many years at the time of their rituals. These longer-term couples are less inclined to invoke the "forever" element of the romantic love ideology in accounting for their participation in a public commitment ritual.

Some ritual participants described their ceremonies as bringing a sense of relief, an ability to relax in the security of the relationship. When I asked Brenda Davis to describe the effect of her union ceremony on her relationship with her partner Kim, she described such a sense of security and well-being:

It felt different to be married. We talked about it, we're married now, it just feels different. It was like that [book] title, "Waiting to Exhale," I felt like I got to exhale. Like I was married now and I didn't have to do all that, whatever I had to do before I was married. And it kind of relaxed me in a way. I was very happy. I got permission to be happy in a way that I hadn't been happy up till then. It felt good to be in a couple. I think it changed, in that I no longer questioned anything about the relationship.

Sarah Robbins also reported this kind of qualitative change in her relationship with Abby after their union ritual. "I did feel more comfortable, I felt a little more settled," she explained. "And I felt like it was more real, this is a serious relationship."

And just as these rituals sometimes have the power to bring a sense of relief or security to committed couples, the memories of the ritual were perceived as a resource to sustain partners and their families through difficult times. Ethan Levinson and Peter Tyler candidly shared with me that their relationship had been under some stress recently, and both agreed that the memory of their ceremony had provided comfort during "harder times" in their relationship. Ethan remarked, "If we hadn't had that, there would still be things to look back to about why we're together and everything, but having that most meaningful and perfect day is really something to think back to." And Betty Freeman offered poignant evidence of how the memories of ritual can sometimes sustain family bonds in difficult times, describing how her partner Mandy's 11-year-old daughter, who lives with the couple, would sometimes close herself in her bedroom and watch the videotape of their ceremony if Betty and Mandy were having an argument.

Reality and equality

When Sarah Robbins commented that her relationship felt "more real" after her commitment ritual with Abby, she echoed the sentiments of many study participants who emphasized the notion of wanting a ceremony to make their relationship "real" to others, to impress others with its seriousness, and to more firmly establish the couple's identity as a couple and a family. Gerry Halloran and Heather Pryor are an upper-middle-class white suburban couple who had a commitment ceremony after four years together. Heather, a 43-year-old writer, explained that the ritual was mainly for the benefit of their friends and family, since the couple had already exchanged rings earlier in their relationship and already felt deeply committed to each other. "So [the ceremony] is more, to me, a confirmation in front of the people we cared about that this is real, we're committed to each other, and I think that's what it accomplished," Heather commented. Judith Klein and Carol Moore had their ceremony after six years together, and Judith felt that the ritual changed people's perception of them as a couple. She commented that "I kind of see a difference in them perceiving us as 'these guys are a done deal, this isn't a joke, this isn't a phase, they had a wedding, they're serious.' There are people now who would perceive us as final, as firm, as solid." Kevin Forrest and Brad Schuster described the motivations for their ceremony, which took place after they had been together for about a year, in a similar way. Brad, a 47-year-old white communications executive, had been in a ten-year relationship that ended with his partner's death. He wanted his relationship with Kevin to be different, to be more recognized by others. Brad commented:

I wanted the ceremony so people would know we're a couple and would treat us like that. When I was in the other relationship, my friends would invite me, his friends would invite him, holidays we would go our separate ways a lot of the time, so nobody had to acknowledge the fact, and this way they had to . . . They treated us like roommates or friends, and this way they know we're a family.

Kevin, a 47-year-old accountant who had formerly been married to a woman and did not come out as gay until he was 40, agreed that the ceremony would help define the nature of their commitment for his family. "I thought it would be very nice for my family to acknowledge that we are a couple," Kevin remarked.

While much of the reality-making function of public rituals is directed at others, especially friends and family attending the event, couples also described the importance of these rituals for making their commitment seem more real and more serious to themselves. When asked about the meaning of her commitment ceremony, Linda Sanchez said that "it made me know I'm committed." Mandy Walker had been in two prior marriages to men before her relationship with Betty Freeman. She explained the meaning of her ceremony with Betty in this way: "Well, that was my first marriage as far as marrying a woman, and I took my vows to be very, very serious. And when I made that commitment with Betty, I took it to be that we were going to be together for the rest of our lives, no matter what, you know, through the good times and the bad times, we had to stick it out." For Brian O'Toole, his public ritual with his partner Larry symbolized a new level of commitment that the couple had reached. "I think it represented that the commitment had evolved," Brian remarked. "At least for me, it wasn't that I wasn't committed [before], it was just that I had been burned too many times and wanted to be sure. And so a sense of trust and readiness had developed that we could do that."

In addition to impressing upon others and themselves the nature and seriousness of the couple's commitment, some participants hoped their ritual would help friends and relatives see the essential equality of gay and straight committed relationships. Jacob Berger and his partner Joe Neufeld, together for twelve years, did not have their ceremony until nine years into the relationship. Jacob, a 34-year-old white entrepreneur, felt the ritual was a way to signal to others that their commitment was equivalent to that of a heterosexual marrying couple:

We knew we were going to spend the rest of our lives together. I think we sort of realized, we wanted to make a sort of public declaration regarding our committed relationship because we wanted people, in addition to the two of us, to realize that we were so committed to each other that we wanted to be together for as far as one can see when one gets married. I guess we wanted people to view our relationship on the same level as they would view a straight couple getting married.

Tim Daniels, who insisted on calling his ceremony with his partner Andrew a wedding, described same-sex rituals as a way to assert the fundamental similarity of gay and straight relationships. Embracing the normalizing potential of these rituals, Tim remarked:

I think we're at a time in our history where gay and lesbian people need to start standing up and saying we're no different from you, and if you get married and you have a wedding, that's what we want too. We just want the same thing. We don't want to separate ourselves out from the rest of society. I live next door to you . . . just because my partner happens to be same-sex has nothing to do with our lives. We all get up in the morning and go to work, we have lives that are very similar.

Diane Wilson echoed Tim's assertion that public commitment rituals are a way for same-sex couples to demonstrate their basic similarity to straight people. "I think it's important for people, if you are in a committed relationship, to stand up and say so in front of other people," said Diane, a 50-year-old white attorney. "Because, I think the more people that other people meet who are in these relationships realize that your lives aren't different – I'm talking about heterosexual people – that your lives aren't really different from theirs." Diane went on to talk about being out as a lesbian parent at her son's exclusive private school, where she and her partner were the only openly lesbian parents. "I think it's important for people to see that, yes, we have kids, we have dogs, we have cats, we have jobs, just like everybody else, and we have committed relationships."

The publicness of public rituals

The publicness of these rituals was a significant part of what made them work as cultural resources for the couples. Most obviously, the rituals were an opportunity to show friends and family that their relationship was "real," serious, stable, committed. But, somewhat paradoxically, the public witnessing of the commitment by others also made it more real and more permanent for the couple themselves. The comments of many couples suggest that the witnessing of the commitment by third parties is an important part of establishing the reality of the commitment, and the publicness of the rituals enhanced the rituals' perceived power to fortify relationship stability.

Becky Rodgers, a 39-year-old white store manager, described how the act of declaring her commitment to her partner Natalie in front of their circle of friends enhanced the reality and importance of the commitment: "It became much more a reality, and much more important, when I had to say those things in front of witnesses, and then it became much more of a commitment." Ethan Levinson also highlighted the importance of the public witnessing in his union ceremony with his partner Peter, commenting that "there is something very meaningful about a public commitment . . . without those people your relationship really can't exist."

In many cases, participants believed that the public witnessing of their commitment would strengthen their relationship and make it more difficult for the couple to break up in the future. In this respect, the public rituals represent what sociologist Howard Becker (1966) calls a "side bet," something of value that is staked on maintaining a consistent line of behavior in the future, thereby bolstering commitment. As Becker notes, such "side bets" are not always conscious and deliberate strategies, but are sometimes recognized after the fact as an incentive for maintaining one's commitment. In the case of public commitment rituals, couples may not consciously plan them as a kind of side bet, but retrospectively they may recognize them as such. Specifically, participants in public rituals come to the realization that they have staked their honor and the respect of their friends and family on remaining committed to their partner, and the cost of defaulting on their commitment will be to face the embarrassment of backtracking on that public declaration of commitment.

Kim Pierson alluded to this aspect of public ritual's power when she described how thinking back to her ceremony with Brenda had helped her get through difficult moments in their relationship:

Well, I guess it is part of marriage, because that's the one thing I keep thinking about whenever I think, God, this is too hard. It's like, wait a minute, I got married . . . We stood up in front of everybody and said we were going to work on this and try to make it last . . . I stood up in front of people and meant it when I stood up there, so it's something that you work on, always.

Peter Tyler, recalling the presence of his best friend's 75-year-old mother who had traveled a great distance to attend his ceremony with Ethan, half-jokingly confided: "When we've had fights and I think, oh, this is not going to work, I think of Mrs. Martin, and I think, how can I possibly go to Mrs. Martin, I had her come all the way to Seattle, and say it didn't work out?"

For some couples, the religious context of the public witnessing to commitment is significant. Claire Bruno, a 41-year-old white social worker, conceived of her holy union with her partner Sue Bruno (who took Claire's surname on their wedding day) as a kind of promise that the couple was making to their religious community. Claire explained:

If you make a promise to another person, and you break that promise, it's a bad thing. But to make a promise before God and the community of faith that you're part of makes that promise something that you owe not just to that person but to that whole community. It's a much more solemn and much more steady commitment.

In Claire's view, the religious context of the commitment deepens the significance of the public witnessing.

Some ritual participants envisioned an active role for those who had attended their ceremony in keeping the couple together in the future. Larry Clemens and Brian O'Toole had their holy union ceremony after three years of relationship. Larry felt that the publicness of their ritual was an important part of its overall meaning. "There's something binding about making a public statement," Larry observed. He went on to explain:

Part of what we're asking our witnesses, or guests, to do is to hold us accountable to this commitment, that if we were to have a difficult time and decided we wanted to break up, it's their responsibility to say to us, "Hey, wait a minute, you made a commitment and I can't let you walk out of that unless you have fully examined what you're doing."

So the binding force of the couple's commitment is enhanced by the side bet of the *public* ceremony. Although it may seem counterintuitive, this most intimate of decisions and commitments takes on its full reality and permanence for some couples only in the context of public witnessing and social support.

Tradition and growth

While most of the motives and meanings that participants attribute to their rituals are oriented toward their future as a couple, some participants also described more past-oriented motivations, including the desire to take one's place in larger traditions and the impulse to fulfill previously imagined aspects of one's personal biography. Christine Pasminski and Amanda Dimarco celebrated their commitment thirteen years ago in a small, intimate ceremony in their home, attended only by a priest and Christine's sister and her lesbian partner. Christine and Amanda did not let the relative rarity of such ceremonies at that time deter their quest to participate in traditions they found meaningful. "We had really decided that we wanted to make a commitment," Christine explained, "and knew that this was our life and that there was nothing else, and believed in the tradition of marriage and weddings and that kind of thing; so we just decided." Judith Klein also conceived of her ritual with her partner Carol Moore in terms of participation in tradition, viewing the ceremony as "validating our relationship as one of many of those out there in the world, in a way that we . . . understood was a really pretty traditional kind of thing. It was what we knew. We wanted to have one of those too!" Beyond an expression of traditionalism, her comment reveals a desire, also expressed by other ritual participants, to join the mythical collective of married people, and thereby to achieve a sense of normalcy and equality with straight married couples.

In some cases, participants described their ceremonies as the fulfillment of lifelong aspirations, and in a few cases those aspirations included an explicitly religious component. Janis Sobirov, a 28-year-old white teacher, saw her desire for a union ritual with her partner Cindy in the context of lifelong dreams of a religious wedding. Janis explained:

I always wanted to get married and have a wedding, and have a nice dress, and flowers, and a big party . . . When we met, we said we wanted to get married and have this formal ceremony where everybody could witness to it, the promises we made to one another, before the people and before God. That's very important. That's something we'd always talked about.

Whether projecting forward in imagining the couple's life together in the future or looking back to past dreams and longstanding traditions, most participants described the meaning of their rituals in highly personal terms. A number of participants situated the ritual event in the context of developmental or life-cycle processes generally, or as part of their ongoing "coming out" process as gay or lesbian.[8] Brenda Davis told me she felt like she was "letting go of that last little bit of homophobia" by having her ceremony with Kim Pierson. "In getting through this wedding, and doing it as publicly as we could, everyone from every part of our life in every way, we just came out, and pulled them all together to celebrate this, and they did," Brenda remarked. Tim Daniels also described his ritual with Andrew Minnelli as a growth experience and an extension of coming-out processes:

I think the wedding process helped us come a long way, both of us, in our growth in loving ourselves more. Andrew went through the whole process of coming out with his mom, coming out with his siblings. I don't think he ever would have done that, to tell you the truth, there had to be a real good reason for it. Because when I first met him, he said he had no reason to come out to his mother. That wasn't something at this point in her life she needed to know. So I think the whole thing kind of rolled out for us lots of different ways, that we loved ourselves more, and we kind of took our place in the world, as who we are. We stopped apologizing for who we are, to anybody. Andrew still was not out with a lot of his friends, and a lot of business associates and stuff like that. And over the year and a half that we were engaged, he started doing more and more of that. So I think it was just a really good growth experience for both of us, individually and as a couple.

Like Andrew, other ritual participants were also motivated by their impending ceremonies to come out to close friends and relatives. William Austin came out to his father in a letter about six months before his ceremony with Ken Glascott. Although his father's reaction was "a disaster" and he refused to attend the ceremony, William did not regret coming out to him after nearly two decades of silence. And in a single conversation, Gerry Halloran told her mother that she was a lesbian and that she was having a ceremony with her partner Heather.

A few participants described how their ceremonies represented a sort of "coming out" for friends and family as well as the couple themselves. Jacob Berger was dismayed that, as the event drew near, his parents had not invited their closest friends to his ceremony. "It became clear to me that they were completely closeted," he explained. With only three weeks remaining before the wedding, Jacob confronted his parents and insisted they invite some of their friends, and they agreed. George Brodie, a 41-year-old white dentist, felt that his family and friends became more open about his sexual identity as a result of his ceremony with his partner Anthony Parisi. George commented:

People got more comfortable, a lot more comfortable actually. And it actually prompted people to take steps of coming out themselves, not gay people but family and friends coming out about us or having gay family members. Within my family there have been conflicts about people who don't accept us. It prompted my family to take a more active role and not put up with that BS.

Other participants talked about the meaning of their ceremony in life-course terms without specifically referencing the coming-out process. For some, the idea of getting married and settling down represented a natural and understandable progression to the next phase of adult life. Kim Pierson explained that the idea of getting married would never have made sense to her when she was in an earlier phase of her adulthood:

I didn't feel the need to get married until I found the right person, and then I thought marriage sounded pretty damn good at that point. But when I was dating around, I was like, "Why would anybody want to get married? What's in it?" And I think just with age and with finding the right person, that part is gone and it's like marriage sounds pretty good, family sounds pretty good, and all of those things I didn't want sound pretty good now.

Kevin Forrest offered a similar interpretation of the appeal of same-sex marriage for some segments of the gay community, commenting that as you get older "you have a different perspective on life."

Men were more likely than women to frame a public ceremony as part of their coming-out process or, more generally, part of their development toward a more mature life phase. The role of the ceremony in the coming-out process was not something participants contemplated in advance of their ritual; rather, it emerged in the process of planning and enacting the ritual. Some women also spoke of their ritual as part of their coming out, but for male participants the ritual often marked a more clearly defined shift from one level of "outness" to another. Several male couples talked about the occasion of the ritual prompting them to come out to friends, co-workers and family members, and to shift into a new relationship with the wider gay male community. Prior to planning their ritual, these men had lived more closeted lives, choosing not to be out to co-workers, clients and close family members, including parents and siblings. Not coincidentally, some of these men tended to compart-mentalize the gay aspects of their life prior to entering the current committed relationship. For example, partners Tim Daniels and Andrew Minnelli told me (in separate interviews) that their relationship had led to a shift in the role of being gay in their individual lives and practices. "I basically led two lives," Andrew commented on his pre-Tim days, explaining that he had a daytime/work life and a nighttime/personal life, with no overlap between them. The occasion of their ceremony, however, prompted Andrew to tell friends, co-workers and family members about his gay identity and his relationship with Tim. And Tim commented that his relationship with Andrew had helped him to integrate his gayness into other parts of his life. Although he was out to his family prior to becoming involved with Andrew, Tim remarked that prior to his relationship with Andrew,

I still kind of saw being gay as something that I wanted to do after dark. You know, like go out to the bars, or go to bookstores. I mean, I was doing all kinds of crazy things in the world. I shouldn't say that. I don't mean "crazy," because I think the people that are there are there, and they're not crazy for doing it, but there's that element of danger that exists in all that.

When I asked Frank Pasternak, a 41-year-old white engineer, about his life prior to becoming involved with James Logan, he exclaimed, "Oh, I was a slut! I have to say I was very promiscuous." Later, Frank stated that he had decided to let go of some of his gay male friends because they were not supportive of his monogamous commitment to James.

Coming out and being out are central issues and lifelong processes for both lesbians and gay men, and both male and female study participants talked about their rituals in the context of their coming-out process. But men's greater tendency to frame their relationships and their rituals as part of their coming-out story is suggestive. While lesbians face some of the same decisions and pressures around coming out to co-workers, straight friends and family, gay men's coming-out process has an added dimension because it occurs in a somewhat different social context. Lesbians generally are not discouraged from forming committed relationships by other lesbians, nor are they regarded as anomalous when they do so; in fact, there is a stereotype within gay and lesbian culture of lesbians entering into serious relationships too quickly. (An old lesbian joke goes: What does a lesbian bring on the second date? A U-Haul.) Gay men, by contrast, must negotiate not only a straight society that may reject their gay identity, but also a gay male culture that they perceive as indifferent or even hostile to committed relationships, and that they themselves may have treated as a discrete, compartmentalized aspect of their lives in the past. Thus the idea of a public ritual as part of their coming out, or as a transition to a different relationship to gay male culture and to their own gay identity, may be particularly salient for gay men.

A few people also situated the proliferation of same-sex ceremonies within a narrative about the development or "evolution" of the gay community as a whole. Referring to the gay and lesbian community, Brenda Davis remarked: "I think we're evolving. As we become less homophobic ourselves, I think we're going to need those things, need the ritual and the validation." And Cindy Dahl, a 45-year-old white retail clerk who began her coming-out process in her early 20s, reflected on the changes she had seen over two decades in the community. "I've seen a lot of how the gay and lesbian community has evolved," Cindy remarked. "When I first came out, holy union wasn't too much around then. It's a bigger part of the gay life style." Of course, not all gays and lesbians interpret such trends as "evolution." Ethan Levinson and Peter Tyler mentioned some older male friends of theirs who came out several decades ago and found the idea of Peter and Ethan's ceremony "quaint," but "distasteful" on ideological grounds, a hopelessly assimilationist act. "There's also a generational piece," Ethan noted. "Being gay meant something wildly different when they were young."

The personal as political

Few ritual participants made any mention of overtly political motivations or meanings implicated in their deployment of the symbols of weddings and marriage. Anita Lindstrom did view her participation in a union ceremony with her partner Peggy Wong as political, but in terms of the politics within her religious denomination rather than in terms of broader cultural politics. Active in organized efforts to shift the denomination's position on gays toward greater acceptance and recognition, Anita commented: "I think it was also . . . for me, really making a statement . . . that we have the same blessing, that we get a piece of the tradition, of what the church has done for straight couples. So, I mean, it felt really political in that sense." Similarly, Jacob Berger, who married his partner in a traditional Jewish ceremony officiated by a Reform rabbi, felt it was "empowering" and "political" to have the people attending his ceremony sign the couple's ketubah, because this act created an obligation for their guests to support the couple's definition of themselves as married.

Anna Roth and Carrie Woodward were one of the few couples who described making any conscious effort to inject political meanings into their ritual. They decided to wear the rings they exchanged on the ring fingers of their right hands, to symbolize that their marriage is not legally recognized. They discussed with their minister the importance of making the point somewhere in the ceremony that their union was not legally recognized. In conversations with family members, they had come to realize that many of their relatives were unclear about whether same-sex marriage was legal in Illinois or elsewhere in the United States. Carrie, a 28-year-old white program director, drafted the text of the community blessing used in the ceremony. The first part of the blessing was a generic request for the assembled guests to support the couple in difficult times. The second part explicitly referenced the lack of legal recognition for the relationship, with the minister stating: "Because gay and lesbian marriage is not legal, there is no legal document that makes this commitment binding. The only statement that makes this ceremony represent a bond of commitment between Carrie and Anna is their standing in front of you today, making that declaration." Reflecting on the meaning of their ceremony, Carrie wove together many of the themes and motivations expressed by other study participants, while adding a political dimension:

It's kind of like about standing up in front of people and saying "this is my relationship, it's serious, it's about us being committed to each other, and it's the same as your marriage." And it was a political act, but it was also an emotional act to declare my commitment to Anna publicly, and to her. And that's what it meant, it's like, we're married!

For Carrie, the ceremony was simultaneously "emotional" and "polit-ical," a chance to express a serious personal commitment, to assert its equality to heterosexual marriages, and to challenge social conventions around intimacy and marriage.

Anita, Jacob and Carrie's comments on the political aspects of their rituals were exceptions to the rule. Most study participants did not talk politics when they talked about their rituals. Certainly it is possible to give a political reading to participants' interest in having their relation-ships be taken seriously, in having them viewed as equal to straight marriages, in establishing permanence in their relationships, in partici-pating in traditions that often exclude gays and lesbians, and in fur-thering their own coming-out process. But except for the few cases just described, participants themselves did not describe these events using the language of politics but rather in highly personal and sometimes psychological terms.

Same-sex rituals as cultural objects

Same-sex commitment rituals are what sociologist Wendy Griswold (1987, 4) calls cultural objects, or "shared significance embodied in form." These rituals convey meaning through what participants say and do within the ritual and through the deployment of a variety of symbols. Same-sex commitment rituals can be read or interpreted as cultural objects by examining the variety of specific meaning-laden elements that come together to constitute the event. The couple's vows, because these are often written by the couple themselves (some-times with the aid of the officiating clergy), represent the most direct statements made by the partners in the course of the ceremony. Other ritual elements, such as music and readings, various visual cues and the remarks of the clergy, also convey particular meanings about the significance of the event and the intentions of its creators. The various meanings packed into the cultural object of the ritual can be directly examined and compared to the formulations of meaning offered by ritual participants in the in-depth interviews. To interpret the "shared significance" captured in these events, I observed four commitment rituals in person and reviewed videotapes, audiotapes, transcripts and related artifacts (such as photos and programs) of the other rituals held by study participants.

Most of the ideas and sentiments captured in participants' vows are quite consistent with the descriptions of the ritual's meanings offered in the interviews. Generally the vows are rather generic, in the sense that they could just as easily appear in a heterosexual wedding ceremony as in a same-sex ritual. The vows almost always capture at least some aspects of the romantic love mythology. Typical elements include a pledge to support one's partner through good and bad times; the notion that one's partner is one's special love or perfect match (possibly destined by fate or God); promises of nurturance, support, sharing, help and availability to one's partner; attitudes of respect and honor toward the partner; honesty and faithfulness in all aspects of the partnership; and the notion of a lifetime commitment. Overlaying all of these specific pledges and sentiments are the general values of partnership, companionship and friendship.

The vows of Diane Wilson and Martha Petrillo, written by the couple, encapsulate many of these core themes. First Martha said to Diane: "Diane, I choose you to be my friend and lover. Your love and support have surrounded me like a warm breeze. I promise to be your friend, lover, and confidante. I will be here for you emotionally and spiritually as we grow and age together." Then Diane vowed: "Martha, building our life together has brought great joy and satisfaction to me. I promise to love and cherish you for the rest of my life. I will be faithful to you and try to be truly a partner in your life."

Frank Pasternak and James Logan, together for thirteen years, celebrated their commitment ritual after seven years together. Frank and James recited identical vows to each other, stressing their commitment to a nurturing lifelong bond. They composed their vows based on examples provided by their minister. The vows read: "I, (Frank/James), take you, (James/Frank), as my one true love, as my heart's companion, and spouse. I pledge to you my devotion as your partner in life, and honesty as your friend. I promise to respect and support your chosen life's work, and honor your individual needs and wants, a bond I will nurture with kindness, honesty, forgiveness and faith. This is my solemn vow."

The vows that seemed least typical or generic were those spoken by Betty Freeman and Mandy Walker. Whereas most couples' vows were carefully rehearsed, generally either memorized or read off of a written copy, Betty and Mandy seemed to give unscripted responses when the minister asked each of them, "Have you anything to say to your beloved?" Mandy told Betty: "I want you to know that this is the happiest day of my life, and I want to thank you for loving me, for being there for me, and we're going to have a beautiful life together, the love of a lifetime. And I'm here for you, through the bad times and the good times, forever. I love you." Then Betty told Mandy: "I've waited a long time to find the right one, and I know that you're the right one, because I feel it in my heart, and you've been here all the time." At the other extreme in terms of formality and traditionalism were the vows of Brad Schuster and Kevin Forrest: "In the name of God, I, (Brad/Kevin), take you, (Kevin/Brad), to be my mate for life, to have and to hold from this day forward, for better or worse, for richer or poorer, in sickness and in health, to love and to cherish, until we are parted by death. This is my solemn vow."

Same-sex vows are remarkable for how unremarkable they are. They contain no particular references to the couple's special situation as a same-sex pair; they could easily be incorporated into a standard heterosexual wedding. Regardless of their length, formality or originality, the vows consistently voice the same aspirations that participants described in the interviews, especially the desire for permanence and the assumption of new identities as spouses or life partners.

Some couples did use other components of the ritual to make at least oblique reference to their difference from heterosexual marrying couples. Most often they made such references through the selection of readings or music for inclusion in the ritual, rather than through more direct statements about the unconventionality or political implications of the event. For example, several couples chose Old Testament readings from the Book of Ruth and the First Book of Samuel, readings that describe intimate (but not necessarily sexual) commitments between members of the same sex – in the first case, Ruth and Naomi, in the second, Jonathan and David. Other couples chose non-religious texts that were not explicitly "gay" but could be given a "gay reading" (a selection from *Cyrano de Bergerac*, for example), and some used readings by gay or lesbian writers with explicit gay content or relevance (such as the poetry of lesbian poet Adrienne Rich or the prose of lesbian novelist Jeanette Winterson). As part of his prepared remarks in his ceremony with Peter Tyler, Ethan Levinson spoke about the status of same-sex love and relationships throughout the course of history. Many couples also chose music that could be given a gay reading, such as the song "Somewhere" from the musical *West Side Story*, which has lyrics that express yearning for a time and space in which love that is deemed socially unacceptable can be freely expressed. Some couples used recordings by gay-identified or gay-friendly musicians such as Melissa Etheridge and Sweet Honey in the Rock. Ken Glascott and William Austin made a definitive nod to their gay identity through the choice of a rainbow color scheme for their ceremony and reception. The rainbow colors are displayed on the gay pride flag and are recognizable as a gay symbol to anyone familiar with gay and lesbian culture.

By far the most explicit references to the couples' distinct identity as same-sex pairs, and to the potentially subversive cultural and political meaning of the rituals, came in the remarks of the officiants. Sometimes the couples were not even aware that the officiants planned to make such statements. Often these remarks focused on the injustice of the fact that the ritual was not accompanied by legal recognition of the union. One of the most striking examples of this kind of statement came from the rabbi who performed Judith Klein and Carol Moore's ritual. He called their ceremony "a profound political act, an act of resistance and defiance and dissent," and went on to state:

As a political act of liberation, this moment has its roots in the marches and demonstrations of the courageous women who fought for suffrage and the right to vote in the 1920s, and it has its roots in the sit-ins in the South in the 1960s. It has its roots in that solemn and sacred moment at Stonewall, and it has its roots in every act of courage and faith that have been milestones in the eternal struggle for liberation and freedom.

Other clergy also drew comparisons between the struggle for full recognition of gay and lesbian relationships and various historical oppressions. The Reform rabbi who performed the ceremony for Jacob Berger and his partner explicitly described the status of their union within Judaism and compared the current oppression of gays to the long history of the Jews, highlighting the similarity in the outsider status of Jews and gays. He also used their ceremony as the occasion to announce that his own congregation would soon be adopting a resolution to recognize the couple as part of the congregational family and establish a task force to address gay and lesbian issues within the congregation. One of the Christian ministers who officiated at the holy union ceremony of Peggy Wong and Anita Lindstrom noted that the couple, as people facing discrimination, had become adept at "living while waiting," and drew an explicit comparison to the plight of African-Americans who had learned to "live while waiting" during their struggle for full civil rights. This minister quoted from Martin Luther King, Jr.'s famous final public address, in which he assured his supporters that justice would arrive someday: "I've been to the mountaintop . . . And I've seen the promised land."

Other officiants discussed the obstacles faced by same-sex couples in a society that is mostly hostile to their relationship. In his homily on the meaning of love, the Methodist minister who officiated at the holy union ceremony of Frank Pasternak and James Logan stated:

The love between two men, the love between two women, in this culture, for some people, is not OK. And so what we have is people who love each other experience rejection based on that love. And if you look at the history of how people who love each other and are of the same sex have been treated, you will find parents have disowned their children, parents have institutionalized their children, people have taken their grandchildren away from their children, people have imprisoned them, castrated them, caused them to have electroshock therapy, even killed them. And they've done that in God's name. And they've done that in the name of love. And what I want for you to hear today is that that's not love.

He went on to extol the couple for choosing to love each other and providing an example of real love, not mere romantic infatuation, for their friends and family: "Frank and James, you have modeled for us love, and we thank you for letting us see it."

In my interviews with clergy, some explained their approach to addressing the political dimensions of these ceremonies within the ritual. The Unitarian minister who officiated at Anna Roth and Carrie Woodward's ceremony told me she raises this issue with couples in pre-ceremony counseling sessions and gets a range of responses:

I do ask same-sex couples whether they want anything of a political nature in the ceremony, whether they want it acknowledged that this is not your traditional wedding, or whether they just want to treat it like any wedding and go forward. And I get a mix of responses. I frankly cannot recall *any* couple that has said, "This is a political issue for us, we're doing this because we feel that we should have the right to get married, God damn it, so we are." Some people, you know, comment on it, are aware of it, but pretty much universally the reason people want to get married is sort of the standard reason people want to get married. They want to spend the rest of their lives together and they want to make that commitment in front of their community, in front of their families and friends, or even just to one another but have it witnessed. They want that statement to be made clear in some ritual kind of way, and it rarely feels particularly different in intent than the straight couples. Sometimes people say, "No, this is not political, we don't want you to talk about it, we just want you to do it." Sometimes people say, "Yeah, say something about what it means for two people of the same sex to be getting married, and this is going to be on people's minds so you may as well acknowledge it." And, yeah, it's not unusual for me to say something that acknowledges that this is a brave act, that is saying in the face of laws and prejudices that yes, who we are is OK and this is something that's worthy of honoring, but I can't say that I've ever made a big sort of political point about it . . . I've never had the experience where the politics of it have been uppermost on people's minds.

By contrast, the MCC minister who performed the union ceremony of Allen Lembas and Ricky Suarez told me he routinely includes comments about the social justice aspect of the event in his welcoming remarks at the start of the ritual:

A large part of my welcome and opening statements talks about how this is, not only is this a holy union, but it's also a statement of justice, because of the fact that society and other churches don't recognize gay and lesbian weddings, that what we're doing here today is a statement about what we believe in justice-wise. And I talk about that because often they have, of course they have heterosexual friends present and visitors, and I just want to point out that fact to them, and remind them what they're doing.

In this instance, the minister's comments are aimed primarily at heterosexual guests, but also serve as a reminder to the couple themselves of the larger social significance of their public declaration of commitment.

These public commitment rituals are cultural objects that combine highly traditional and overtly political content. The direct statements made by ritual participants in the form of vows tend to express quite generic sentiments and promises, indistinguishable from typical heterosexual wedding vows. Readings and music are sometimes used to symbolize the oppression faced by the couple or to highlight their sexual identities, but it is the officiants rather than the couples themselves who inject the most overtly political content into the rituals.

The officiants actually inhabit a somewhat ambiguous position with respect to these rituals, part co-creators of the cultural object along with the couple, part receivers of the cultural object, insofar as they often try to be quite open to letting the couple decide what the ceremony will contain; they, like the guests, may have their own reactions to the resulting cultural object. Some clergy confided that they personally questioned some of the choices couples made in constructing these rituals, but they did not want to impose their own views and preferences on the couples. One pastor of a Metropolitan Community Church[9] (MCC) congregation expressed his frustration with what he saw as slavish adherence to (heterosexual) wedding traditions: "Even in gay and lesbian couples, there's a tendency to say, 'Oh, here's how it's done.' There's supposed to be this traditional walking up with the parents, and so forth. And I say, 'You know, there are no sacred cows, you can do anything you want.'" Another MCC minister, who had performed over fifty same-sex commitment ceremonies, observed that many female couples seemed to gravitate to gendered roles in planning their ceremonies:

I try to indicate that they need to be however they want to be, and one will show up in full bridal regalia and the other one's in a tuxedo. And while I'm willing to do that, for me personally that's really stereotyping things, that one clearly has to be the bride and the other clearly has to be the groom, you know? We've been liberated, we're freed, and let's think about this on an equality level or whatever, but I must say . . . it often isn't, it's not an equal thing.

This minister also expressed concern about same-sex couples' tendency to spend large amounts of their savings on having an expensive, formal ceremony and reception. "I wish the couples could understand," he commented, "that if you had pizza and beer in your living room, but it was a ceremony, that God would still be there, that it would still be blessed, that it would still be as meaningful as if you save for three years and blow a wad of money that you can use on something else."

So the officiating clergy are co-creators of these rituals, having considerable input into their content and often taking the opportunity to highlight the political significance of the event. But at the same time they are also among the receivers of these cultural objects, and as such they form their own opinions and reactions to these events.

The reception of same-sex rituals: responses of guests

If all cultural objects have both creators and receivers (Griswold 1987), the people who are most clearly the receivers of the cultural object of same-sex rituals are the friends and family who attend these rituals. I rely primarily on the accounts of the couples and the clergy to gauge guests' responses to these events, supplemented by my own observations of the rituals, both in person and on videotape. What the couples tend to highlight in particular are the feelings of support and affirmation they received from their guests. Many couples related with delight how they were pleasantly surprised at the outpouring of emotion they saw from their guests, particularly their straight friends and family. Jacob Berger described the heightened emotions that characterized his ceremony with his partner Joe three years ago:

People to this day – Joe's parents' friends – to this day talk about our wedding. People who weren't there come up to us and say, "I've heard about your wedding"! Because it was really heartfelt. People say that they had never been to a ceremony where there was so much feeling, and so much emotion, and so much love, not just between the two of us, but everybody there was so supportive . . . people were crying. It was this major thing!

Judith Klein recalled watching the video of her ceremony with her partner Carol and being struck by the emotion she saw on her parents' faces: "We were looking at the video, and my parents were *genuinely* smiling, and *genuinely* walking me down the aisle, and not uncomfortable, because they can be very uncomfortable people, and none of that was happening."

Others pointed out that straight guests seemed to be particularly affected by these rituals. "The most reactions we've had have been from the straight people who were there," Gerry Halloran commented. Her partner Heather concurred. "They're the ones, when we see them, they always bring it up," Heather observed. "That was so cool or neat. 'Romantic' is one of the words they use." Heather speculated that their ritual made a particular impression on the straight guests because it seemed unfamiliar to them: "The straight people, it was like it almost meant more to them than just a 'normal' wedding. Like it was something really unusual and special, and it was the only one they'd ever been to." Peggy Wong made a similar observation about the impact of her ceremony with Anita Lindstrom on the heterosexuals who attended:

Heterosexuals that had never been to a holy union ceremony of a committed gay or lesbian couple, I think they were really very touched. Just because it was untraditional, they could not anticipate what was coming next. The words of things that were read were different. I remember [Anita's] aunt saying that the words just meant so much more. Heterosexual people saying that it just meant so much more, because they know that we are up against a lot as a lesbian couple.

In Peggy's view, it was the novelty and unpredictability of the ritual, as well as the obstacles facing the couple as lesbians, that made the ceremony particularly moving for some straight guests.

Ethan Levinson and Peter Tyler described how the tears began to flow near the beginning of their ceremony and many guests continued to cry throughout. "Many, many people who came have told us since that this was the most beautiful ceremony they'd ever seen," Ethan noted. And Peter's mother confided afterwards that she had been especially moved. "My mother came up to me afterwards," Peter said, "and had a very difficult time putting it into words, but basically she said, 'This was so much more moving than your sister's wedding.'"

Of course, weddings are often emotionally charged events for both the marrying couple and their families and friends, regardless of the couples' sexual orientation. But participants' repeated emphatic comments about the high level of positive emotion that characterized their ceremonies suggest that same-sex events may be different in degree if not in kind when it comes to emotionality. The comments also indicate that same-sex couples value this public display of affirmation and goodwill. Some couples may attach significance to emotional display as a signal of the ritual's success. The couples themselves may not be completely objective in their assessment of the distinctiveness of these emotional displays, so it is interesting to note that one of the clergy I interviewed, a Unitarian minister who routinely performs both straight and same-sex weddings, also commented on the difference. She said she saw an "added sweetness" in the same-sex ceremonies, noting that "there's something very lovely about a wedding and people's family being supportive, but there is a particular quality about same-sex couples being there and having their families there, that affirmation and community support has a kind of special power to it that's particularly moving."

Swidler (2001) identifies love's heroic ability to overcome obstacles as one of the components of the romantic love mythology, but notes that most couples no longer face serious obstacles in their choice of marriage partner. Taboos against marrying outside one's class, race or age range have largely fallen away, stripping decisions to marry of possible heroism. But the taboo against partnering with someone of the same sex remains. Perhaps guests' highly emotional and enthusiastically supportive responses to same-sex rituals reflect a recognition that these are couples who do still face social resistance to their love. Guests may embrace the rare chance to celebrate this part of the romantic love mythology and to throw their support behind the romantic underdogs.

Of course, joyful support is not a universal response to these events, and the guests who actually attend same-sex rituals are a self-selected group who are predisposed to show support. When I asked study participants to describe people's reactions to their ceremonies, they consistently chose to highlight these reactions of affirmation, support and even joy. But pressing for details, I often discovered that couples also had to contend with various disappointing reactions to their ritual, including people who refused to attend or cancelled at the last minute and straight couples who chose not to bring their children. Vicky Staples and her partner Annette Royce held a public commitment ritual after eleven years together. Their relationship included two separations lasting several months, and the couple described their past struggles with issues of jealousy, trust and differing temperaments. When Vicky, a 37-year-old white computer programmer, told her mother about their plans for a public ceremony, her mother said she would attend, but Vicky assumed that meant she *might* attend. Her mother phoned three hours before the event to say she was not coming. "I was disappointed but I was not surprised," Vicky remarked, noting that her mother seems to hold their past relationship difficulties against Annette.

Several other participants told of parents and siblings who refused to attend or in some cases refused to even acknowledge the invitation. Jacob Berger described how a lasting rift with his older brother formed as a result of Jacob's commitment ceremony. Jacob had been the best man at his brother's wedding several years earlier, but his brother holds highly conservative views and wanted nothing to do with Jacob's ceremony. The brother told other family members he could not even respond to the invitation to Jacob's ceremony, because to respond would be to acknowledge the existence of the occasion. A year later, when Jacob's sister married, the older brother attended and the family acted as if nothing had ever happened, enraging Jacob. He ultimately called a family meeting to tell his parents and siblings how angered and disappointed he had been with their tolerance of his brother's behavior.

The negative reactions to same-sex rituals, unlike the positive reactions, tend to be to the idea of the event rather than to the event itself. Sarah Robbins described to me the reaction of a close lesbian friend, who had actively participated in their ritual by performing songs. This friend told Sarah after the ceremony that it was a lovely ritual but she did not see the point of the event, could not see what had changed as a result of Sarah and Abby having the ritual. Carrie Woodward described how her mother was rather unsupportive in advance of the ritual, insinuating that it was not a "real" wedding, lamenting the fact that she would never be "the mother of the bride," and even half-joking that Carrie would have been better off marrying her ex-boyfriend. Yet when the event arrived, she was "really happy and seemed very supportive," according to Carrie. Vicky Staples noted with amusement that her aunt, who "doesn't like anything," came to her ceremony and presented the couple with a beautiful handmade gift.

Some of the negative reactions described by participants came not from close family and friends but from larger institutions. Linda Sanchez initially called a Catholic church about performing her ceremony with her partner Maria, but her phone message was never returned. Paul Colvin, 63, and Dwight Winfrey, 57, had been active for a while in Lutherans Concerned (LC), a group targeting gays and lesbians with Lutheran affiliations, when their twenty-fifth anniversary was approaching. They decided they wanted a holy union ceremony to mark the anniversary, and approached LC about it. According to Paul and Dwight, the LC leadership was receptive but was eager to keep the ceremony "low-key." After several months of negotiation, the couple and the LC leaders agreed on a service that satisfied everyone. The union ceremony would be part of a larger, regular worship service at their host church, and the minister who served as advisor to LC would officiate. But shortly before the scheduled date, the church leaders found out that the Lutheran bishop would be visiting on that date, and the LC leaders decided at the last minute, without the couple's input, to have a lay member of the group officiate the holy union portion in place of the minister. Paul and Dwight felt betrayed by this last-minute change. Paul explained:

We talked about this later on, as time went on we talked to them, that what had happened and what they had done, how it really affected us inside, because while they were an organization that was supposed to advocate and support gay and lesbian people in the church, what they had done was to deny us, by pulling the pastoral support away from having it happen.

The couple became disenchanted with LC and with the denomination in general. Within a few years they had left the Lutheran church and joined an MCC congregation, and later held their "recommitment" ceremony in their new church.

Sue and Claire Bruno recounted the most dramatic negative reaction to a public commitment ritual. They held their ceremony in an MCC church in a conservative region of the country. Because such a ceremony was considered unusual in that area, one of the local newspapers decided to run a story on it, with the couple's full cooperation. Initially Claire and Sue were pleased by the response to the news story; strangers approached them in public to congratulate them on their union. But the publicity ultimately came at a cost. Sue lost her lease for office space shortly after the story ran, and she was convinced it happened because of the publicity. And Claire was fired from her job and was told it was because she was "too out."

Many participants did encounter personal and institutional responses to their commitment rituals that were unsupportive or even hostile. But these couples seemed to take these reactions in stride and chose to emphasize the positive rather than negative responses they had received. Despite sometimes rather dramatic rejections and disappointments, overall the couples described many more positive than negative reactions, and most couples seemed to attach great significance to the sense of affirmation they received from the invitees who did choose to attend and support their commitment.

Blurring the distinction between creators and receivers

Although I first described the guests at public rituals as "receivers" of the cultural object of the same-sex commitment ritual, attending a wedding or similar ceremony is actually a form of active participation in a ritual. Just as the clergy are both co-creators and receivers of this cultural object, the guests too are both participants and receivers. In fact, there is usually some moment in the ritual when the officiant asks the guests to formally voice their support for the couple and their relationship, often called a community blessing. For example, the MCC minister who performed the holy union of Cindy Dahl and Janis Sobirov said the following immediately after the couple exchanged their vows: "I ask all of you gathered here tonight, do you know and care for Janis and Cindy, and give them your blessings now as they enter into this new relationship, and do you promise to give them your love and understanding in both times of joy and times of difficulty? If so, answer 'We will, with God's help.'" Moments like these, or similar ritual components (such as the candle-lighting ritual in which each guest approached the couple and offered their personal wishes), draw the wedding guests into the event and transform them from passive spectators to active co-creators of the ritual.

A defining feature of rituals as a cultural form is that participation is both conscious and voluntary (Rothenbuhler 1998, 10–11). Even when people feel a strong social obligation to participate in rituals (i.e., when their participation is not substantively voluntary), they always retain the option not to participate. So, as Rothenbuhler puts it, "[f]ormal voluntarism has a substantive implication" in the case of rituals, because much of the meaning of rituals derives from participants' choosing to be a part of them, rather than from the content of the ritual itself (1998, 11). This is a crucial feature of rituals in the context of same-sex commitment ceremonies, because it means that whatever private misgivings guests may have about affirming the couple's commitment, they become co-creators of the ritual by their mere presence at the ritual, as receivers of the cultural object. Even if they feel a strong social obligation to attend, their presence is still voluntary in a formal sense and it is therefore a signal of some degree of approval or at least acknowledgement of the couple's relationship and commitment.

As noted earlier, couples repeatedly emphasize the public nature of these rituals as key to their meaning. This emphasis on the publicness of the rituals makes sense given some of the motivations behind the rituals. Although participants sometimes describe the significance of the rituals in the rather predictable language of the romantic love ideology, they also make statements that suggest the couples are partly using these events to engage in a form of cultural problem-solving. They view these rituals as a way to tackle the problem of invisibility or lack of recognition for their intimate commitments, the problem of stigma attached to devalued difference, and the problem of achieving permanence that challenges all couples in today's cultural climate, but perhaps is more challenging for same-sex relationships because they lack many of the social and legal supports that straight couples take for granted. For some gays and lesbians, the rituals are even a way to address issues of self-acceptance and internalized homophobia. The couples feel they need the guests to be there and to witness the event, because this witnessing makes their commitment more real and more serious, and also because couples believe the public witnessing increases their own sense of accountability. The presence of the guests also at least indirectly contributes to the goal of making these rituals equivalent to straight weddings, and thereby making these relationships equivalent to straight marriages. Because the cultural object of the commitment ritual is a collective production of the couple, the clergy and the guests, any private concerns individual guests may harbor about the value or propriety of the relationship or the event are largely irrelevant. Aside from anything the receivers (guests and clergy) might say or do within the ritual, their mere presence is a form of participation that confers approval and recognition for the couple's relationship and implies that the event bears some similarity to a heterosexual wedding.

Same-sex commitment in its social context

What makes certain cultural practices political? Should same-sex commitment rituals be viewed as political acts? Do these cultural practices constitute resistance against dominant social structures? Do they represent meaningful moments of individual agency? And might they contain the seeds of broader structural change? I will argue that same-sex commitment rituals should be read as political action even though the couples holding these ceremonies for the most part do not think of them in political terms. I focus my discussion of politics, resistance, agency and change on public commitment rituals, but some of the argument may apply to other commitment practices as well (for example, use of marriage-related terminology). Specifically, I contend that it is the conscious and voluntary nature of participation in rituals generally, combined with the social context of same-sex commitment rituals specifically, that renders these rituals political acts, moments of resistance, in spite of the fact that the couples themselves usually do not describe their meaning in political terms.

The notion of resistance assumes conditions of inequality and refers to behaviors through which subjugated social actors somehow challenge or push against the conditions of their subjugation. Resistance can take both symbolic and material forms. Scholars of resistance are divided on whether resistance must be intentional and whether it must be recognized as resistance by others (Hollander and Einwohner 2004). Jean and John Comaroff (1991) argue that it is most useful to conceive of resistance as a spectrum of social action, ranging from "organized protest, explicit moments and movements of dissent that are easily recognizable as 'political'" to "gestures of tacit refusal and iconoclasm, gestures that sullenly and silently contest the forms of an existing hegemony" (31). Resistance often falls between these two extremes, occurring through actions that "hover in the space between the tacit and the articulate, the direct and the indirect" (31). James Scott (1990) offers the concept of infrapolitics to capture one end of the spectrum, the "wide variety of low-profile forms of resistance that dare not speak their own name" (19). Infrapolitics consists of petty resistances that are small-scale, ambiguous, and often disguised or invisible to those in power. Scott argues that infrapolitics should be understood as the elementary form of politics, "the building block for the more elaborate institutionalized political action that could not exist without it" (201).

Relevant to the idea of resistance through cultural practice is recent work by social movement scholars on the cultural dimensions of political protest and social change (Johnston and Klandermans 1995). Some of this work has focused on gay men and lesbians, and particularly the importance of collective identities for mobilizing political resistance, valorizing marginalized groups, and pursuing social change through strategies of education and critique (e.g. Bernstein 1997, 2002; Taylor and Whittier 1992). Sometimes cultural strategies of protest and resistance assume forms that bear little resemblance to more familiar modes of social movement action such as marches, rallies and sit-ins. For example, Leila J. Rupp and Verta Taylor (2003) studied drag queen performances as a form of political protest. Based on intensive ethnographic observation of drag shows and interviews with the performers, Rupp and Taylor conclude that the drag shows represent a clear challenge to hegemonic understandings of gender and sexuality. Through a combination of songs, comic banter and visual cues, the drag queens challenge the normalcy of heterosexuality, dominant notions of masculinity and femininity, and the social and political exclusion of sexual minorities. Even though the primary purpose of the shows is entertainment, they are undeniably moments of political resistance as well, and their political message reaches people who might never attend an overtly political event. Based on this case, Rupp and Taylor argue that cultural performances act as political protest when they are characterized by contestation of existing power relations, intentionality to resist on the part of the performers, and affirmation of a collective identity that links the cultural performance to a broader collective struggle against injustice (Rupp and Taylor 2003, 217–220; also see Taylor, Rupp and Gamson 2004; Taylor and Van Dyke 2004).

Same-sex commitment rituals, like the drag shows analyzed by Rupp and Taylor, fall somewhere in the middle of the spectrum of resistance and political protest. On one hand, they are not the kind of large-scale protests that have a collective character and primarily political aims. Couples largely avoid framing their commitment rituals as political events and instead describe their significance in fairly personal terms. They are social events but not organized collective action. On the other hand, they do not fit well within Scott's notion of infrapolitics. Although these rituals are somewhat mundane, personal, small-scale moments of resistance, they are also highly visible one-time events, meant to call attention to themselves, rather than ongoing practices veiled in strategic invisibility.

In this and other respects, there are close parallels between same-sex commitment rituals and the drag performances described by Rupp and Taylor (2003). Both types of cultural performance clearly contest dominant cultural conceptions – in the case of drag, ideas about gender and sexuality, in the case of commitment rituals, ideas about marriage and family. In both cases, the publicness and visibility of the cultural performance is key to its political impact. Rupp and Taylor note that drag shows reach audiences who might not attend more overtly political events (such as gay rights marches) and effectively break down the distinction between the performers and the audience, thereby driving home the political message that differences of gender and sexuality should not divide people. Likewise, commitment rituals frequently involve guests who might have no other connections to gay politics or culture. The structure of the ritual makes the "audience" active co-creators of the cultural performance, and the visible celebration of same-sex love invites guests to recognize the basic similarity between same-sex and heterosexual relationships and commitment.[10] The creators of both same-sex rituals and drag shows also connect their performances to a broader collective identity – the gay and lesbian community – through words, visual symbols and the selection of performance elements (for example, songs with lyrics that can be given a gay reading). On their surface, these two kinds of cultural performance might appear quite distinct: the tone of drag shows is playful and sometimes confrontational, whereas the tone of commitment rituals is serious and emphasizes harmony over direct confrontation. Yet the two kinds of cultural performance operate quite similarly as forms of middle-ground resistance and cultural protest.

Previous studies of same-sex commitment rituals have wrestled with the question of whether these rituals constitute resistance. In their books on same-sex marriage, both Ellen Lewin (1998) and Gretchen Stiers (1999) ask whether same-sex marriage rituals represent attempts to assimilate into mainstream society or acts of resistance against dominant definitions of marriage and family. Lewin concludes that ritual participants are engaging in a form of "unconscious resistance" (241). Lewin asserts that her findings warn against a simplistic view of resistance and accommodation as opposed categories of action, arguing that same-sex commitment rituals are "simultaneously conservative and subversive," conservative in their validation of norms of fidelity, domesticity and love but subversive in their attack on gender conventions and heteronormativity (243). Likewise, Stiers' central argument "is that same-sex ceremonies and marriages should be conceptualized both as acts of resistance to traditional marriage and wedding norms and as acts of accommodation to these same standards" (6). I agree with these authors that same-sex rituals represent a blend of resistance to heteronormativity and accommodation to norms of love, marriage and family. But I want to push the question of resistance a bit farther, to argue that the social context of these rituals makes them political and resistant in a particular way.

Same-sex couples decide to have public commitment rituals for seemingly quite personal reasons, including the urge to celebrate their love and commitment in a public way, the desire to make their relationship "real" to themselves and others, the hope of enhancing the stability of their relationship, the impulse to fit in and be seen as fundamentally similar to heterosexual couples, and the interest in participating in meaningful traditions. But the very act of deciding to have a *public* ritual, and inviting friends and family to attend and clergy to officiate, forces others to make what amounts to a political decision, because merely showing up constitutes active participation in ritual. Showing up is a way of affirming the reality and seriousness of the event, and offering a signal of support, regardless of any undisclosed hesitations. Attendance and participation in ritual are fundamentally collective and social, and thus the meaning of that participation escapes the control of individual guests. In the case of same-sex rituals, attendance and participation are also fundamentally political, because of the broader social context in which these rituals are situated. The social context is one of widespread disapproval of same-sex relationships as morally wrong and undeserving of social support.

Although gays and lesbians in the United States have made significant progress over the last several decades in terms of both social acceptance and legal protection, they still face a social and legal environment that is often intolerant, hostile and even life-threatening. Gays and lesbians confront routine symbolic violence in popular culture, despite gains made in improving visibility. More generally, gays and lesbians live their daily lives in a climate of "cultural and psychological heterosexism" (Herek 1990, 1995), in which dominant sex and gender ideologies normalize heterosexuality and justify anti-gay prejudice. In most religious denominations, same-sex behavior is defined as intrinsically sinful, "out" gays and lesbians are denied the opportunity to serve as clergy, and same-sex marriage is prohibited. At the most personal level, gays and lesbians who decide to come out to friends and family face the threat of permanent rejection. On the legal front, anti-gay discrimination in the areas of employment, housing, public accommodations, education and credit remains legal in most states, and efforts to prohibit employment discrimination through national legislation have repeatedly failed. The brutal murder of college student Matthew Shepard in 1998 drew national attention to the problem of hate crimes targeting gays and lesbians, but did not result in changing the federal hate-crimes prevention law to cover crimes motivated by sexual orientation bias.[11] Despite the arrival of legal same-sex marriage in Massachusetts, same-sex couples in the United States do not have access to the same legal rights and privileges available to opposite-sex married couples. Gay and lesbian parents also fare poorly in the legal system, sometimes losing custody of their children because of their sexual orientation. In short, American gays and lesbians continue to live in a climate that is both socially and legally hostile to their identities and their relationships.

In this general social context, same-sex wedding rituals represent a form of political resistance, regardless of how their primary creators (the couples) describe their intentions. In the context of a society that devalues gay and lesbian people and relationships, conducting an event that acknowledges and validates same-sex intimate commitment and implies its fundamental equivalence to heterosexual marriage constitutes a clear form of symbolic political resistance.

Beyond the reality of a hostile mainstream social climate, the social context of same-sex rituals matters in a second sense. Not only are same-sex rituals political because they occur in a generalized context of disapproval of homosexuality, but also because they actively construct a social context for naming and recognizing the couple's commitment. This is accomplished through the participation of people other than the couple, including officiants and guests. The publicness of public rituals – their visibility, and the way they force others to decide whether they will give their support and recognition to the couple – distinguishes them as a particular kind of resistance. Some of the other cultural practices of commitment described in this chapter, such as private rituals and the use of marriage-related terminology in private settings, can also be read as political resistance, but in a way that more closely resembles the infra-politics described by Scott. Public same-sex commitment rituals, by contrast, hold the middle ground along the spectrum of resistance be-cause they are events that draw others into collectively producing a social reality that contests dominant norms and institutions.

The kind of middle-ground resistance represented by public same-sex rituals raises interesting questions about agency, intentionality and pro-cesses of structural change. My argument is that gays and lesbians are exercising agency through the middle-ground resistance of same-sex rituals, and there is certainly some intentionality behind their decision to contest dominant norms of marriage and family. At the same time, there is little direct evidence that these couples have as their main purpose the transformation of the social structure of marriage. Instead, same-sex couples describe more personal motivations: to celebrate their commitment and strengthen their relationships, but also to assert the reality of their commitment, its essential similarity to heterosexual mar-riages, and its rightful place within traditions that have historically excluded or ignored same-sex love. Almost none of the study partici-pants described the purpose of these rituals in more general political terms, as a way to redefine the institution of marriage, for example, or further the cause of gay and lesbian rights and equality.[12] Members of couples often spoke as though they simply wanted to enter the existing institution of marriage, not to challenge or change it in any radical way. They rarely acknowledged that their appropriation of the cultural prac-tices of marriage strikes many people as a fundamental transformation of the institution.

In Chapter 1 I briefly described Sewell's (1999) argument about the dialectical relationship between culture as meaning system and culture as practice. It is the structural features of culture (its meaning-system qualities) that make innovative cultural practices possible. Cultural structures consist of both schemas and resources, but their schemas are open to multiple interpretations and their resources can be deployed for a variety of purposes. Extrapolating from Sewell's earlier essay on social structure (1992), we might say that the possibilities for cultural agency are embedded within cultural structures. Weddings are one particular cultural structure, encompassing a range of material and nonmaterial resources (from cakes and gifts to the religious authority of officiants) and invoking various meanings or schemas (romantic love, commitment and marriage itself). Same-sex rituals represent cre-ative cultural agency because they put the schemas and resources that constitute weddings as a cultural structure to new ends, namely the recognition and celebration of same-sex intimacy.

This redeployment of the schemas and resources of weddings in service of same-sex commitments has the potential to transform the institution of marriage, even though the couples themselves do not voice aspirations to institutional transformation. The cultural object of the same-sex commitment ritual decouples the institution of marriage from heterosexuality and evokes an affirmation of intimacies that are more typically ignored, devalued or stigmatized. By appropriating the schemas and resources of weddings to celebrate same-sex love, these rituals put the dominant understanding of marriage at risk. Of course it is possible that heterosexuals attending or officiating at these rituals continue to think of marriage as a fundamentally heterosexual institution. But there is a good deal of indirect evidence (based on couples' descriptions) that many guests who were skeptical or ambivalent about the rituals were drawn in by their cultural power and became enthusiastic participants. Such participants may be likely to understand weddings and marriage somewhat differently as a result of their experience. And the private thoughts and opinions of individual guests or officiants are less important than the fact that they have joined the couple to collectively construct an event that both borrows from and challenges the dominant cultural forms of marriage. This mutual (re)construction of the cultural structure of marriage becomes part of the social transcript of weddings and marriage regardless of the thoughts, beliefs or intentions of any particular actor. Indeed, I have noted how the couples' own accounts of the purpose and significance of their rituals are highly personalized. Weddings and marriage are cultural structures that some same-sex couples choose to appropriate in service of personal aspirations toward recognition, acceptance and inclusion.

Even though the couples usually do not describe their cultural practice in political or institutional terms, I suggest that the rituals have the potential to produce a cumulative effect across time and place, leading to a significant transformation of the cultural structure of marriage. The effectiveness of same-sex rituals in changing the cultural structure of marriage depends partly on the frequency and visibility of such rituals. As public same-sex rituals become more commonplace, diffused across gender, class, racial and geographic lines, they impact more people directly (as guests/participants and thus co-creators of the rituals) and indirectly (through media coverage of the practice and second-hand accounts of specific rituals, for instance). Such processes of aggregation and diffusion, I would suggest, often contribute to the gradual transformation of dominant cultural structures like marriage. James Scott makes a similar point regarding the impact of infrapolitics: "Under the appropriate conditions, the accumulation of petty acts can, rather like snowflakes on a steep mountainside, set off an avalanche" (1990, 192, footnote omitted). While Scott is referring to the cumulative impacts of disguised forms of material resistance such as poaching and foot-dragging, a parallel argument can be made for the cumulative symbolic impacts of more overt symbolic resistances, including the middle-ground resistance of same-sex rituals.

What might be the conditions under which middle-ground resistances such as same-sex commitment rituals lead to structural or institutional change? Perhaps such processes of change are particularly likely when relatively powerful social institutions – such as marriage – attract the "wrong" social actors. The cultural practices that partially constitute marriage have a strong pull on many people, including some who are excluded from marriage as a legal institution. This is true not only of contemporary same-sex couples, but of other excluded relationships as well. American slaves were forbidden legal marriage but constructed wedding rituals for themselves outside the law. And polygamists, both historically and in the present, draw on the cultural trappings of marriage to enact their "plural marriages," despite the absence of legal recognition and even the threat of criminal prosecution. Neoinstitutional theory emphasizes the strong reproductive tendencies of dominant social institutions, but does less well at accounting for processes of institutional change. The cultural practices of commitment among same-sex couples, and especially the practice of public rituals, point to one possible avenue of institutional change: powerful institutions may draw in social actors for whom the institution's benefits are not intended. As these excluded actors appropriate those elements of the institution that are least easily restricted (in the case of marriage, its cultural practices), the institution itself begins to transform. Marriage can no longer be a straightforward celebration of heterosexual coupling when gays and lesbians increasingly adopt its cultural practices. One can think of parallel examples concerning other sorts of institutions. For example, the institution of the professional career lost its tight association with maleness when women began to force their way into various male-dominated occupations and declared their professional ambitions (even as they remained formally excluded from specific professions and training opportunities).

Perhaps wedding rituals, and by extension marriage itself, are examples of cultural structures that are almost "too" powerful, in the sense that they have strong self-reproducing tendencies but also sometimes pull the "wrong" people into their reproduction. This is a somewhat counterintuitive point: those cultural structures that are the most powerful in terms of their self-replication may also be particularly vulnerable to transformation, because they are likely to elicit the participation of actors who are in some sense inappropriate to the cultural structure in its present form. Their participation sets in motion a process of institutional change.

I am describing a specific type of institutional change, related to changes in the boundaries of institutions and to access by seemingly inappropriate actors. This model of institutional transformation clearly would not account for all instances of institutional change; institutions may decay or innovate without any significant change in the kind of actors who participate in the institution. An important challenge for future theorizing and research is to specify the conditions under which this particular kind of social change happens. I have implied that such change may be particularly likely with powerful institutions: such institutions have something to draw the interest of the "wrong" actors in the first place. Might it be possible to identify more precisely the kinds of institutional power that have this draw? There are different possible sources of institutional power, including richness of resources (symbolic or material) and social centrality (connections to other important institutions or the participation of many social actors or particularly important social actors). Perhaps all powerful institutions are not alike in this regard. Maybe social institutions that are already experiencing rapid change of other kinds are most likely to incorporate new actors who in turn further change the institution. Such a description would certainly apply to the institution of marriage in the United States in recent decades.

To argue that same-sex couples holding public commitment rituals are practicing a form of politics says nothing about the desirability of the kind of social change these practices might produce. As we shall see in the next chapter, not all people in committed same-sex relationships are eager to embrace the cultural practices of commitment associated with the marriage model. Some gays and lesbians choose not to celebrate their commitments in public rituals because the cultural form (the ritual or "wedding") appears to imitate heterosexual cultural practices in an unreflective way. Others experience ambivalence, lack of interest or antipathy toward the institution of marriage itself. And some same-sex couples who have not held public rituals view these rituals positively but find themselves unable or unprepared to participate in them for a variety of reasons.

3   How do I love thee? Questioning the marriage model

Marriage is a great institution, but I'm not ready for an institution yet.
— Mae West

A casual observer of recent media coverage of same-sex marriage developments might easily get the impression that all gays and lesbians (or at least all those in relationships) are enthusiastic proponents of marriage in both its cultural and legal forms. In February 2004, hundreds of same-sex couples waited in line for hours on the cold, rainy streets outside San Francisco's City Hall for the chance to obtain marriage licenses of dubious validity. Around the country, same-sex couples have been willing to construct commitment rituals ranging from the traditional to the innovative, the small-scale to the grandiose (including "mass weddings" performed at recent gay rights marches in Washington, DC and elsewhere), even with the knowledge that these rituals would not bring any change in legal status for the couples. When Vermont began offering civil unions in 2000, it turned out that the large majority of people who flocked to this new legal status were out-of-staters, couples drawn to the chance to have a government formalize their commitment even though their new status would not be recognized in the states where they lived. And the scenes from Massachusetts on May 17, 2004 were dramatic and emotionally charged: hundreds of same-sex couples leaped at the opportunity to enter legal marriages and obtained their marriage licenses against a backdrop of cheering crowds of supporters.

But the picture is more complex than coverage of recent events suggests. Gays and lesbians have been debating the desirability and importance of same-sex marriage for years, and this intracommunity debate reflects deeper tensions and oppositions within gay and lesbian communities, conflicts over the political and cultural goals of the gay and lesbian movement and over the tactics used to accomplish those goals. In particular, the marriage question reveals a fault line among gay and lesbian activists and commentators, a divide between those who embrace a rights-oriented approach to social change, viewing assimilation as the ultimate goal of gay and lesbian activism, and those who advocate a liberationist or "queer" ethic focused on deconstructing fixed sexual categories and transforming dominant cultural understandings of intimacy, sexuality, family and the state.

This chapter describes the intracommunity debate on marriage among gay and lesbian activists and commentators and examines the perspectives of the couples in my sample who chose not to embrace marriage as a cultural model of commitment through public ritual. I compare and contrast the views of these couples with the discourses of the intracommunity debate, as well as with the views of heterosexual couples who choose to cohabit rather than marry. My findings indicate that couples who decide against public commitment rituals sometimes stake out a principled position against marriage, paralleling some of the critiques of marriage in the intracommunity debate, but more often express mere ambivalence or lack of interest toward marriage as a cultural model of relationship. And some of these couples, while choosing not to hold public commitment rituals, adopt other cultural practices linked to marriage, which also suggests an attitude of ambivalence rather than outright opposition toward marriage. Many of these couples occupy an ambiguous middle ground on the marriage question, one that is not well represented in the intracommunity debate on marriage but somewhat resembles the position of many heterosexual cohabitors who neither fully embrace nor flatly reject the institution of marriage.

The marriage debate among gays and lesbians

Discussions on "the marriage question" within gay and lesbian communities are not new, but they take on heightened significance in light of recent legal and political developments in the United States and abroad. Over the years, the marriage debate has found a home in both the popular gay press and academic forums. This intracommunity debate on marriage first gained prominence in 1989 with the publication of a now-classic pair of "pro" and "con" articles by Tom Stoddard and Paula Ettelbrick in *OUT/LOOK* magazine. At the time, Stoddard was the executive director of the Lambda Legal Defense and Education Fund, a national civil rights group specializing in gay-related impact litigation, and Ettelbrick was Lambda's legal director. In his piece, Stoddard (1992) asserts that same-sex marriage is a worthwhile movement goal for practical, political and philosophical reasons. The practical benefits at stake include tax benefits, a range of government benefits such as Social Security and veterans' benefits for spouses, legal protections such as inheritance rights and the power to make medical decisions on behalf of one's spouse, and access to health insurance through a spouse's policy. In political terms, Stoddard argues that same-sex marriage is the single best way to end discrimination against gays and lesbians. And Stoddard claims that a philosophical commitment to equality dictates legal recognition of same-sex marriage, noting that the *right* to marry should be available to all citizens, even if some gays and lesbians would prefer not to participate in the institution of marriage.

In her companion piece, Ettelbrick (1992) warns that marriage will not liberate gays and lesbians; rather, it will force them into the mainstream, make them invisible and undermine some of the most cherished goals of gay liberation, including recognition and respect for a diversity of family forms and intimate relationships. Ettelbrick fears that the fight for same-sex marriage will force gays and lesbians to compare themselves to the heterosexual norm, demonstrating their similarity to straight couples and in the process perpetuating the socially elevated status of married people and of couples in general. She postulates that marriage will most appeal to those gays and lesbians who are already closest to the straight mainstream (white middle-class men) and will further marginalize the more marginal members of the community who are more likely to reject the marriage alternative (women, people of color, the working class and the poor). In the process, marriage will create a new form of inequality within the gay and lesbian community, granting social legitimacy to the married at the expense of those who choose another path.[1]

Other voices joined the debate on both sides, often reiterating the points laid out in the Stoddard–Ettelbrick exchange and sometimes adding new insights. Marriage advocates have elaborated on the perceived benefits of marriage for gay and lesbian couples and communities and for American society as a whole. Attorney Evan Wolfson, former director of Lambda Legal's marriage project and current head of Freedom to Marry, a same-sex marriage advocacy group, shares Stoddard's zeal for marriage as the path to full social equality. "Inclusion at the level of marriage is uniquely revolutionary, conservatively subversive, singularly faithful to true American and family values in a way that few, if any, other gay and lesbian victories would be," Wolfson argues (1994, 580). Wolfson situates the fight for marriage rights within the broader history of civil rights movements, asserting that "the freedom-to-marry movement is about the same thing every civil rights struggle has been about: taking seriously our country's promise to be a place where people don't have to give up their differences or hide them in order to be treated equally" (2004, 185). Journalist Andrew Sullivan, one of the most vocal proponents of same-sex marriage, goes so far as to claim: "If nothing else were done at all, and gay marriage were legalized, ninety percent of the political work necessary to achieve gay and lesbian equality would have been achieved. It is ultimately the only reform that truly matters" (1996, 185).

The marriage advocates argue that marriage is a dynamic, socially constructed institution; it has no essential nature but rather can be shaped to meet the changing needs of society. Historian George Chauncey points to several changes in marriage over the past century that have made marriage more imaginable and appealing for gays and lesbians. These changes include the establishment of marriage as a fundamental legal right, trends toward egalitarianism within marriages, increasing use of marriage to allocate public and private benefits, and the declining influence of religious authorities on marriage policy (Chauncey 2004, Chapter 3). Same-sex marriage, advocates claim, holds the potential to further transform the institution of marriage by destabilizing prescribed gender roles and downplaying the connection between marriage and reproduction (Hunter 1991; Eskridge 1993; Pascoe 2000). Gay author Jonathan Rauch argues that marriage must expand to include same-sex couples or it risks losing its status as "the gold standard for committed relationships," especially when other options such as cohabitation and domestic partnership seem increasingly appealing to heterosexual couples (2004, 94). Philosopher Richard Mohr (1994) suggests that same-sex marriage might also teach the broader society about the flexibility of the institution of marriage, for example by illustrating that sexual monogamy and merging of finances are not essential components of marriage relationships. Marriage advocates claim that legal marriage will bring various emotional benefits for same-sex couples, such as strengthening commitment and increasing social and familial support for the couple (Graff 1996; Sullivan 1996). Some commentators have suggested, rather provocatively, that these benefits will be particularly important for gay men, steering them toward stable long-term relationships and away from a culture dominated by sexual promiscuity (Eskridge 1996; Rauch 1996, 2004).

Gay and lesbian critics of marriage, by contrast, view marriage as fundamentally incompatible with the defining principles of queer life and activism and argue that the costs of pursuing marriage outweigh its supposed benefits. Law professor Nancy Polikoff echoes some of Ettelbrick's concerns when she suggests that "the desire to marry in the lesbian and gay community is an attempt to mimic the worst of mainstream society, an effort to fit into an inherently problematic institution that betrays the promise of both lesbian and gay liberation and radical feminism" (1993, 1536). Polikoff worries that entry into the institution of marriage will rob the gay and lesbian movement of the power to critique the flaws of the institution and will derail efforts to unhook various economic and social benefits from marriage. She also dismisses the idea that same-sex marriage will make gender roles irrelevant to marriage, pointing out that historical examples of same-sex marriage relationships typically feature clear gender roles. Philosopher Claudia Card (1996) expresses concern that legal marriage will make same-sex couples stay together for the wrong reasons while further glorifying the monogamous dyad, a relationship form that does not fit the reality of many gay and lesbian relationships. Sociologist Suzanna Danuta Walters (2001b) shares Card's discomfort with reinforcing the romantic/sexual couple as "the single true model for intimate life," and argues that a focus on marriage also reinforces an ideology of familialism that undermines more broadly conceived "values of community and care" (354–355). Based on his research on gay and lesbian domestic practices, sociologist Christopher Carrington (1999) attacks the goal of legal same-sex marriage, arguing that marriage will lead more gays and lesbians to take the risk of specializing in domesticity and then trap them in unhappy relationships. Carrington argues that marriage will increase the expectations for accomplishing domesticity without providing the resources that average gays and lesbians would need to accomplish domesticity. He also asserts that "participation in marriage will legally reinforce inequality within lesbigay relationships and drive social wedges between single and married lesbigay people," and that the pursuit of marriage is "a strategy that is willing to sell out the interests of the typical lesbigay family, and of the broader lesbigay communities, in order to obtain the privileges of married heterosexual society for a few, mostly affluent lesbigay families" (1999, 224).

Queer theorist Michael Warner (1999) offers the most thorough and persuasive critique of the pursuit of same-sex marriage in his book *The Trouble with Normal*. Warner views marriage as an inherently stratifying institution: "Marriage sanctifies some couples at the expense of others. It is selective legitimacy" (1999, 82). Warner rejects the idea that it is possible to advocate for the right to marry without thereby advocating the institution of marriage itself. He sees marriage as a normalizing and disciplinary institution that is antithetical to many of the core tenets of queer thought, including the destructiveness of the mythology of romance and marriage, the existence of a diverse range of sexual and intimate relationships deserving respect and protection, resistance to using the norms of straight society as standards for measuring gay relationships, and opposition to state regulation of consensual sex and sexuality generally. Like other marriage critics, Warner fears that legal marriage would intensify stratification within lesbian and gay communities and produce adverse consequences for the unmarried. More broadly, Warner questions the state's interest in fostering stable, long-term coupling, arguing that the "claim that the state has an interest in fostering long-term coupling is profoundly antidemocratic" (1999, 112).[2] He sees marriage as a way of bundling privileges, benefits and statuses that might more logically be available separately to a range of intimacies and relationships. Echoing Polikoff's point, Warner predicts that same-sex marriage will further erode support for the idea of unbundling the existing package of marriage benefits and making them more available to everyone who needs them.

Warner scorns those marriage advocates who see marriage as a way to produce "good gays" through "normalization of queer life" (1999, 114) and reads the desire for marriage as representing a desire for an "intensified and deindividuated form of coming out" (132). He appreciates same-sex commitment ceremonies for their ability to "turn banal privacy into public-sphere scenes" (132), calling attention to the non-universality of the marriage institution and forcing reactions in situations where the social scripts are not already written. But these ceremonies also appear safer than simply coming out, because "[m]arrying makes your desire private, names its object, locates it in an already formed partnership" and thus makes gay sexuality less threatening to the straight world (133). Warner reads gays' desire for marriage as an understandable but unfortunate form of false consciousness, one that is reinforced by the taken-for-granted quality of the institution and reflects the increasingly assimilationist bent of gay and lesbian politics.

The tensions evident in this intracommunity debate on marriage reflect deeper divisions within gay and lesbian communities and movements along the fault line of assimilation vs. liberation. For those on the queer/liberationist side of the divide, the desire for marriage represents a problematic effort to integrate into mainstream society without challenging its oppressive power structures. Critics view the institution of marriage as fundamentally flawed, both because of its patriarchal history and because it grants the state undue control over sexual behavior and intimate commitments. They dismiss the idea that gays and lesbians will fundamentally alter and improve the institution of marriage by becoming part of it. For those on the assimilation/equality side of the divide, however, the lack of marriage rights symbolizes one of the few remaining barriers to full social and legal equality for American gays and lesbians. Marriage supporters argue that the institution of marriage has changed over time and will continue to evolve, such that participation in marriage signifies the chance to reshape an important social institution into a more egalitarian form, rather than capitulation to an inherently oppressive and stratifying arrangement.[3]

This intracommunity debate has mainly focused on the public policy question of *legal* recognition of same-sex marriage, rather than on the value of adopting marriage as a *cultural* model for intimate same-sex commitments. Still, it provides a useful starting point for looking at the diversity of viewpoints among gays and lesbians on the question of marriage as a cultural model for relationship. My interview sample includes twenty-two study participants in committed same-sex relationships who have not held a public commitment ritual with their partner. Is their choice not to hold a public ritual motivated by the same concerns about marriage voiced by the marriage critics in the intracommunity debate? Are these couples worried about imitating heterosexuals, supporting an institution with patriarchal roots and buying into the romantic love mythology? Do they voice concerns about creating new inequalities among gay and lesbian people, eroding respect for diverse family forms or trapping couples in unhappy relationships? Or does their decision against public ritual reflect other kinds of concerns?

Deciding against public ritual

Alex Gellar and Robbie Caputo met in college through their volunteer work for a campus gay organization. They became involved when Alex was a junior and Robbie a sophomore, and they have been a couple for six years, including one year of long-distance relationship after Alex graduated and moved to Chicago. Alex is a 27-year-old African-American stockbroker who grew up in a lower-middle-class family in Harlem. Robbie is a 26-year-old white accountant from a working-class Midwestern family. Robbie says he has known he was gay since he was six or seven years old. Alex struggled with his sexual orientation during his college years, and met Robbie only months after deciding he was gay. In some respects, Alex and Robbie view themselves as a married couple. Alex usually uses the term partner to refer to Robbie, but sometimes with friends or with Robbie he will call him his husband. "We do everything together," Alex told me. "I think we do everything that a married couple does." Robbie usually refers to Alex as his partner, but will sometimes call him his husband to make sure people understand the nature of their relationship, or to be provocative with people he considers homophobic. The couple recently purchased a home together, a step that both view as a symbol of the depth of their commitment.

Alex and Robbie considered having a public commitment ceremony a few years ago, when Robbie was planning to convert to Alex's faith, but they put the idea of a ceremony on hold after Robbie changed his mind about converting. Both friends and family members have asked about a ceremony and sometimes urged the couple to have one, but Alex and Robbie are hesitant. In separate interviews, each man talked about a combination of reasons for holding off on a public ceremony. Alex is not firmly opposed to the idea, but does not have much enthusiasm for it either. Cost is one factor. With their recent home purchase, Alex feels they cannot afford a ceremony at this point. The lack of legal recognition is another factor. Alex thinks he would be more excited about the idea of a ceremony if it would bring a new legal status to the couple. He also wonders whether the time for a ceremony may have passed in their relationship, and does not believe such an event would change or deepen their mutual commitment. "I think it would be nice to have one," Alex remarked, "but it's like, what's the point?" He explained:

I mean, we've been together six years, it's clear that we're going to be together. Having a ceremony isn't going to change my views toward Robbie, it's not going to make me say, "Oh, I've had a ceremony, now I've got to stay with him." I think I've already said that. I've said, "Now we've bought a house, we need to stay together." But it's not going to change things.

Alex believes it might be useful to have some tangible marker of their commitment, perhaps an exchange of rings at some point in their future, but feels it does not need to be a "huge ceremony." However, if legal marriage became available to them, Alex thinks he and Robbie would have a ceremony right away.

Robbie shares his partner's ambivalence about a public ritual of commitment. Robbie feels he got much of the support and warmth he would expect from a commitment ceremony from the housewarming party he and Alex held after moving into their new place. "Having a housewarming party, for me, was almost like having a commitment ceremony, because of all the people showering all these gifts on us as a couple, for our home, as a symbol of our togetherness," Robbie recalled. "It was pretty moving for me; I almost cried." Like Alex, Robbie feels that the lack of legal recognition accompanying same-sex commitment ceremonies is a problem. Robbie said he would want to be clear about the kind of recognition he sought or expected from such an event. He expressed a fear about expecting a kind of recognition that a non-legal ceremony cannot provide:

I totally have this thing, if you're doing it to show other people or whatever, it would be difficult to hear someone say, "Oh, you had a ceremony but you're not really married, you're not legally married." So I would be really concerned about doing this for some type of recognition. If you're looking for recognition from outside . . . Basically, if a heterosexual couple gets married, they get a legal recognition. If you're looking for that legal recognition, don't do it for that reason. If you want the recognition of your chosen friends and family, that's fine, but you're not going to get the legal recognition and it can hurt you if that's what you're looking for.

Robbie also has some qualms about importing a heterosexual relationship norm into the gay community. Although he and Alex have chosen to have a monogamous relationship, Robbie recognizes that this is not a choice that works for all gay men. "Maybe we're not, maybe some people aren't meant to be in these monogamous unions," he explained, "and maybe there are other structures that fit, and we only know this heterosexual marriage thing, and I would be afraid to try to go have a same-sex marriage ceremony, just to try to copy off of what they're doing, just because that's the norm for them."

Susan Lemus and Bess Hardin have been together four years. They met through their involvement with a lesbian theater group, but when they first became acquainted both women were involved in other relationships. Eventually those relationships ended and Bess and Susan's casual friendship began to shift toward something more involved. During their initial period of flirting, they recall being the talk of the theater group and being teased about their growing attraction. When they began to date, both women expressed a desire to move slowly; Bess recalls being concerned about getting into a "rebound" relationship. But they vacationed together after four months of dating, and decided to move in together after less than a year. Susan, 29, is a white graduate student from a lower-middle-class background. Her parents divorced when she was 10 and her mother raised her and her siblings in a strict fundamentalist version of Christianity. Susan embraced this religious viewpoint as a teenager, but during college she got in touch with her own attraction to women and discovered that homosexuality and religious belief were not necessarily at odds. Susan said coming out was "wonderful for my own sense of self-worth," but she experienced rejection by her mother who "thinks it's wrong, thinks I'm sick." Bess is a 37-year-old white veterinarian who came out relatively late in life, at age 29. She grew up in a middle-class family headed by her minister father, and says she is the "black sheep" of her family for moving away from her home state of Alabama. She does not feel close to her family of origin and has not come out to them. Bess and Susan live together in a home owned by Bess. They agree that they have had two "minor crises" in their four years together, both concerning financial issues. Because of the large disparity in their incomes, they have decided to keep all of their finances separate for now. Bess pays all the bills and Susan makes a monthly payment that covers less than half of their joint expenses. Susan does more of the household chores, which she considers fair given her lesser financial contribution to their shared expenses.

Neither Bess nor Susan is interested in a public commitment ritual. They exchanged rings privately after they had been together for about a year, and both agree that the ring exchange signified their commitment to a monogamous partnership. They decided to write each other letters in conjunction with the ring exchange, outlining their beliefs about the meaning of their commitment. And they celebrated the ring exchange with dinner at a favorite downtown restaurant. They chose identical rings and wear them on the traditional wedding-ring finger, a decision meant to signal their involvement in a committed relationship, despite the fact that they do not think of their rings as wedding rings. Neither woman has much investment in marriage as a model for their commitment. Both avoid marriage terminology in referring to their partner or their relationship. When someone inquires about marital status, Susan usually responds, "No, I have a partner." Bess is more adamant in her rejection of a married identity: "I feel very strongly about marriage, and I would never say I was married."

While Susan and Bess have not completely foreclosed the possibility of a public commitment ritual in their future, such a development seems unlikely given their reservations about marriage and their lack of enthusiasm for a public ceremony. Susan feels such a ritual would be more for their families than themselves, and this is not a compelling motivation given her difficult relationship with her fundamentalist Christian mother and Bess's emotional distance from her family of origin. Their recent attendance at a female couple's commitment ceremony gave Bess and Susan the chance to reaffirm their rejection of marriage as a model for their own commitment. Susan described the couple's ceremony as "beautiful," "cool" and "kind of a rebellious thing to do," but also expressed dismay at the couple's close adherence to the marriage model, such as their use of the terms wife and wedding. "The whole thing about marriage as an institution is very loaded, and I think it turns us off," Susan explained. Bess observed that some same-sex couples appear to embrace "the trappings of heterosexuality" in a bid for social acceptance. She acknowledged that "there are no homosexual traditions for this type of thing," but said she would prefer to see gays and lesbians invent their own new traditions instead of uncritically adopting the "heterosexual model."

A range of beliefs and concerns underlies same-sex couples' decisions not to use public ritual to celebrate or define their intimate commitments. Some study participants point to other ways of enacting commitment, such as private rituals that include only the couple or alternative forms of public celebration, such as housewarming parties, that reaffirm the couple and their shared life. For some people, a public ritual does not seem to make sense in the context of their own life course, or in the context of their relationship's evolution. Some study participants describe specific obstacles that make a public ritual difficult or unappealing, such as concerns about their sexual identity being revealed to family or co-workers, lack of time or money to put together a public celebration, or a partner who does not want to participate. For others, the choice not to have a public ritual stems from unanswered questions about the purpose of such an event. And a few study participants explained their lack of interest in a public ritual as a principled questioning or rejection of the marriage institution.

Not very long ago, the vast majority of same-sex couples in the United States probably "chose" not to have public commitment rituals, and in fact this was less a conscious choice than a decision reached by default. Public commitment rituals were not a commonplace and culturally visible practice for same-sex couples two or three decades ago. But there is strong anecdotal evidence suggesting that the popularity of these rituals has mushroomed in gay and lesbian communities in recent years. As a result, even if public commitment rituals remain a minority practice within the gay and lesbian population, they are now popular and visible enough that most committed same-sex couples are confronted with the option of having a public ritual and will give conscious thought and discussion to the possibility. Thus it makes sense to explore with committed couples who choose not to have such rituals how they arrive at their decision. The perspectives of these couples enrich our understanding of the role of marriage as a cultural institution in the lives of gay and lesbian couples. It is in the cultural realm that same-sex couples have the most choice and control about whether to "do marriage." Most American same-sex couples cannot choose whether to enter marriage as a legal institution or whether to have a particular religion recognize their union, but they can make choices on their own about holding public commitment rituals and using other cultural practices that connect their own commitment to the institution of marriage.

There are other ways to enact marriage culturally besides through a public commitment ritual, and some of the study participants who had not held a public ritual had used one or more of these other marriage-related practices to mark their commitment, including exchanging rings, exchanging vows privately and applying marriage terminology to their relationship. So, the couples in this study cannot be neatly divided into "marriage" and "non-marriage" people. However, it makes sense to look more closely at those study participants who had not participated in public rituals, for two reasons. First, weddings are the single most significant cultural practice associated with marriage. They are public, often spectacular, occasions, usually drenched in symbolism and typically marking the transition to the status of legally married for heterosexuals. Some observers have documented how weddings seem to be taking on heightened cultural importance even as the institution of marriage becomes less stable (Ingraham 1999; Otnes and Pleck 2003). So for same-sex couples, the decision to hold a wedding-like public commitment ritual represents an embrace of the most widely recognized and easily understood cultural practice associated with marriage. By the same token, the decision *not* to stage such a ritual represents a choice to refrain from the most powerful cultural symbol of marriage. Second, the people who have not opted for a public ritual appear to be somewhat less invested in marriage as a cultural model for committed relationships, compared to those who pursue a public ritual. The study participants who had not held a public ritual were also less likely to use marriage-related terminology to refer to their partners or their relationship and less likely to respond affirmatively if asked whether they were married. These differences suggest that the couples who decided against public ritual may have a different take on the desirability or usefulness of marriage as a cultural model for their own commitment.

Alternatives, obstacles and issues of timing

Many study participants described fairly specific reasons for not participating in a public commitment ritual with their partner. Among the most commonly cited reasons were other commitment practices shared privately between the couple or other kinds of public celebration that served some of the same purposes a public commitment ceremony would. Several people also described specific obstacles that prevented a public ceremony, such as lack of time, money or family support. And for some, the idea of a public ritual posed timing issues. An event meant to symbolize the couple's commitment did not seem appropriate to some couples because they had been together for a long time. For others, the concern about timing emerged from their feelings about how their relationship was going or the lack of community support at this particular stage in their relationship.

As I described in Chapter 2, many same-sex couples engage in cultural practices other than public commitment ceremonies to express their mutual commitment, and some of these practices do draw on the symbolism of marriage. When I asked study participants why they had not held a public commitment ritual, several people pointed to these other practices and described them as sufficient for meeting the couple's need for an expression of commitment. The most common form of commitment practice mentioned as an alternative to public ritual was a private ring exchange, which sometimes occurred in the context of a private ceremony of some kind, involving only the couple themselves. Joel Hauser and Christopher O'Neal are white middle-class professionals in their 30s. Joel, an engineer, and Christopher, a retail manager, met in a bar five years ago and moved in together after dating for about a year. After three and a half years together, they exchanged rings with each other during a trip to Europe. Both partners feel that this private ring exchange was enough. "We had our own private little moment where we exchanged rings in Italy," Joel commented, "and that's all we really need." Christopher concurred: "Yeah, we never wanted a ceremony."

Other couples described doing a ring exchange within the context of a private ritual. Jenny Pyrdol and Sandra Drewitt have been together for thirteen years. They bought a home together after the first year of their relationship. When I asked about a public commitment ritual, Sandra, a 41-year-old white therapist, noted that the couple had decided not to hold a public ritual but had exchanged rings privately. Jenny, a 55-year-old white entrepreneur, explained:

I'm not really interested [in a public ceremony], she wasn't really interested. What we did do, in the first year we were in the house here, was exchange rings that we picked out specifically with each other. And we had diamonds – the ring she has is a diamond that belonged to my mother, and I have diamonds that belonged to her mother and her father. So what we did was take something that both of us had given to the other, and these [rings] were just settings, and we liked the settings and had the diamonds put in. And we had a little mini-ceremony . . . and said what it meant, and it was just really informal.

When I asked Jenny to elaborate on the meaning of their private ceremony, she stated, "A simple and true commitment. That's it. It's really nothing fancier than that." Other couples described similar private ceremonies centered on a ring exchange. Gary Weaver and Jeff Muldoon exchanged rings under a tree in a local park. Barry Sargent and Howard O'Hara conducted a private ritual in their home and now keep a small box that contains mementos from their ritual and reminders of the significance of their commitment. Susan Lemus and Bess Hardin exchanged both rings and letters describing their views on commitment.

For some couples, housewarming parties serve as a meaningful alternative to a public commitment ceremony. I have already noted Robbie Caputo's observation that his housewarming party with his partner Alex "was almost like having a commitment ceremony" because it provided an opportunity for the couple to celebrate their shared home and life, and for their friends to affirm the value of their relationship. Likewise, Susan Lemus and Bess Hardin pointed to their housewarming party as an event that served some of the same functions as a commitment ceremony:

BESS: A few months after we moved in together, we moved into a new apartment. We decided that we would move in together into a new place, so that it would be ours, not her moving into my place. And when we did that, we had a huge housewarming party. And that was kind of like, in a way, it had the feeling of a ceremony. We sent out these invitations that we made ourselves, and, not that we really thought about it, but a lot of people that saw the invitation, because it was all about our love for each other and we were moving in together . . .

SUSAN: It was like a housewarming and . . .

BESS: Well, a lot of people said to me later, "We couldn't tell if it was a commitment ceremony or a housewarming!"

SUSAN: There was no ceremony or anything . . . And it was really nice, but I think in a way, it kind of served a similar purpose, because all your friends, the people you work with come, they see where you live, they acknowledge you.

Bess and Susan's account suggests that their housewarming was an occasion that not only served as an alternative to a public commitment ritual, but even blurred the boundary between commitment ceremonies and other communal events that can provide affirmation to same-sex couples.

Some study participants explained their choice not to hold a public commitment ritual by reference to specific obstacles to such an event. Two male study participants, whose partners were not interviewed for the study, said their partner's lack of interest was the only significant obstacle. Ted Grasskamp, a 46-year-old white nurse, cites his partner Damien's reluctance in explaining the fact that they have not held a public commitment ritual. Ted and Damien have been a couple for seven years, and have maintained separate residences throughout their relationship. Ted is eager to have a ceremony, believing it will strengthen their relationship and send an important message about same-sex commitment to the wider community, but Damien is not enthusiastic. Still, Ted reported that he had gotten Damien to agree to have some kind of public ceremony by their tenth anniversary. Justin Tanner, a 47-year-old white administrative assistant, has been with his partner Frederick for six and a half years. Justin and Frederick attend a gay-friendly synagogue in Chicago. Justin discussed the idea of a commitment ceremony with their rabbi, who was encouraging, but when he raised the issue with Frederick he got a chilly response. Justin explained that Frederick is not out to many of his friends, family, neighbors and co-workers, and would feel ashamed if some of these people found out he is gay. Justin recalled Frederick telling him, "When everyone I know is dead, then we'll have a ceremony."

Other study participants also described issues related to being out in explaining their decision not to have a public celebration of their relationship. Paula Dunham, a 51-year-old white high school teacher, has been with her partner Sally Mitchell for thirty years. Sally said she is not against the idea of a ceremony, but Paula said it is not a priority for the couple. Paula is not out at work, except to a few close friends, and would not consider having a ceremony while still in her teaching job. "I'm afraid somebody . . . I don't know what . . . I have a hang-up with that," she explained. Bess Hardin and Susan Lemus both pointed to the fact that they were not out to all of their family members as a consideration when contemplating a public commitment ceremony. Susan knows her conservative Christian mother would not support her, and her mother has forbidden her from discussing her sexuality with younger siblings still living at home. Bess feels little closeness to her own family of origin, and has chosen not to come out to them. Neither woman could envision their family members attending a public ritual and showing support for their relationship.

Several people mentioned lack of time and money as obstacles to holding a public ceremony. Ralph Scripps and his partner Jack are new parents to twin baby boys. Ralph, a 42-year-old white researcher, described the process of becoming parents as long and expensive. The couple explored different options, including domestic and international adoption, and eventually decided to use a surrogate mother. Jack had proposed to Ralph about two years ago, and family members began pressuring them to have a ceremony when they learned of their parenting plans. "Things have just steamrolled out of control," Ralph explained, "and we've had no time and no money to actually put that into play, and that's why we haven't had a ceremony." Ralph added that he and Jack have somewhat different visions of what a ceremony would look like: Jack would like a large, lavish affair whereas Ralph would prefer something small and simple. "I don't think that we can afford, with the boys and stuff like that, to have a big ceremony," Ralph commented, "and he's like, well, if we're going to do it we've got to do it right." Ralph also noted that gays and lesbians face an added pressure to make their ceremonies "bigger than life" because they cannot simply follow the script for a legally or religiously sanctioned ceremony. "The more meaningful you create the ceremony, the more meaningful your relationship, you know?" he observed half-jokingly. "If you just have, OK, we're going to get hitched four weeks from now, whoever can come, come, whoever can't, oh well, it just seems like then you're doing a disservice to your relationship to not make a big deal of it. So I think it's a hard task to do. It's not simple." Partners Gary Weaver and Jeff Muldoon, together seven and a half years, also cited cost issues as an obstacle to having a public ceremony. Gary, a 38-year-old white psychotherapist, said he and Jeff have talked about having a ceremony in connection with their tenth anniversary. "We just don't have any money," Gary commented, "and we'd like to do it nicely, and have something that we'd like to invite people to, and we just couldn't afford it right now." In a separate interview, Jeff also cited money as the main reason they have not yet held a public ritual.

A number of study participants described timing and life-course issues that made the idea of a public ceremony seem unappealing or inappropriate. Some of the couples who had been together for a period of years felt it might be too late in their relationship for such a ceremony to make sense. Paula Dunham and Sally Mitchell's thirty-year relationship was one of the longest represented in the study. Sally, a 66-year-old retiree, said the couple had enjoyed attending the commitment ceremony of two female friends but Sally felt "it might be a little bit embarrassing at this stage" for her and Paula to hold such an event. Likewise, Gary Weaver wondered whether a ceremony would be appropriate after more than seven years with his partner Jeff. Although Gary thought they would have had a ceremony already if they could afford one, the passage of time has made the idea seem less fitting. Gary observed:

A ceremony would be kind of redundant. It would suggest that . . . You know, when heterosexual couples marry, until they're married, they're not married, and then they're married, and the wedding is really an event, it really marks a transition for them. I'm not sure what kind of transition it would mark. I don't see how we would be more married. So it kind of feels redundant.

Like Gary and Jeff, Barry Sargent and Howard O'Hara are considering having a public ceremony in conjunction with their tenth anniversary, about a year away. They had talked about a public ceremony in the early stages of their relationship, but Barry was not out to his family at that point. They exchanged vows privately on their fifth anniversary, but neither feels sure they will decide to hold a public ritual for their tenth. Howard is a 46-year-old white corporate trainer who left the Catholic priesthood when he became involved with Barry. Howard feels some-what drawn to a public ritual, but also feels the couple does not have the kind of communal support that would make a ritual meaningful. "I think if we had a ceremony," Howard remarked, "I would want to have a religious element to it, and to have a religious element I would feel like we needed to have some real involvement in a religious community that could support that and celebrate that, and we don't." Howard noted that many friends had been urging him and Barry to have a public ceremony, but "it hasn't felt like the right time yet."

A few study participants placed their lack of interest in a public ceremony in the context of their personal and relationship history. Silvia Mendez and Marisol Ochoa have been together for four years. Neither woman has much interest in a public commitment ritual. Silvia, a 44-year-old biracial retail executive, married a man when she was only 15 years old, had two children with him, and was divorced by age 19 despite pressure from family members to stay in the marriage. When I asked her whether this history was relevant to her current feelings about a commitment ritual, she commented:

I felt like I couldn't get out of a marriage. And I know that those constraints were largely based on roles, that I was a mom, and I was a woman, and he was a man, and we belonged in a family, and I couldn't get any support for divorcing him. So it's hard for me to disassociate the trapped feeling that I had in my marriage. And it forces you to look outside. You know, why do we need this institution, what's the purpose?

Marisol, a 37-year-old Latina fundraiser, also described how her own relationship history had affected her interest in a commitment ceremony. Marisol was with her first female lover for several years and believed the relationship would be permanent, but her lover eventually left her for a man. Silvia had also been in a long-term relationship with a woman prior to Marisol, one that she expected to last a lifetime. Marisol explained that past relationships have made both of them more cautious in thinking about their own commitment:

Coming at this relationship being older, you know, we have more realistic views of what relationships are. Yeah, I want to be with [Silvia] forever, you know, but sometimes we say, a "we'll see" type thing. We're being real, because she thought she had forever, and I sort of thought I had forever, and it really rocked my world when that changed.

Bess Hardin also described the impact of an earlier relationship on her current views of commitment. She was with her first female lover for four years before the relationship came to a "very ugly end," and Bess spent about a year grieving the relationship. In her current relationship with

Susan, Bess feels committed, but her ideas about the meaning of commitment have changed. Bess explained:

I think Susan and I agree that we feel we have a monogamous relationship and that we're committed to a long-term relationship together. In my previous relationship . . . we talked about forever, that we would be together forever, and there would never be anyone else and all that. And one thing I think I learned from that relationship is that I don't believe in that anymore, I don't believe in relationships lasting forever. It may last forever, but I don't believe in talking that way.

The perspectives offered by Bess, Marisol and Silvia suggest that some people's current lack of interest in a public commitment ritual can be best understood in the broader context of their relationship histories and the unfolding of individual life courses.

Ambivalence and indifference

While many study participants pointed to quite specific reasons for not holding a public commitment ritual, others expressed a more generalized ambivalence or indifference toward the idea, or uncertainty about the kind of message or meaning that would attach to such an act. Sometimes people located the source of this ambivalence within themselves, citing personality factors such as shyness or just a general lack of interest in weddings and marriage. For others, the ambivalence had a more social source, stemming from their lack of clarity about what kind of message a public ritual would send to others or how it would be received. A few people highlighted the lack of legal recognition accompanying such rituals in describing their ambivalence or lack of interest.

Joel Hauser and Christopher O'Neal share a general indifference to the idea of a public commitment ritual. Their private ring exchange in Italy met their need to ritualize their commitment, and a public ceremony "would be more for our friends than ourselves," Joel observed. Joel and Christopher could not recall ever sitting down to have a conversation about the idea of a public ceremony. "We just kind of knew from talking with other couples when we were out that we both kind of felt the same way about it," Joel explained. Barry Sargent and Howard O'Hara are still contemplating the possibility of a public ritual, but Howard thinks they are both ill-suited to such an occasion in personality terms. "The ceremony thing for me is, in part, that I'm a terribly introverted person, and Barry is fairly introverted too," Howard stated. "You know, the thought of having a public celebration of our relationship just sends me into my introversion in a big way." For Marisol Ochoa, the issue is not shyness but the lack of any personal ambition connected to weddings and marriage. "I think growing up I just never thought I would get married," Marisol commented, "that whole thing just didn't make sense to me, so . . . that ceremony thing is just something that's never been in my psyche of what I wanted."

Gary Weaver, by contrast, is more ambivalent than indifferent. He feels some attraction to a public ritual, but is not sure where it comes from. As noted above, Gary worries that a public ceremony would be "redundant" since he and Jeff have been together for over seven years and the ritual would not mark a significant transition in their relationship. In discussing the possibility of a public ritual connected to his tenth anniversary with Jeff, the following exchange occurred:

Q: If you do eventually go ahead with that, given that you don't see it marking a transition per se in the relationship, what would be the significance of the ceremony to you?
A: That's a good question, and if I knew an answer to that better, it would make me want to have a ceremony more. I think, so that when people say, "Have you had a ceremony?" we can say, "Yes, we really are married." You know, it kind of feels like, when I call myself married but I've never had a ceremony, you know, maybe I'm not really married or something.
Q: It's like a litmus test for other people?
A: Kind of, kind of! We were talking last night, actually, about who we think of when we think of our family . . . Maybe a wedding would help us feel more like we are a family, you know, our own nuclear family.

Gary's comments simultaneously capture both his feeling of being drawn to a public ritual as a way to create a stronger sense of family and his ambivalence about whether a public ritual would really hold any significance for him. His remarks also demonstrate that his ambivalence is rooted in both personal and social considerations: will a ceremony make him and Jeff feel more like a family, and will it make them "really married" in the view of others?

Other study participants shared Gary's questioning attitude about what kind of social recognition public rituals might deliver to same-sex relationships. Some felt that a public ceremony would effectively enhance others' perception of their commitment, without really deepening the commitment between the partners themselves. Barry, a 29-year-old white manager, feels a public ceremony would do nothing to strengthen his relationship with Howard. "I feel like everyone we know thinks of us as a couple, that's definitely true," Barry commented, "but to have a public ceremony would just sort of solidify it, more so for other people than for us, which I guess is why I don't feel as invested in doing it. I feel like we're very committed to each other, there's no doubt in either of our minds what our commitment is, and so I don't really feel the need for it for us." Robbie Caputo's hesitations about a public ceremony, and the kind of social recognition same-sex couples seek through such rituals, were described earlier. Robbie said that "one of the valid reasons" for having a public ceremony would be "to allow other people to celebrate our union," but he is concerned about "looking for recognition from outside" through a public ritual. Part of his ambivalence results from the lack of legal recognition accompanying such rituals ("you're not going to get the legal recognition and it can hurt you if that's what you're looking for"), but Robbie also framed his ambivalence about social recognition more broadly, as a question about whether external validation should be pursued. "Part of my thing right now, one of the things I'm working on," Robbie explained, "is trying to figure out where in my life I am looking for recognition, from outside society or from structures to validate me." Robbie also voiced concern about same-sex couples imitating the practices of heterosexuals ("we only know this heterosexual marriage thing, and I would be afraid to try to go have a same-sex marriage ceremony, just to try to copy off of what they're doing"), a concern that was also articulated by Bess Hardin when she described the commitment ceremony of some friends who "took the heterosexual model" in designing their ritual. "It just makes me bristle," Bess commented, "to think, you know, why do we have to do that?"

Other study participants echoed Robbie's concerns about the lack of legal recognition for same-sex commitment rituals. For Jenny Pyrdol, the lack of legal recognition renders same-sex ceremonies virtually meaningless. When I asked Jenny why she had no interest in a public commitment ritual, she explained:

I think it's a sham, an imitation of something you can't do. I would attend somebody else's [ceremony] if it's important to them, but it's completely unimportant to me. It means nothing legally, which is what marriage is. We've made a commitment, which is what some married people do effectively as well, but without any benefits to it I just think it's a sham.

Pam Jackson used similar language in describing her lack of interest in a public commitment ritual. Pam, a 40-year-old biracial administrator, has been with her partner Dorothy Purnell for five years. Pam and Dorothy have discussed the idea of a public ceremony, but Pam has no interest because of the lack of legal benefits:

To me, if it's not legal it's a farce. I would like to be protected under the same laws heterosexual couples are, and I think that's very important in terms of our rights and our stability, but I think it's a farce. Why do it? That would be like me doing a rain dance! I don't know what I'm doing, and even if I did, it would just be stupid to me.

Pam went on to say that if Dorothy really pushed the idea, she would probably accommodate her, but the idea of a ceremony without legal recognition seems "really confused" to her. "We can, if push comes to shove, prick our fingers and go, 'OK, we're married!'" Pam joked. "I mean, it's about as legitimate as that." Some study participants who remain open to the idea of a public ritual also cited concerns about the lack of legal benefits as a factor in their thinking. Robbie's partner Alex, for example, suggested that he would be more enthusiastic about the idea of a ceremony if it would bring some change in legal benefits or status. "If we had a ceremony and we came back and Robbie's insurance accepted me for domestic partnership . . . that would be really cool," Alex said. "Or if we could file jointly on our taxes and get some tax breaks or something like that, that to me would be definitely worth having a ceremony and going through the rigmarole, but I don't know what the benefit is." Alex does not appear to share Pam and Jenny's view that the lack of legal recognition renders same-sex rituals a "farce" or a "sham," yet the absence of legal benefits contributes to his ambivalence about the appeal of such a ritual for himself and his partner.

Critiques of marriage

While most study participants who had not held a public commitment ritual described specific reasons for their decision or a more generalized ambivalence or indifference toward the idea, a smaller number leveled critiques against the institution of marriage itself. These critiques of the marriage institution made various arguments against the marriage model, including a questioning of monogamy as the basis for intimate relationships, a repudiation of marriage's history as a patriarchal property relationship, and a rejection of the current debased state of the marriage institution in an era of unstable marital commitment. Some people also expressed skepticism toward the idea of lifetime commitment, thereby offering at least an indirect critique of marriage as a cultural model of close relationship.

Robbie Caputo was the only study participant to offer a critique of monogamy in the context of explaining his ambivalence about the idea of a public commitment ritual, but several other people also described their questioning of monogamy at other points in their interviews. Recall that Robbie made the following observation in explaining his mixed feelings about a public ritual: "Maybe we're not, maybe some people aren't meant to be in these monogamous unions, and maybe there are other structures that fit, and we only know this heterosexual marriage thing." Other study participants also raised questions about the value of sexual monogamy for same-sex relationships or for any long-term committed relationships. Pam Jackson, for example, recalled that when she first became involved with her partner Dorothy, they discussed the nature of their commitment and Dorothy introduced her to some couples who had sexually open (nonmonogamous) relationships. Pam was bothered by the idea at first, but has come to accept that sexual monogamy may not work for all couples:

I have to say that initially it really bothered me. And I have to say, in the last year, not because I have any desire to see anyone else or anything, but I do see why couples may do that. I can kind of see where there is a funny place for that to work. I don't think it necessarily works, somebody's still going to feel bad out of the two, somebody's going to come up short, but I can still see where that might work for some people.

Barry Sargent also described an evolution in his thinking about the necessity of sexual monogamy in gay relationships. He recalled that he used to have a strongly negative opinion of open relationships, but as he got to know more gay couples in such relationships his attitude became more tolerant. "I sort of figured, well, if it works for people and they want to define it that way . . . and I still feel that way, that if people want to define it that way, then that's their prerogative," Barry explained. But recently he has become more skeptical about the viability of open relationships, since "everyone we know who has a relationship like that either has a really, really tumultuous relationship, that is just up and down all the time, or it just doesn't work." Yet Barry holds to his belief that gay couples should feel free to experiment with other forms of relationship that might work better for them.

Gay critiques of sexual monogamy have existed since the birth of the gay liberation movement at the end of the 1960s, a movement that was itself influenced by both the women's movement and the American counterculture. Some gay liberationists argued that sexually monogamous gay relationships represent a destructive and self-hating attempt to imitate heterosexual marriages.[4] A number of studies have found relatively high rates of sexual nonexclusivity among gay male couples (Blumstein and Schwartz 1983; McWhirter and Mattison 1984; Kurdek 1988, 1991; Peplau and Cochran 1988; Peplau, Cochran and Mays 1997; Adam 2003). Adam (2003) notes that "[n]on-monogamy is not an indicator of relationship failure among gay men," since studies have found no major differences between open and closed relationships in terms of relationship quality, and some studies even suggest a positive relationship between sexual openness and relationship duration. Many of these studies were conducted prior to the advent of AIDS, and gay relationship practices may have shifted somewhat in response to the AIDS threat. But Adam's (2003) recent study of gay men in relationships of at least one year's duration found that complete sexual exclusivity was practiced in only about a quarter of the relationships. In my interview sample, reported rates of sexual exclusivity were much higher than these studies would suggest: only one male couple (and none of the female couples) reported a sexually open relationship at the time of the interview. One other male couple had practiced nonexclusivity at an earlier point in their relationship.[5]

A few female study participants referenced the history of marriage as a gendered, patriarchal institution in explaining their lack of interest in marriage as a cultural model of relationship. Silvia Mendez, who attributed some of her lack of interest in a commitment ceremony to her own history of early marriage and divorce, commented: "The institution of marriage is really about chattel, it's about property . . . so I'm not sure, I'm not too hip on that part of it!" Bess Hardin and Susan Lemus also grounded their critique of marriage in the institution's history as a gendered property relationship:

BESS: The institution of marriage is, to me, an institution of ownership. Traditionally, it was when a man acquired a woman, as part of his, he was in possession of her or something. That's where the whole dowry thing came from. And so I don't, in my own life, in my own relationship, I really don't want to participate in that. I want it to be more of a partnership.

SUSAN: Yeah, neither of us possesses the other. We're both here because we want to be.

BESS: Right. Plus, I see it as a very heterosexual institution, and so therefore I don't really . . . I'm not heterosexual, I don't identify as heterosexual, and I don't have any desire to participate in this heterosexual institution.

Silvia, Bess and Susan were the only study participants who described their questioning of marriage in terms that were clearly linked to a feminist understanding of the history of marriage as a site of gender oppression.

A few people also questioned the idea of a lifetime commitment, which might be considered a defining feature of marriage, in theory if not in practice. This questioning sometimes occurred in the context of reflecting on past relationships, as when Marisol Ochoa remarked: "I want to be with [Silvia] forever, you know, but sometimes we say, a 'we'll see' type thing. We're being real." Likewise, Bess Hardin attributed a shift in her thinking about lifetime commitment to the breakup of her previous relationship. When Bess observed that she no longer believes in talking about "forever," her partner Susan concurred: "Life is really long, and both of us have changed so much from the time we were born to now, and other things could change too, so to promise forever, I agree with you, I don't know how someone could really do that." Joel Hauser recalled that after he and his partner Christopher exchanged rings privately, people asked them whether the rings symbolized a lifetime commitment. "And our answer to that is we hope so, the way we feel right now, but you never know," Joel said. Remarks like these, challenging the idea of making a lifetime commitment to a partner, do not directly critique the institution of marriage, but they do cast a critical gaze on one of marriage's defining principles.

Finally, one study participant based her critique of the institution of marriage not on history or on the defining features of the institution (sexual exclusivity and lifetime commitment), but on how marriage is actually practiced in the present. Sandra Drewitt argued that the institution of marriage has been undermined by people's failure to take their marriage vows seriously in a world of widespread and easy divorce. Sandra explained that she did not want to participate in an institution so debased by its current participants:

I . . . think the institution of marriage is pathetic, really. Because it's easier to get divorced than it is to get married, it's cheaper to get divorced than it is to get married. I think people don't adhere to what it's supposed to be, if they would adhere to their vows. You know, well, if it doesn't work out we'll just get a divorce. I really don't believe that people believe that if they sign that piece of paper they'll work harder. You know, there's all this research out there, that if you just live together, people just walk away, but if you're married . . . that's crap. The only time people work harder is because they have children . . . If they don't have children, they can just pay their $650 to a lawyer and they walk away. So I think the institution of marriage is kaput.

Sandra's critique of marriage is not leveled against marriage as an ideal, but instead against the way contemporary (heterosexual) couples have corrupted the marriage ideal through their lack of true commitment to the institution and to each other.

In sum, the people in this study who had not held a public commitment ritual identified a variety of reasons for not holding such an event. Many of these reasons were quite specific: other events such as housewarming parties or private exchanges of rings made a public ritual seem unnecessary; particular obstacles stood in the way of such an event, such as lack of time or money, partner's lack of interest or not being out to some friends and family; a public ritual did not seem to fit into the relationship's evolution or into the individual personal histories of the partners. Beyond these rather specific reasons, a number of study participants also expressed a more generalized ambivalence or indifference toward the idea of a public ritual. Some people were unsure what the purpose of such a ritual would be, or felt they were not the kind of person who would participate in such an event. Others simply felt no need for such an occasion. Some felt the event would be mainly for other people rather than for the couple themselves, noting that it would not change their relationship or enhance their commitment. And a few felt that the lack of legal recognition accompanying such rituals made them unreal and therefore unappealing. A smaller number of study participants framed their lack of interest within a critique of the institution of marriage, by challenging the value of some of the defining features of the institution (sexual monogamy and lifelong commitment), decrying marriage's history as a patriarchal property relationship, or lamenting the current instability of the institution.

Individual study participants typically cited several different reasons for their decision not to participate in a public commitment ritual. For Bess Hardin, for example, the reasons ranged from the personal to the ideological. Bess and her partner Susan had done a private exchange of rings and had held a housewarming party when they moved in together; both of these occasions made a public ritual seem unnecessary. Bess has not come out to her family of origin, so the idea of a public ritual that includes family participation does not make sense at this stage in her life. Her painful breakup from her previous lover has caused Bess to rethink the idea of promising forever to a partner, no matter how strong the current feelings of love and commitment. And Bess is turned off by marriage's history as a "heterosexual institution" and a property relationship that oppressed women. Like Bess, Alex Gellar also described an array of reasons for hesitating to move forward on a public ritual with his partner Robbie. After so many years with Robbie, Alex cannot see the point of such an event. He believes a public ritual would not bring any significant change in their commitment to each other, a commitment that has already been solidified by their joint purchase of a home. The cost of such an event also deters Alex, and the fact that it would not bring the tangible benefits that accompany legal marriage further dampens his interest. Most study participants were like Bess and Alex in identifying a mix of considerations against having a public ritual. Only a few cited one simple reason: for both Ted Grasskamp and Justin Tanner, their partners' reluctance to participate in a ritual was the only reason offered; for new parent Ralph Scripps, lack of time and money was the sole obstacle.

In general terms, what emerges from these accounts is less a resounding rejection of the marriage model than a vague sense that public ritual does not fit into these couples' lives at this stage in their relationship or their individual life courses. Many of these individuals told me they did not object to the idea of public commitment rituals, and several described attending the rituals of other couples and finding them quite moving. For many people, the question about public commitment rituals was less "why not?" and more "why?" They felt no compelling desire to participate in such an event (with only a few exceptions), and did not have a clear sense of any purpose that would be served by a public ritual. Some individuals emphasized issues of timing, others wondered who such an event would really be for, and a few specifically objected to the lack of legal recognition for these rituals. The various specific reasons people described were often connected by a sense of ambivalence and uncertainty. A few study participants were anxious to sweep away the obstacles that prevented them from holding a public ritual, and a few others positioned their lack of interest in a broader critique of the institution of marriage. But most occupied a mushy middle, at once acknowledging possible interest in a public ritual and expressing ambivalence and uncertainty about such an act. If these mixed feelings toward public ritual are taken as a measure of people's feelings about marriage as a cultural model for intimate commitment, the dominant theme that emerges is not a decisive rejection of marriage as a cultural model, but a questioning ambivalence about importing the marriage model into their own lives at this point in time.

The intracommunity debate on marriage that has unfolded in academic publications and popular media outlets highlights the viewpoints of a particular slice of the gay and lesbian community (namely scholars, activists, journalists and professional commentators) and focuses on the policy question of legal recognition. But many of the views articulated in the intracommunity debate address marriage in general terms, and some of the concerns raised by marriage critics could apply to gays and lesbians embracing marriage as a cultural model. But in my interviews with an admittedly small number of same-sex couples who have chosen not to hold public commitment rituals, I heard only faint echoes of many of the concerns raised in the intracommunity debate. A few female study participants identified marriage's history as a gendered and patriarchal institution as being central to their choice not to enact marriage culturally through public ritual. Other study participants wondered whether marriage (and its requirement of sexual monogamy) was a good fit for all same-sex relationships, and some expressed qualms about imitating a heterosexual norm. Some took a highly realistic view of relationships and distanced themselves from the romantic ideology of "forever" that underpins marriage as a cultural form. But only a minority of the study participants who had not held a ritual advanced these kinds of explicitly critical explanations. More common was a vague ambivalence or indifference.

My findings are based on too few couples to draw broad conclusions, but they suggest that the discourses of the intracommunity debate on marriage portray highly polarized positions on marriage that may not reflect the way ordinary gays and lesbians think about marriage. Interestingly, some of the critiques of marriage articulated in the intracommunity debate did not appear in any of the comments by study participants. None of the people choosing against ritual mentioned concerns about how cultural practices of marriage might erode social support for a diversity of family and relationship forms (although the questioning of the monogamy requirement could be read as an indirect critique of the marriage model's foreclosure of other models of commitment). Nor did any of the study participants talk about the danger of cultural practices of marriage producing new inequalities among gays and lesbians. In fact, these couples' ambivalence toward marriage as a cultural model of relationship may have more in common with the perspective of heterosexual couples who choose unmarried cohabitation than with the views of participants in the intracommunity debate who critique marriage mainly on ideological grounds.

Heterosexual cohabitation and the retreat from marriage

Social commentators and social scientists have identified what they call a retreat from marriage among heterosexuals. Specific manifestations of this trend include high divorce rates, lower marriage and remarriage rates, later age at first marriage and the dramatic rise in cohabitation over the past few decades. All of these developments can be read as evidence that Americans are more hesitant to marry than in the past or place less value on the institution of marriage. Thus, it is interesting to compare the gay and lesbian couples in this study who choose not to fully embrace marriage as a cultural model of relationship with those heterosexuals who choose to distance themselves from marriage in some way. Since twenty of the twenty-two people in my sample who had not held a public commitment ritual were cohabiting with their partner, the most obvious comparison group is unmarried heterosexual cohabitors. Are there parallels between the motivations and beliefs of the study participants who question or reject the marriage model and heterosexuals who choose cohabitation over marriage?

Of course, gays and lesbians who question or reject marriage as a cultural form face a different set of options than heterosexuals who cohabit instead of marrying. Most gays and lesbians have access to *only* the cultural dimension of marriage, whereas heterosexuals who choose not to marry are simultaneously declining both the cultural and legal dimensions of marriage. This is a crucial distinction, since some gays and lesbians express ambivalence toward the cultural practices of marriage precisely because they are not accompanied by legal recognition, and some heterosexuals may choose not to marry primarily to avoid the legal constraints and responsibilities of marriage rather than to reject marriage in cultural terms. Still, the comparison of these two groups is useful to give a rough sense of the similarities and differences among heterosexuals and homosexuals who distance themselves from marriage despite being in a committed relationship.

Heterosexual cohabitation rates have risen sharply in recent years. The proportion of American women age 19–44 who had ever cohabited jumped from one-third in 1987 to almost one-half by 1995 (Bumpass and Lu 2000, 32). Cohabitation has now become a typical prelude to marriage: only one in ten marriages was preceded by cohabitation in the late 1960s and early 1970s, but by the early 1990s cohabitation preceded the majority of marriages (Smock 2000, 3). Cohabitation is usually not a long-term relationship status for heterosexual couples in the United States, with half of all cohabitations lasting a year or less and only one in ten lasting five years or more (Bumpass and Lu 2000, 33). Although cohabitation often precedes marriage, the proportion of cohabitations that turn into marriages has been declining. By the 1990s, only about one-third of cohabitations transitioned to marriage within three years, compared to almost two-thirds of cohabitations in the 1970s (Manning and Smock 2002, 1065–6).[6] So it appears that cohabitation may be serving as a kind of "trial marriage" for heterosexuals less often now than in the past. Compared to people who do not cohabit, cohabitors on average have somewhat lower education and income, and are somewhat less traditional in the sense that they are more liberal, less religious and more committed to the ideal of gender equality (Smock 2000, 4).

Surprisingly little research has been done to determine why straight cohabitors choose to live together without marrying. Blumstein and Schwartz (1983) collected survey and interview data from married couples, cohabitors and gay and lesbian couples in the late 1970s. They found that most of the heterosexual cohabitors approached cohabitation as a trial marriage, but about one-fifth were what they called "ideological cohabitors," committed to cohabitation as a way of life and a permanent alternative to marriage. The ideological cohabitors were more likely than other cohabitors to have been previously married, and some of their preference for cohabitation resulted from their past negative experiences with marriage and divorce. Some of the ideological cohabitors reported that they did not see the point of getting married, did not want to commit to a monogamous relationship, or wanted to stay in their relationship for the right reasons rather than out of a feeling of obliga-tion. The ideological cohabitors were concerned with maintaining their own independence and limiting their partner's dependence on them, and expressed skepticism regarding relationship permanence.

More recent research on the motivations of cohabitors suggests a move away from using cohabitation as a stepping stone to marriage. In one of the few recent studies that asks heterosexual cohabitors to de-scribe their decision to cohabit, sociologist Sharon Sassler (2004) con-ducted in-depth interviews with cohabitors aged 20–33 in the New York City area and found that most cited finances, convenience or changes in their housing situation (such as a roommate moving out) as their pri-mary reasons for moving in with their partner. Sassler concludes that researchers should no longer assume that most heterosexual cohabitors regard living together as a precursor to marriage. Instead, many straight couples may now begin living together without firm plans to marry each other, but also without firm convictions against marriage. Recent re-search on low-income couples with children finds these couples have positive views of marriage but feel they must wait to marry until they have achieved more financial and emotional stability (Gibson, Edin and McLanahan 2003). For such couples, cohabitation functions as a marriage substitute they perceive to be dictated by socioeconomic circumstances rather than as a repudiation of marriage.

No recent studies have provided an in-depth look at American couples who explicitly choose cohabitation as a permanent alternative to mar-riage, but a 2000 study of New Zealand cohabitors focused on this part of the heterosexual cohabiting population, comparable to the "ideo-logical cohabitors" identified by Blumstein and Schwartz over two decades ago. Elizabeth (2000) conducted in-depth interviews with nine-teen cohabitors who framed their decision to live together as a rejection of marriage. The main theme that emerged in their accounts of the preference for cohabitation was the desire for freedom and choice in their intimate lives, as opposed to the compulsion and constraint they believe typify marriage relationships. These marriage resisters stated that the lifetime commitment required by marriage was unrealistic and could potentially trap people in loveless relationships that did not foster individual growth. They also argued that the gendered roles and expectations of marriage were constraining for partners.

Another kind of heterosexual relationship outside marriage is domes-tic partnership, which differs from cohabitation in granting legal re-cognition and limited rights and benefits to unmarried couples. Over the past two decades, dozens of localities and a few states have imple-mented domestic partnership policies, which make available some marriage-related benefits to unmarried couples who register their relationships with the government. Many of these policies are available only to same-sex couples, but some are available to other kinds of relationships, including straight cohabitors. Marion Willetts (2003) conducted interviews with twenty-three heterosexual cohabitors registered as domestic partners in four US cities to find out why they had chosen domestic partnership instead of marriage. Most of the heterosexual licensed domestic partners cited the ability to obtain a particular economic benefit such as health insurance without having to get married. Several previously married cohabitors pursued domestic partnership as a way to obtain some legal recognition without remarrying. A number of other cohabitors registered as domestic partners in order to document their commitment to each other or to outside individuals and organizations. And a few female cohabitors reported that they chose domestic partnership because they rejected marriage as a conformist institution that robs women of their individual identities.

This brief review of the limited research on the motivations of unmarried heterosexual cohabitors and domestic partners suggests some significant parallels with the perspective of committed same-sex couples who choose not to hold public commitment rituals. Again, it is important to emphasize that heterosexuals who decline to marry are facing a different set of options than most same-sex couples, who at this point have the option to decline only the cultural dimension of marriage, since the legal dimension is unavailable to them. Still, there is notable overlap in how heterosexual unmarried partners discuss their choice not to marry and how same-sex couples explain their choice not to enact marriage culturally through public ritual. It appears that most people in both groups (gay and straight) are distancing themselves from marriage mainly due to a mix of circumstance and general ambivalence or indifference toward the institution of marriage, rather than as a result of explicit ideological opposition to marriage. For heterosexuals, the ambivalence often includes a discomfort with the idea of assuming the legal obligations of marriage, whereas for people in same-sex relationships it is sometimes the very lack of legal obligation and recognition that creates ambivalence toward the cultural dimension of marriage. Because most people in both groups do not express a decisive rejection of marriage, the possibility of moving toward marriage in the future often features in the background of their relationship lives. In other words, many same-sex couples leave the door open to a future embrace of the marriage model through public ritual, just as many heterosexual cohabitors and domestic partners retain the option of getting married later in their relationship.

For a minority in both groups, feelings about marriage go beyond ambivalence or indifference to outright opposition and critique. Among both gays and straights, the people who consciously and decisively reject the marriage model appear focused on the broad cultural meaning of marriage rather than on the specific requirements of marriage. Both gay and straight marriage critics describe a few core concerns with marriage. These include marriage's history as a patriarchal institution of property and gender oppression, a concern that appears to be articulated more often by women; its requirement of sexual monogamy, sometimes perceived as an unnecessary or unnatural constraint; and its expectation of lifetime commitment, which strikes some people in committed partnerships as a desirable but possibly unrealistic goal.

The social characteristics of ritual participants and nonparticipants

How do same-sex couples who choose not to use public ritual to celebrate their commitment compare to the couples who do? Are there clear patterns of difference in terms of the social characteristics of these two groups? Is it plausible that such differences might partly explain their different approaches to the cultural enactment of commitment? The two groups in my study were not randomly selected, so we cannot assume that they are representative of the broader populations of same-sex couples who do or do not participate in public commitment rituals. Any differences between the two groups in this study must be viewed as suggestive evidence of the possibility of general differences between these two types of couples. Nonetheless, there are several notable differences, as well as some interesting similarities, in the social characteristics of these two groups, and these patterns provide a starting point for thinking about the possible relationship between social location and the use of cultural practices to enact commitment.

I collected a broad range of basic background information in the in-depth interviews, including demographic characteristics such as gender, age, race/ethnicity, occupation, place of residence and social class, as well as attitudinal information such as general political views. I also collected information on people's relationship histories, including past heterosexual marriages. And I gathered some background information that was specific to their social location as sexual minorities. These background questions were meant to provide a sense of the study participants' embeddedness in gay and lesbian communities, cultures and movements. Thus, in thinking about possible differences between the social characteristics of couples who held public rituals and those who did not, we can consider both general social characteristics as well as aspects of social location that are specific to a person's identity as a sexual minority.

There are a few notable differences between the two groups in terms of their general social characteristics. Ritual participants were more likely than nonparticipants to be female, suburban and previously in a hetero-sexual marriage. On average, ritual participants also had lower socio-economic status and less interest in politics. Taken together, these patterns suggest the possibility of some significant social differences between same-sex couples who participate in public commitment rituals and those who do not.

It was much easier to find female couples who had participated in public commitment rituals than male couples, as I noted in Chapter 2. In combination with national survey data finding that women more often participate in such rituals, my experience suggests that same-sex couples holding public commitment rituals are disproportionately female. Since recent estimates put the population of self-identified gay men at roughly twice the size of the population of self-identified lesbians (Laumann et al. 1994), the gender imbalance among the ritual participants is all the more striking. By contrast, I had little trouble locating equal numbers of men and women in recruiting ritual nonparticipants for this study.

Beyond gender, the ritual participants and nonparticipants differed on several other important social characteristics, including socioeconomic status. Using a combination of criteria, I coded all study participants as upper middle class, middle class or lower middle class/working class.[7] Ritual participants were more likely to be lower middle class/working class and less likely to be upper middle class compared to nonpartici-pants. Roughly half of the people in both groups fell into the middle-class category. Among the rest, nearly half of the nonparticipants were upper middle class, compared to only about one in five ritual partici-pants, and about a third of the ritual participants were lower middle class/working class but only one nonparticipant fell into this category. Significant educational differences between the two groups paralleled these class differences. About one-third of the people in both groups had a college degree as their highest education level, but only one-third of the ritual participants had a graduate or professional degree, compared to more than half of the ritual nonparticipants.

In the intracommunity debate on marriage, some marriage critics assert that well-educated and prosperous gays and lesbians are the most interested in marriage and the most likely to benefit from it. It may be the case that the greatest *financial* benefits from legal marriage would flow to the most well-off, but the socioeconomic differences within my sample suggest something different with respect to the relationship between socioeconomic status and interest in the *symbolic* benefits of marriage. My findings suggest that relatively less-educated couples of modest financial means may have a stronger interest in using public ritual to enact commitment and capture some of the symbolic benefits of marriage that these rituals may provide.

Ritual participants and nonparticipants in this study also differed in terms of where they live and the political views they hold. While about half of the ritual participants lived in the city and the other half in the suburbs, about two-thirds of the ritual nonparticipants were city dwellers. The groups also differed in terms of their political views, with ritual participants demonstrating less interest in political matters. Nearly a quarter of the ritual participants described themselves as apathetic or apolitical, whereas none of the ritual nonparticipants expressed a complete lack of interest in politics. Given the average voter turnout in recent elections, the ritual participants seem to more closely mirror the general population in terms of their interest and involvement in politics.

The two groups also differed in the likelihood that their members had previously been in a heterosexual marriage and in the meanings they attached to those previous marriages. Ritual participants were about twice as likely as nonparticipants to have previously been in a heterosexual marriage. When ritual participants spoke about these prior marriages, they often did so in the context of contrasting them to their current relationship, sometimes directly comparing their heterosexual wedding to their same-sex commitment ritual. Several of the women who had been married to men said they married too young, sometimes as a way to escape living in their parents' home. Several study participants described their same-sex ritual as an opportunity to have a wedding that was consciously chosen rather than a convenient escape hatch or a nod to social expectations. Diane Wilson said she was nervous before her ceremony with Martha Petrillo, because it was her second time around. "But I was very excited about it," Diane commented, "because I felt like this was the one I really wanted to do, in a lot of ways. This is the one that's really for me and who I am." James Logan, a 36-year-old white corporate manager, married a woman in his early 20s, partly in response to family and religious pressures. James said he was glad he was able to leave that marriage and correct his mistakes while he was still fairly young. He also remarked that he had enjoyed being married to his wife and he viewed that marriage as a model for his relationship with his partner Frank. James conceded that heterosexual marriages are not perfect, but said "there's a couple things that work."

The few ritual nonparticipants who had previously been in heterosexual marriages attached a rather different meaning to their marriage history. Silvia Mendez, who married a man at age 15 and got divorced four years and two children later, resented the lack of social or familial support for deciding to end her marriage, and the feeling of being "trapped" in the marriage. She asserted that this personal history (along with her view of marriage as a property relationship) contributed to her lack of interest in participating in a commitment ritual with her partner Marisol. Dorothy Purnell married at 18, had her only child at 22, and remained with her husband for fifteen years, mostly for the sake of their child. She commented that part of her lack of interest in having a commitment ritual with her partner Pam might stem from having gone through the wedding process with her former husband.[8]

While there were patterns of social difference between the ritual participants and nonparticipants in this study on some dimensions (gender, social class, education, place of residence, political views and marriage history), on other dimensions they looked more similar than different. The two groups were close in terms of their average age (41 for ritual participants and 42 for ritual nonparticipants). Even though ritual participants sometimes described their decision to hold a public ritual as part of their coming-out process or as part of their individual transition to a new stage of adulthood, they were not older than the nonparticipants on average. This lack of age difference between these groups may reflect the competing influences of cultural-historical context and the effects of life-course progression at the individual level. Members of older cohorts of gays and lesbians often came of age sexually during the late 1960s or 1970s, a period when both gay and mainstream culture emphasized sexual liberation and sometimes questioned the value of monogamy. So, although moving toward middle age might prompt some gays and lesbians to give more serious consideration to "settling down" and having a public commitment ritual, gays and lesbians currently in their 40s, 50s and 60s also may have absorbed cultural messages in the earlier years of their adulthood that make them less attracted to marriage as a cultural model for commitment.

The two groups of couples also look quite similar in terms of social characteristics and practices relating to their sexual identity. If public commitment rituals are viewed as an assimilationist cultural practice, one that attempts to erase the distance between same-sex couples and mainstream heterosexual society, we might expect the ritual participants to be somewhat less embedded in gay and lesbian social networks, subcultures and movements. However, despite being more likely to live in the suburbs and less likely to take an interest in politics, the ritual

participants did not appear to differ substantially from ritual nonparticipants in terms of social networks and practices that tie them to gay and
lesbian communities and cultures. Ritual participants were no more or
less likely than nonparticipants to include other gays and lesbians in their
primary social networks, and no more or less likely to engage in a range
of gay-related practices such as reading gay publications, attending gay
and lesbian cultural events, belonging to gay and lesbian organizations or
donating to gay and lesbian causes.[9] Thus, the ritual participants in this
study do not appear to be less connected to gay people, groups and
issues.

Nor do ritual participants appear to differ from nonparticipants in
terms of their degree of outness or their expression of aspirations to
assimilate into mainstream society.[10] Most people in both groups described a high degree of outness in their daily lives, meaning they were
out to most or all people in their family, friendship and work relationships. Only a few people in each group led closeted lives, revealing their
sexual orientation to few friends, family or acquaintances. Living in a
suburban area and expressing lack of interest in politics – both characteristics that were more frequent among the ritual participants – might
be expected to reduce people's level of outness, since suburbs are perceived to represent a less welcoming environment for gays and lesbians
than cities, and since many gays and lesbians think about coming out as
at least partially a political act. So it is perhaps a little surprising that the
ritual participants on average appear to be no more closeted than those
who chose not to hold a public ritual. (Of course, a certain level of
outness is required to hold a public commitment ritual or even to see
that as a possible and desirable option. Thus, the ritual participants in
this study may be somewhat more out than other gays and lesbians with
similar social characteristics such as suburban residence and low interest
in politics.) Ritual participants and nonparticipants were roughly equally
likely to express assimilationist views in the course of the study interview,
with about a quarter of each group articulating goals or concerns related
to establishing social normalcy or fitting into mainstream society. So,
although some commentators have interpreted same-sex commitment
rituals as assimilationist cultural practices, and some study participants
expressed concern that these rituals could be read as attempts to "imitate" straight society, my interview data do not support the idea that gays
and lesbians participating in public commitment rituals have a greater
interest in assimilation than other gays and lesbians.

In summary, the ritual participants and nonparticipants in this study
differed on some social characteristics and not others. Specifically, the
ritual participants on average were more likely to be female, had lower

socioeconomic status, were more likely to live in the suburbs and were less likely to be interested in politics, compared to the ritual nonparticipants. Also, the ritual participants were somewhat more likely to have been in a heterosexual marriage in the past, and the ritual participants attached a different meaning to their past marriages than the nonparticipants who had been married. Ritual participants and nonparticipants did not seem to differ much in terms of their embeddedness in gay and lesbian communities, cultures and movements. People in both groups appeared equally likely to be a part of gay and lesbian social networks, to attend gay and lesbian events or read gay and lesbian publications, and to participate in gay and lesbian social movements through volunteer work or financial donations. The two groups also appeared quite similar in terms of their degree of outness and their interest in assimilating into mainstream society, with the majority in both groups being out to most of their family, friends and co-workers, and only a minority in both groups making comments that reflected a strong desire for assimilation to mainstream society.

Thus, it seems that the characteristics that distinguish the ritual participants from the nonparticipants are general social characteristics such as gender, socioeconomic status and residential location, rather than characteristics that are specific to their identity as sexual minorities such as embeddedness in minority communities, outness or desire for social assimilation. On these latter characteristics, the two groups in this study appear more similar than different. Again, it must be emphasized that the participants in this study were not randomly selected, so any observations about their social characteristics and comparisons across the two groups provide only suggestive evidence that might guide future research. And this study included only people currently involved in a committed same-sex relationship, so the perspectives of gays and lesbians who are single, dating, or involved in casual or new relationships are not represented here. With these caveats in mind, my findings are suggestive and cautionary. The findings suggest that the differences between gays and lesbians who are drawn to the cultural practice of marriage and those who are less attracted to marriage may relate more to general social location than to ways of living in the world as a sexual minority. And the findings caution against simplistic assumptions about the kind of gay or lesbian who is likely to be drawn to marriage as a cultural model of commitment. Although public same-sex commitment rituals can be interpreted as assimilationist cultural practice, my findings suggest that the couples who are drawn to marriage as a cultural model are no less likely to be embedded in gay and lesbian communities and cultures, no less likely to be out and no more likely to voice assimiliationist concerns than other gay and lesbian couples. The world of gay and lesbian couples does not neatly divide into those who embrace marriage and those who reject it, and choices about enacting marriage culturally through ritual do not clearly correspond to different ways of "doing gayness" or different values and aspirations regarding the relationship between minority sexual identities and mainstream society.

This chapter has examined the perspective of same-sex couples who define their relationships as committed but have not held a public commitment ritual. A range of beliefs and practical considerations motivated their decision not to hold a public ritual. Several study participants articulated an explicit critique of marriage as an institution, but more people explained their lack of interest in public ritual in terms of a vague ambivalence or indifference toward the idea, and many also cited specific obstacles to holding a public ritual. The overall picture that emerges from these couples is less a defiant rejection of marriage as a cultural model than a mixture of ambivalence, indifference and inability to surmount particular obstacles to holding such an event.

In some respects, the perspective of these same-sex couples parallels the motivations of heterosexuals who choose unmarried cohabitation or registered domestic partnership over marriage. Heterosexual couples of course have the option of legal marriage, so their decision not to marry is not only (or even primarily) a decision about marriage as a cultural model, whereas most same-sex couples who choose not to have a public ritual are refraining only from the cultural practice of marriage. Still, there is a good deal of overlap between the two kinds of couples in their thinking about marriage. The limited research on the motivations of straight cohabitors and domestic partners indicates that a minority reject the institution of marriage on ideological grounds (i.e. rejecting patriarchy, monogamy or the idea of lifetime commitment), but more describe an ambivalence about marriage that may have a variety of sources, and some consider marriage a possibility in the future. Some of the members of same-sex couples who had not held a public ritual expressed a partial embrace of marriage as a cultural model in other ways, such as holding private rituals or using marriage terminology to refer to their partners or their relationship. Among both opposite-sex and same-sex couples, then, the decision not to "marry" (in the legal sense or the cultural sense) sometimes represents a wholesale rejection of marriage as a social institution, but more often reflects ambivalence or practical considerations shaped by current life circumstances, with the option of marriage left open for the future.

The intracommunity debate on marriage might give the impression that gays and lesbians fall into two discrete and warring camps, for and against marriage. But my findings show that the couples in this study cannot be neatly divided into those who embrace marriage and those who reject it. Some people who had participated in a public commitment ritual expressed reservations about the institution of marriage, and some couples who did not use public ritual found other ways to adopt marriage as a cultural model for their relationships. These two groups of couples differ somewhat on basic social characteristics including gender and socioeconomic status, but they appear quite similar in terms of their involvement in gay and lesbian life, their embrace of a public gay or lesbian identity, and their concerns about assimilation into mainstream society. Future research should address whether the differences and similarities observed in this study are found more generally among gay and lesbian couples, and should compare how committed couples think about marriage as a cultural model to the perspectives of gays and lesbians who are single or in less committed or "marriage-like" forms of relationship.

While the people interviewed for this study had a range of views and practices concerning marriage as a cultural model of commitment, they were quite unified in their support for some form of legal recognition for same-sex relationships. In the next chapter, I describe the reasons study participants gave for wanting legal marriage (or some equivalent legal status), and I explore the relationship between same-sex couples' cultural enactments of marriage and their aspirations for legal recognition and equality.

4   Making it legal: marriage, law and legality

> Law is the quintessential form of the symbolic power of naming that
> creates the things named, and creates social groups in particular. It
> confers upon the reality which arises out of its classificatory operations
> the maximum permanence that any social entity has the power to
> confer upon another, the permanence which we attribute to objects.
> — Pierre Bourdieu (1987)

The previous two chapters examined the range of cultural practices used
by same-sex couples to enact their intimate commitments, and found
considerable variation among couples in their adoption of marriage as a
cultural model of relationship. Some couples embraced the marriage
model wholeheartedly, others were more hesitant or selective in their
use of marriage-related terms and practices, and a few sought to distance
their own relationships from marriage. This chapter examines same-sex
couples' views and attitudes regarding legal recognition of their relationships, and finds similar variation. Although the people in this study
shared broad agreement on the desirability of legal recognition for
same-sex couples, they varied in their views about the form such recognition should take, the reasons legal recognition is important and the
priority that should be given to legal marriage as a gay rights issue.

My interviews with the couples in this study reveal that the law
represents a significant cultural force and resource for some but not all
people in same-sex relationships. Law and culture are closely intertwined in the way many gays and lesbians perceive and enact marriage
in their own lives. I will argue that some of the cultural practices described in the previous chapters, especially public commitment rituals,
can be read as an effort to compensate for the absence of legal recognition of same-sex relationships by constructing a kind of *legality* for these
relationships outside the official law of the state. At the same time, I
describe how some people in same-sex relationships assign a unique
cultural power to the law of the state, the power to render their relationships socially normal and culturally equal to the commitments of
married heterosexual couples (also see Hull 2003). Looking at what

same-sex couples think and say about legal marriage provides a window onto how law and culture mutually constitute the institution of marriage. Couples sometimes use cultural practices to create a sense of legality in their relationships even in the absence of official law, and some gays and lesbians perceive the law of the state as a unique and powerful cultural resource.

Currently, American same-sex couples' access to legal recognition depends on their place of residence, and nowhere in the United States do gay and lesbian relationships enjoy the same legal treatment as heterosexual marriages. At this writing, Massachusetts provides the most comprehensive legal recognition for same-sex couples, granting them marriage licenses and access to all of the *state-level* rights and benefits of legal marriage. However, same-sex marriages formed in Massachusetts are not recognized by the federal government, and many of the significant protections and benefits of legal marriage flow from federal laws and programs. Another limitation to Massachusetts same-sex marriages concerns their "portability," or married couples' ability to have these marriages recognized when they travel in or move to other states. Most states have passed laws (in some cases even amended their state constitutions) to explicitly state that they will not recognize same-sex marriages from other states. States' refusal to recognize these marriages will be subject to court challenges around the country in the years ahead. American same-sex couples also have the option of entering a legal marriage in Canada, but these marriages also are not recognized by most state or federal authorities in the United States.

Three other states run a close second to Massachusetts in providing legal recognition to same-sex relationships. Vermont's civil unions law, passed in 2000, gives couples who enter civil unions a legal status equivalent to marriage in all but name as far as *state* law is concerned. Connecticut passed its own civil unions law, closely paralleling the Vermont statute, in 2005. And the recent expansion of California's domestic partnership system, which took effect in 2005, likewise renders same-sex domestic partners legally equivalent to married couples under state law in almost all respects. The civil unions and domestic partnerships available in these three states face the same limitations as Massachusetts same-sex marriages in terms of lack of recognition by the federal government and most other states. A few other states – Hawaii, New Jersey and Maine – have statewide domestic partnership systems that offer a more limited set of benefits to registered couples.[1]

Beyond statewide forms of recognition, same-sex couples in some parts of the United States have access to limited legal recognition from local governments, and some employers make spousal benefits available to employees who designate a domestic partner. Sixty-four cities, counties and government agencies around the country had implemented domestic partner registries by the end of 2003 (HRCF 2004, 25). These registries often have mostly symbolic value, but in some cases they entitle registered partners to visitation rights in health care and correctional settings. Over 8,000 employers, including 46 percent of the Fortune 500 companies, provide domestic partner benefits including health insurance coverage to employees. Among public employers, eleven states and 188 local governments offer their employees domestic partner benefits that include health insurance. The large majority of these employer-sponsored domestic partner programs are available to both same-sex and opposite-sex couples (HRCF 2005, 15–22). In addition, several city and county governments, and one state, have passed "equal benefits ordinances" requiring firms with large government contracts to offer domestic partner benefits (HRCF 2004, 16).[2]

Although these various forms of partnership recognition offered by governments and employers deliver some marriage-related benefits and protections to same-sex couples, none provides the full package of rights and obligations that constitute legal marriage. Until relatively recently, most gay rights activists and organizations focused all of their efforts in the area of partnership recognition on measures such as domestic partnership, but with the dramatic successes in Vermont and especially in Massachusetts, the political ground shifted and most gay rights organizations now insist that nothing short of full legal marriage is acceptable.[3] But what, exactly, does the institution of legal marriage actually do?

Considering the legal consequences of marriage for same-sex couples, law professor David Chambers (1996) identifies three broad functions of laws related to marriage: recognizing and promoting spouses' emotional attachments, regulating parenting relationships and regulating married couples as economic units. These categories provide a useful framework for considering the possible benefits of legal marriage for same-sex couples and the harms resulting from lack of access to legal marriage.

State and federal laws honor the emotional attachments of legal spouses in various ways. Prominent examples of these kinds of laws include laws that empower spouses to act as decision-makers for mates rendered incompetent through short-term medical emergencies or longer-term mental or physical deficiencies, as well as laws that provide for surviving spouses to receive some or all assets when their spouse dies without a valid will. Same-sex couples can achieve some of these benefits through prudent advance planning (health care powers of attorney, wills, etc.), but the benefits of some other laws in this category cannot be realized through private contracting. For example, the government grants preferential treatment to foreign-born spouses of US citizens under federal immigration law. The federal Family and Medical Leave Act allows spouses, but not domestic partners, to take leaves from work to tend to sick partners. And evidentiary rules that protect spouses from testifying against each other in court and that treat marital communications as confidential are also unavailable to unmarried partners. These sorts of government-conferred benefits, intended to protect and foster emotional attachments between intimate partners, can only be acquired through legal marriage.

Laws regulating parenting relationships also give special treatment to married couples. State laws generally serve to expedite legal adoption of stepchildren by stepparents, but in the case of unmarried same-sex partners there is no expedited process for partners to adopt each other's children. Workers' compensation and Social Security survivors' benefits accrue to minor stepchildren upon the death of a stepparent (even when no adoption has occurred), but these benefits are not available to children upon the death of their biological parent's same-sex partner. Compared to married couples, same-sex couples also face formidable challenges in establishing both partners as legal parents of children who come into their lives through artificial insemination, surrogacy, adoption or foster parenting.

Finally, a wide range of laws regulate the economic relations within married couples or between married couples and the state. Married couples can file joint tax returns (reaping financial bonuses or penalties depending on their incomes), nonworking spouses can obtain Social Security benefits through their spouse, and married partners enjoy exemption from gift and estate taxes. The state regulates economic relations between spouses primarily at the time of divorce, when the government steps in to manage a forced allocation of assets between the parties and to determine the need for alimony or maintenance payments. State laws also generally protect the financial interests of spouses upon their partner's death, through inheritance laws that guarantee some minimum share of the estate to the surviving spouse. And state laws regulate economic relations between married couples and other third parties to a limited degree, for example by giving surviving spouses the right to recover economic losses in wrongful death suits. Same-sex couples can use private contracting to specify how they will divide their assets in the event of a breakup, but courts are sometimes unwilling to enforce such private agreements. Most of the other laws regulating the married couple as an economic unit cannot be replicated by same-sex couples through private contracts or domestic partnerships.

Given the advantages of legal marriage over other forms of relationship recognition in all of these areas, it is perhaps unsurprising that all of the couples in this study voiced support for legal recognition of same-sex couples and that most study participants thought that recognition should take the form of marriage or its exact legal equivalent. Indeed, the specific legal and financial benefits of marriage were the most frequently cited reason for supporting legal marriage among study participants. But many study participants also talked about other reasons for desiring legal marriage, especially issues of rights and equality as well as the perceived symbolic benefits of access to marriage.

Legal marriage: benefits, rights, legitimacy

Although they varied in the reasons they gave and in the importance they attached to the issue, study participants were unanimous in their support for legal recognition of same-sex marriage (or its exact legal equivalent).[4] The specific reasons people gave for supporting legal same-sex marriage included the legal and economic benefits attached to marriage, the belief that access to marriage is a matter of fairness and equal rights, the legitimacy and recognition legal marriage would provide to same-sex relationships, and other positive impacts on the gay and lesbian community generally and on gay and lesbian couples specifically.

Legal and financial benefits

Over two-thirds of the study participants pointed to legal and financial benefits in explaining their support for legal same-sex marriage. In particular, many mentioned the issues of health insurance benefits and the perceived tax benefits of being married. Several study participants expressed frustration that they were unable to get health insurance coverage as a spouse under their partner's insurance policy, or that they could not put their partner on their own health insurance as a dependent. Some people also mentioned particular government benefits that were unavailable because of lack of marriage rights. On taxes, some study participants believed there would be a financial benefit to filing a joint tax return,[5] and others mentioned problems with inheritance taxes and the taxation of domestic partner benefits under employee benefits plans.

Brad Schuster framed his support for legal marriage in terms of a sense of entitlement to the legal benefits of marriage. Earlier in my interview with Brad and his partner Kevin, we had discussed the meaning of their commitment ceremony and they had shown me their photo album chronicling the event. Affirming his support for legal marriage, Brad stated:

It needs to be done . . . Why shouldn't we get the Social Security, and the insurance, and all this other stuff that everybody else is getting if we're doing the same thing? And, sometimes I get a little upset with this [pointing to the photo album from their ceremony], because I think we spent all this money for really nothing legally, I mean legally it means absolutely nothing. And when you fill out legal forms, you still have to check the box that says you're single, because legally you are. In my head I'm not, but on the legal papers I am. So I'm thinking, why not? We're just entitled to these benefits like everybody else.

Many other study participants shared Brad's frustration with lack of access to the legal benefits of marriage. Alex Gellar cited a range of specific complications arising from the lack of access to legal marriage, including issues related to taxes, property transfer and access to health insurance. Like many study participants, Alex worried about interference from blood relatives: "It's ridiculous that I can spend my whole life here with Robbie and have to worry about, you know, when I die is my brother going to come in and try to take all of my property and say that Robbie's not really family and that because I've spent forty years with him it doesn't mean anything? . . . You shouldn't have to live in fear and go through all this stuff you do have to go through to secure your relationship, secure your holdings really." Summing up his support for legal marriage, Alex remarked, "It's financial issues, and somewhat legal."

A number of study participants discussed the complications relating to parenting issues created by lack of access to marriage. The study sample included five couples currently raising children together, two couples who had raised children together in the past, and ten couples who were considering becoming parents or had firm plans to do so (including one woman who was pregnant at the time of the interview). The couples who were currently parenting or considering parenthood were most likely to discuss the practical concerns related to parenting in describing their support for legal marriage. Some discussed the difficulty of establishing legal parenthood for the non-biological parent in couples raising children. Others mentioned the obstacles facing unmarried couples seeking to adopt or become foster parents. And a few noted the problem of obtaining health insurance for children through the policies of partners who have no legal standing as parent. Janis Sobirov and her partner Cindy Dahl are planning to raise a child together in the near future, with Janis hoping to be the biological parent and Cindy planning to become a stay-at-home mom. But Janis' family has not accepted her homosexuality or her relationship with Cindy, and Janis anticipates needing to take extra steps to protect their parenting arrangement. As she explained her support for legal same-sex marriage, Janis stated: "If I had a child, and then something happened to me, we'd have to do all sorts of legal things to make sure [Cindy] could take care of our children, rather than my parents taking our children, and that's ridiculous but that's how it is. And we're going to have to be really careful about that." Like Alex, Janis sees legal marriage as a bulwark against unwanted control and intervention by biological relatives.

Marisol Ochoa, active in Chicago's Latina lesbian community, voiced concern that the lack of access to marriage benefits falls particularly hard on poor women of color. After her partner Silvia remarked that gay men and lesbians feel different impacts from lack of Social Security survivor benefits because women live longer, Marisol added: "And in the lesbian community of color it's even worse. Because lesbians of color are more likely to have children, and so it brings the poverty threshold even lower, and when I think of the friends that we have that are now going through [child] custody battles, and have their girlfriends, what the legal act of marriage would allow for them and their kids, that's when I really believe in it." Marisol also felt personally impacted by the lack of legal marriage. "I opened up today, my Social Security benefits thing came in the mail, and it said if you die your spouse will get this much money a month, it's like a thousand dollars a month! And I'm like, we ain't gonna get shit at that age because we're not legally recognized."

Only one couple included a partner who was not a US citizen, but their story illustrated the difficulties facing binational couples. The immigration-related benefits of marriage were a significant factor in Peggy Wong and Anita Lindstrom's support for legal marriage. Peggy is a native of a southeast Asian country who immigrated to the United States to attend college and only recently obtained her permanent residency status after many years of trying. Peggy and Anita described how the first ten years of their relationship were dominated by problems related to Peggy's immigrant status and the constant threat that she would lose her visa and be forced to return to her native country. At one point, they were separated for a period of several months when she was not allowed back into the United States after visiting family abroad.

Study participants also discussed other difficulties related to health care beyond access to health insurance, including hospital visitation rights and the power to make health care decisions for a partner in the event that the partner becomes incapacitated. Ted Grasskamp had special knowledge of such problems both professionally and personally. Ted's first lover had been in a serious car accident and spent time in the hospital intensive care unit. Despite being his partner, Ted had to request permission from his lover's biological family to visit him in the ICU, and the family retained complete control over health care decisions throughout the ordeal. As a nurse, Ted had also witnessed the misfortunes of other gay couples. He explained:

I work in a hospital. I've seen horror stories beyond people's wildest imaginations. One couple, both with AIDS, as one started deteriorating in health and needed twenty-four-hour care in a nursing home, the family took him away from his partner, put him in a nursing home at an undisclosed location, wouldn't even tell him when he died. I've seen bank accounts frozen within hours after death. I've seen wills not followed. I've seen just horror stories after horror stories. And I had my own horror story too. And that's just not to be tolerated, just not at all.

Alex Gellar expressed fear about the possible interference of homophobic relatives if some kind of health crisis were to befall his partner Robbie, despite the fact that they had established health care powers of attorney for each other.

In fact, several people expressed skepticism about the effectiveness of some of the legal protections they had put in place to safeguard their relationships and financial wishes, including wills, trusts, powers of attorney, partnership agreements and guardianship provisions. They perceived such protections as vulnerable to the whims of judges and blood relatives. Brenda Davis and Kim Pierson drew up their wills and related legal documents around the time of their commitment ceremony. Brenda expressed resentment about the added costs imposed on same-sex couples by the need to establish such protections outside the framework of legal marriage:

It was crazy to have to go and draw up wills and pay for wills, and draw up all these papers for when you're sick, and health whatever, and all the other stuff, power of attorney, all this legal stuff, to get married. And pay those full costs over and above all of that, when everybody else gets to do it for free . . . I'm pretty adamant. I feel very fucked over when those things happen.

For Brenda, the denial of legal marriage represented lack of access to a relatively inexpensive and convenient legal vehicle for establishing a range of protections for her committed relationship. And for most of the study participants, the legal and financial benefits of marriage are part of its attraction, although relatively few people explained their support for legal marriage solely as a matter of access to benefits. Most also framed marriage as a matter of equal rights or a source of social legitimacy.

Equal rights

After tangible legal and financial benefits, the most frequently mentioned reasons for supporting legal same-sex marriage were the issue of fairness and equal rights, and the desire to achieve legitimate status for same-sex couples in society. About half of the study participants framed their support for legal same-sex marriage in the language of rights, fairness, equality or non-discrimination, and half also pointed to the symbolic value of legal marriage, describing marriage as a source of recognition, legitimacy, validation, status or respect.

Many study participants invoked the language of rights in describing their support for legal marriage. Linda "Chico" Sanchez is a 43-year-old transgender individual[6] who has been with his partner Maria for just over a year. When I asked about legal same-sex marriage, Chico remarked:

I strongly feel that [same-sex marriages] should be legalized. We should be allowed the same rights that straight people have, because we have a right to have a family and the right to live like everybody else does. What's wrong with that? We're people too! We're not animals, we're human beings! I think it should be legal.

Chico's concept of rights includes the right to a family life and a certain way of living, "the right to live like everybody else does." Chico views the denial of marriage rights as dehumanizing, putting same-sex couples on the level of animals.

Many other study participants also invoked the language of rights in describing their support for legal marriage. Dorothy Purnell voiced some concerns about what she perceives as the heavy emphasis being put on marriage within the gay rights movement, remarking that "we're not talking about the complexity." Dorothy had been married to a man in her younger years, and she was skeptical that gays and lesbians had thought through all the implications of legal marriage, including the prospect of going through a divorce if a legally recognized relationship ends. But Dorothy supported the goal of legal marriage, and viewed it as a civil rights issue. "I strongly feel that as citizens we ought to have all our civil rights, so I'm in no sense opposed to it," she remarked. Commenting on the immigration problems faced by her partner Peggy, Anita Lindstrom also invoked civil rights to explain her support for legal marriage: "It's a violation of my civil rights as an American citizen, when Joe Blow can bring over his whole family, let alone just marry whoever he wants and get a green card for her." And Peter Tyler called the lack of legal same-sex marriage "state-sanctioned discrimination," adding: "It's a violation of the Constitution to any fair-minded human being. It's largely the last civil rights battle that needs to be fought."

Joel Hauser does not feel drawn to marriage as a cultural model of relationship, yet he feels strongly that gays and lesbians should have access to marriage as a simple matter of rights. Initially he framed the marriage issue as a question of equal treatment, stating that "anybody who wants legal recognition for any type of relationship they have, should be allowed it." He then explained that he viewed the marriage issue in the context of the larger problem of anti-gay discrimination. "One of the big fights is anti-discrimination," Joel commented, "and I think that's all part of anti-discrimination, not allowing same-sex couples . . . the state telling someone, no, you don't have the right." Joel likened the fight for relationship rights to earlier pivotal moments in the gay rights struggle:

You think about Stonewall and the drag queens, if they hadn't done that, we wouldn't have a lot of the rights that we have today. So you have to push for everything you can get, because there's people on the other side pushing just as hard to make sure we don't get anything. I just think the marriage thing is part of anti-discrimination. Because it says they're normal people, we're normal people, we're allowed to live a middle-American normal life, what is perceived as a normal life. And I think that's all part of it.

Again, the concept of rights here transcends the issue of specific legal rights to encompass a broader conception of human rights. For Chico, marriage rights mean being treated as fully human, and for Joel, marriage rights represent freedom from discrimination and the right to live a "normal life."

Like Joel, Claire Bruno places marriage in the context of a broader anti-discrimination framework. But for Claire, the right to marriage is not just one among many anti-discrimination issues that need attention. Rather, Claire sees marriage rights as central to achieving a range of other rights and protections for gays and lesbians. Claire dismissed common reasons for opposition to same-sex marriage, including religious beliefs and concerns about the cost of same-sex marriage to the government. "They just have no [valid] interest in keeping us from having legal rights and marriage," Claire said of opponents of same-sex marriage. She then observed:

The only thing that really has a legal impact for those who are opposed to us having marital rights is that if we have the right to marry, then there's no reason to oppose every other right that we've ever asked for. Hate-crimes protection, housing and employment discrimination, things like that. Because once they have said that the relationship is valid in the eyes of the law, that's where the key turns in the lock. If the relationship is equal in the eyes of the law, then why can't everything else be given too?

Claire sees legal marriage as a rights issue and believes that the attainment of marriage rights will have a positive impact on the other rights claims asserted by the gay and lesbian movement.

Others framed the issue as a matter of basic fairness and equality, without specifically invoking the language of rights. Robbie Caputo, for instance, posed this rhetorical question: "If a man and a woman can just go to Las Vegas and get married, why can't two men and two women?" Frank Pasternak described his anger over the unfairness of paying taxes into a system that will not provide Social Security benefits to his partner. "I pay taxes just like anybody else," he noted, "and I'm paying into a system that essentially does not recognize me, so I find that very offensive." Anthony Parisi stressed the goal of full equality without specifically framing legal marriage as a rights issue:

I would like to see laws passed that would make it equal to heterosexual marriages, the same benefits, the same acknowledgement . . . Even the domestic partnership laws they're talking about, I think they're great, but it needs to be equal, whether it's gay or straight.

Whether they framed it specifically as a rights issue or more generally as a matter of equality, fairness and non-discrimination, many study participants described their support for same-sex marriage in the language of equal treatment. As we shall see in the next chapter, this equality framework stands in sharp contrast to the way the opponents of same-sex marriage frame their arguments against legal recognition of same-sex couples, since opponents of same-sex marriage frequently deny that it is a rights issue and prefer to frame it as a moral issue.

Social legitimacy

Although rights and equality were important ways of talking about the value of legal marriage, study participants were just as likely to talk about it in the language of social legitimacy and validation. About half of all study participants specifically mentioned concepts such as legitimacy, status, respect, recognition or validation in describing their support for legal marriage. Jacob Berger, for example, stated that the concrete legal and economic benefits partly motivated his support of legal marriage, but added: "I think just to have society view our relationship as on an equal par with a straight relationship; that's what we really want." Judith Klein emphasized that legal recognition was important for the validation it would bring in the wider society, rather than for any personal validation of the couple's commitment to each other. Judith remarked:

I don't need [legal recognition] to feel at this moment that my commitment to Carol is any stronger. I don't need that. But what it will do, when it happens, it's a basic civil right, which just shouldn't be denied, but it will also force a lot of people to reckon with the reality of couples that are same-sex. So I kind of want the government to do it, so all these people, they can shut up! And [gays] can say, "See, it's legal, it's recognized." And I'm sure that's what happened when blacks could marry whites, when that became legal, I'm sure that just validated it. Not validated it for the people getting married, just validated it for the people on the outside. So there's going to be some outside equity gotten from it, big-time. I wouldn't mind that, really, I wouldn't mind that at all!

Other study participants expressed confidence that legal recognition would bring more than just the grudging acknowledgement of committed same-sex couples envisioned by Judith. These people saw legal recognition as the key to greater social acceptance for gay and lesbian couples through their normalization by the law. For example, Diane Wilson explained her strong support for legal recognition in this way:

I think [legal recognition] would go a long way to legitimizing our relationships, in the eyes of other people. That we do have committed relationships. The stereotype is that nobody who's gay can possibly have a committed relationship; well, that's not true. I know more people my age who are in committed relationships than not. And I think that would just be the step that would get people over those hurdles. And all that baloney about, you know, people are child molesters and all this stuff. I mean, what kind of crap is that? It's just that gay people, as marginal people in our society . . . well, the fact that you can't have all the same relationship rights as straight people, it just makes people keep thinking like that. And if we had that ability, I think a lot of that would go away . . . [Legal marriage] really would give us the correct status in our society that we need.

Like Judith, Diane spoke of marriage as both a rights issue and a legitimacy issue. In Diane's view, lack of "relationship rights" is closely tied to the perpetuation of anti-gay attitudes and stereotypes in mainstream society.

Anna Roth is a 27-year-old white science teacher. Anna and her partner Carrie are considering having children in a few years. Anna expressed concern about the message sent to children by the denial of married status to same-sex couples. "I think it's important as far as kids are concerned, it's really important," she explained. "I mean, it says something to your kids that you're not legally recognized and other people are. I mean, that to me says this is right and this is wrong in a very clear way to them." Anna's partner Carrie chimed in with an anecdote that vividly illustrated Anna's point. Prior to Anna and Carrie's ceremony, one of their friends had explained to her young daughter, who was invited to the ceremony, that Anna and Carrie were getting married even though it was not legal. When the friend arrived for the ceremony with her daughter, the girl wandered around in the church in amazement, observing the dozens of guests who had arrived for the event. She told her mother that everybody knew "the secret," and when her mother asked her what she meant, the girl explained that she was afraid too many people knew what Anna and Carrie were doing and the police might show up. The child had interpreted her mother's statement that the ceremony was not legal as meaning that it was actually illegal for the couple to have it. For Anna and Carrie, this incident illustrated how the lack of legal recognition sends a message to children that same-sex commitments are inferior or even wrong.

Many study participants seemed hopeful that legal change could produce deeper, transformative effects in society as a whole, naturalizing the presence of same-sex couples in a way that efforts to educate and persuade through argument and information never would. In most cases, what is central to these hopes is a belief that straight society will come to see that gays and lesbians are really just the same as they are. William Austin summed up such aspirations for legitimacy and normalcy when he commented that legal marriage "just gives more credence and validity to your relationship. And if it were just the same as straight America's at this point, it would put you on just the same playing field as far as acceptance, and legally as well."

Some study participants anticipated that the symbolic benefits of legal marriage would extend beyond the married couples themselves to the gay community more generally. In particular, some believed legal marriage would make it easier for gay people to come out, and several specifically mentioned the beneficial effect on young people coming to terms with their own gay identity. A few suggested that marriage would lead to a decline in sexual promiscuity in the gay male community, with the existence of gay married couples creating new models of intimacy and sexual expression. Natalie Konstantos, who now works as an AIDS caseworker, had endured an extremely painful coming-out process in her middle adulthood, at one point considering suicide. She commented:

I think a lot of the cause for suicides in gay teenagers, I think a lot of the cause for suicides in gay people in general, and emotional problems for gay people in general, and promiscuity . . . is because of the social ostracism people experience. And, you can't say anything, so it creates an ambiguity in yourself. OK, if it's not allowed anyway, who cares if you're living with somebody else every week? Nobody cares, nobody recognizes you in the first place, so what difference does it make if you grow up, have a faithful monogamous relationship, get married, have kids, that's never going to happen, so what difference does it make if you have [a new lover] every weekend? . . . The climate that was set, the reason that people got AIDS in the first place, had a lot to do with the fact that they're not an accepted population . . . If you could be married, if you could be on insurance, if you could be socially accepted, a lot of these problems would go away.

Many gays and lesbians would undoubtedly take issue with Natalie's causal narrative, in which social ostracism (rather than a virus) leads to people getting AIDS and the social acceptance fostered by marriage makes problems like AIDS "go away." But her comments are just a particularly stark encapsulation of the views expressed by several other study participants who hoped that legal marriage would reduce the feelings of social exclusion that many gays and lesbians experience and provide incentives for gay men to depart from a stereotypical gay male life style characterized by sexual promiscuity and lack of enduring emotional commitments.

Beyond generalized benefits for the gay and lesbian community, some study participants cited the likely emotional benefits of social recognition for same-sex couples *as couples*. Sarah Robbins said she thought legal marriage would "help support the nurturing of relationships between the women and the men." Sarah thought some of her own hesitation in committing to her partner Abby resulted from the lack of social recognition for their relationship. "For myself, my own issues around intimacy with Abby and making a commitment to Abby also came largely in part from the fact that it wasn't recognized out there, and the issues around my family recognizing it," Sarah commented. Other study participants shared this belief that legal marriage would enhance commitment in same-sex relationships, although they did not always attribute this effect to the social legitimacy conferred by marriage. Gary Weaver, for example, argued that the legal bond of marriage would help same-sex partners stay together because it makes leaving a relationship more difficult and complicated:

I'm really convinced, one thing that keeps straight couples together is how difficult it would be to disentangle legally, and that kind of gives you time to get over some difficult things . . . that's what marriage does for people, it kind of gets you over those times. There's a tie that you would have to consciously break, that you would have to deliberately break, and that's a problem for gay couples, because your relationship has to be able to withstand breaks, because there are breaks that just happen in relationships. And that's why I think marriage is so important, because it gives you extra glue, like elastic, you can go further and further apart and still snap back. I think that's where gay relationships have problems.

For Gary, there is a coercive element to the legal marriage relationship that has beneficial effects on commitment. He views the difficulty of extricating oneself from the legal bond of marriage as an advantage, a source of stability for long-term relationships. Howard O'Hara also thinks legal marriage could have positive effects on same-sex relationships, especially male couples. "I think it's so hard for gay men to develop the skills they need for long-term relationships, to find long-term relationships, to sustain them once they have them," Howard noted. He went on to suggest that legal marriage "would be really helpful for the couples, but even more for the [gay] community, if they could see that and learn to value that." In Howard's view, the question of social legitimacy extends beyond straight society's perceptions of same-sex relationships to include how same-sex couples are valued within gay and lesbian communities.

I have discussed three main reasons study participants gave for supporting legal marriage – legal and financial benefits, equal rights and social legitimacy – and have presented them as distinct bases of support. But close examination of the comments of the study participants suggests that these reasons often overlap and interlock in telling ways. Some study participants discussed *only* benefits, rights or legitimacy in explaining their support for legal recognition, but more often people mentioned some combination of these reasons when they talked about legal marriage. Recall how Judith Klein talked about the value of legal marriage, citing rights and social recognition in the same breath when she remarked that same-sex marriage is "a basic civil right, which just shouldn't be denied, but it will also force a lot of people to reckon with the reality of couples that are same-sex." It is possible to separate these different reasons for analytical purposes, but often the words of the study participants suggest that these reasons are closely interconnected. For example, when Brad Schuster talked about his desire for the benefits that accompany legal marriage, he framed the benefits as a fairness issue, asking: "Why shouldn't we get the Social Security, and the insurance, and all this other stuff that everybody else is getting if we're doing the same thing?" Likewise Anthony Parisi expressed his desire for equal treatment by stating, "I would like to see laws passed that would make it equal to heterosexual marriages, the same benefits, the same acknowledgement." The tangible benefits of legal marriage are important to both Brad and Anthony, then, not only for their inherent value but also as a marker of equal treatment. One's status as an equal citizen is realized by being treated the same way that similarly situated people are treated, including being given the same benefits and protections.

Another instance of the close interconnection of reasons for supporting legal marriage concerns the relationship between equal rights and
social legitimacy. Several of the study participants who based their
support for legal marriage on its expected legitimacy effects linked those
effects directly to equal rights. Recall, for example, the words of Diane
Wilson, who lamented the fact that many straight people saw gay people
in a negative light, even as child molesters, and asserted that "the fact
that you can't have all the same relationship rights as straight people, it
just makes people keep thinking like that." In Diane's view, gays' and
lesbians' lack of "correct status" in society flows from their lack of
relationship rights. Beyond their intrinsic value as a guarantor of equal
legal treatment, then, rights are important as a source of *social* legitimacy
and equality. Likewise, Joel Hauser talked about marriage as an issue of
rights and non-discrimination, but then moved immediately to the issue
of social normalcy, in effect framing marriage rights as the right to be
perceived as "normal people."

The interpenetration of the different reasons for desiring legal recognition is well illustrated in the comments of James Logan. When we
began talking about legal recognition, James focused on legal and financial benefits. He acknowledged that he and his partner Frank would
pay higher income taxes if they were married, but cited the value of
other benefits such as health insurance access, Social Security and
pension benefits. In response to these comments, I asked James, "So
you think the main benefits of legal marriage would be these financial
and legal things?" He responded:

Well, it's beyond that though. It's a cultural recognition. It's a background of the
social fabric that society has woven into an acceptance of marriage in general. I
mean, marriage is as old as this country, as old as society basically, and there's
always been benefits that have been reaped and have been levied into those
relationships that don't inure to two people of the same sex. And it's not fair
. . . That's the structure that society has come up with, so you function in it, but
you should benefit from it as well, that same fabric. It's not just financial.

James moves from talking about marriage as gateway to concrete financial benefits to talking about the "social fabric" of society, which includes
"cultural recognition" and "acceptance" for marriage. He then moves
back to the idea of "benefits that have been reaped and have been levied
into [marriage] relationships," and asserts the unfairness of denying
those benefits to same-sex couples. The social structure favors marriage
in both financial and symbolic ways, and gays and lesbians deserve to
benefit from "that same fabric," and not only in financial terms. So for
James, the question of legal recognition simultaneously involves tangible

benefits, equality and cultural recognition, all of which are interwoven in a social structure that honors marriage by bestowing rights, benefits and social status on the married.

Marriage as a movement priority

Although all of the participants in this study favored legal recognition for same-sex relationships, they differed in terms of the priority they gave to the marriage issue. I asked people how high a priority they thought legal marriage should be, compared to other issues the gay rights movement might address. Some people declined to give an opinion, usually because they felt they were not knowledgeable enough about the movement or gay rights politics to comment. Among those who did respond, about half said marriage should be a high priority and the other half said that other issues are more important or that marriage is not a high priority.[7]

Study participants who felt other issues were more important than marriage pointed to a range of issues deserving higher priority, including general anti-discrimination or civil rights legislation, hate crimes, health issues (including HIV/AIDS and cancer) and the repeal of sodomy laws (which remained on the books in some states at the time of the interviews). Referring to the problem of gay-bashing, Kim Pierson noted: "If you can be married, that's not going to mean anything if you have to hide." Anna Roth said she used to think marriage was "a really low priority . . . frivolous," but her concern about the message that the lack of marriage rights sends to children has changed her views somewhat. "I would put job protection probably first because that's a means of eating," Anna said. "You've got to make money to survive. You don't need to get married to survive, but it's still, it's the same rights that other people have and that's important, that's a really important statement."[8] Several other study participants also said that basic anti-discrimination protections in areas such as employment and housing should take priority over marriage. Teresa Morton, who did not frame her support for marriage in the language of rights, said basic "civil rights" and anti-discrimination measures, along with hate-crimes prevention, should come before marriage as movement goals. "I don't think gay people should have any discrimination," Teresa commented. "I think it should be totally seamless, transparent. That's true civil rights, whether a person is gay or straight, bi[sexual] or transgender." Ralph Scripps also said that "there are certainly things that are more important" than marriage, but argued that marriage should be "fairly high on the agenda for gay rights activists" since it is a "clear-cut, yes-or-no" issue.

People who gave marriage relatively low priority often pointed to other issues they perceived as much more important. Tim Daniels, for instance, said legal marriage was not a high priority in his view, but it was probably in his "top ten." He described a much stronger concern with helping gays and lesbians overcome their internalized homophobia, and his interest in legal marriage was mainly connected to this concern. "I think same-sex marriage is important," Tim explained, "because it will help in that regard tremendously, if same-sex couples are entitled to the same benefits as opposite-sex couples, I think that's going to help, that could help with that [internalized] homophobia thing." Silvia Mendez said she supports legal marriage "as something that gay people deserve to have, or should not be prohibited from achieving because they're gay." But she could not see marriage as the center of a social change agenda. "In terms of a high priority, I don't know, or in the realm of what's important in the world, it's not there," Silvia remarked. "We need to see racism and poverty addressed." Heather Pryor described marriage as "a background issue that needs to be considered." Heather said she already feels married as a result of her commitment ceremony with her partner Gerry, and does not need the government's recognition. Heather explained: "I don't need some big daddy to pat me on the head and say, 'I think what you've done is OK.' I think that is just fascist!" Heather said she believed it was more important to work on increasing social acceptance for gays and lesbians in general.

In fact, several study participants argued that the gay rights movement should try to change the public perception of gays and lesbians before pushing for specific legal remedies like same-sex marriage. As Sandra Drewitt explained:

I think the issue in front of [marriage] is normalizing gays and lesbians, which I think the community as a whole doesn't do a good enough job of that, of normalizing the upper-middle-class people living on Maple Street with a kid, rather than prancing around in the streets in bizarre outfits and that kind of thing, or this whole sexualized identity thing. I think they don't do a good job of that. Look at the papers, look at the magazines.

Sandra's comment was representative of a subset of study participants who expressed dismay at the racy public image of gays projected at large public events like annual gay pride parades and the mainstream media's willingness or even eagerness to portray such images as representative of the gay and lesbian community as a whole. Natalie Konstantos shares Sandra's concerns about cultural acceptance for gays and lesbians. "I would like to see [marriage] made legal," Natalie remarked. "I think the culture, though, still has to move a little closer in that direction . . . I think the climate in the United States has to move a little closer to acceptance before making it legal, otherwise it's going to be a problem." Natalie said she believed that if same-sex marriage became legal, "people would be outraged, and I think there'd be a lot of objection. So I'd like to see the climate move a little closer to acceptance, and then I'd like to see it made legal." Sandra and Natalie's focus on achieving cultural acceptance or normalization is a striking rationale for giving legal marriage lower priority as a movement goal, given that so many other study participants saw the legitimacy and social recognition of same-sex couples within the wider society as one of the primary symbolic benefits that legal marriage would bring. Sandra and Natalie's position reflects a pragmatic political judgment that broader cultural acceptance will have to precede legal marriage, rather than the other way around.

While many people in this study put specific issues ahead of marriage or saw marriage as a relatively low priority for the gay movement, about half of the study participants saw marriage as a top priority and did not specifically identify other issues that should take precedence over marriage. Gary Weaver told me he thought that marriage would become a line-in-the-sand issue for the gay rights movement because it represents such an obvious case of unequal treatment under the law. "I think that marriage has to be way up there," Gary commented. "I think that's kind of our Martin Luther King issue . . . It's very, very easy to see that this is not equal." Vicky Staples said she would rate the priority of marriage "relatively high," and she did not offer any other issues as more important. Vicky outlined two reasons for viewing marriage as a high priority:

One is that it legitimizes our relationships and I think that's very important, because I think that can lead toward some of the other things that we need. The second thing is that I know a lot of gay and lesbian people reject the idea of marriage because it originally was all about property rights, but you know, you can't refuse something that you're not able to have. So anybody who says, 'I'm gay and I'm not getting married' is protesting nothing . . . I can't boycott something that I can't do in the first place. So, I think it's important to have that equal legal standing, so that protests are going to be more meaningful, and those of us who do choose to cement our relationships in this way, it's going to make this a relationship that has standing in society, and from that we can start to show that we are just couples. Now we can make a change. Now, I'm not going to say that we need to assimilate, because I don't believe in assimilation, but I do believe in having the right to assimilate if that's what we choose. I'm not saying that every African-American person should look like every Caucasian businessman or businesswoman, but they should have the right to do that if they want to, and they should have the right to hang on to their culture if they want to, and if I don't have that freedom, then I'm forced to stay in my culture and I can't choose.

Part of Vicky's support for legal marriage comes from her desire for the symbolic benefits of marriage, to have "a relationship that has standing in society." But marriage is also a high priority for Vicky because she views it as a matter of freedom of choice. Working off of an understanding of gay identity and culture as a kind of ethnicity (see Epstein 1987), Vicky argues that gays and lesbians should have both the option to reject legal marriage at the individual level and "the right to assimilate" through marriage if that is their desire.

Some study participants framed marriage as one part of the broad goal of ending discrimination against gays, and did not view it as any more or less important than combating discrimination in areas such as employment and housing. As Jacob Berger put it, "I think ending discrimination is first, and I think the marriage thing is part of that." Others felt legal marriage should be a top priority because it would speed progress on other important issues facing the gay community. These people anticipated a sort of domino effect, in which legal marriage would build momentum for other remedies like hate-crimes legislation and anti-discrimination measures. Recall, for example, Claire Bruno's assertion that legal marriage is "where the key turns in the lock," meaning that once same-sex relationships are legally recognized the state has no valid basis for allowing other forms of discrimination against gays and lesbians. While Claire expected a domino effect in the legal realm, Ted Grasskamp viewed marriage as a top priority because of its potential to change social attitudes. "I think that once we started recognizing, the legal recognition of same-sex marriage, that other things would fall into place," Ted remarked. Ted drew on his own childhood memories of racism in the American South to explain his understanding of the effect of legal change on broader social change:

I look at the way we handled African-Americans. I mean, I remember growing up in the South where blacks sat on the top of the balcony, in the movie theaters, and I remember coming to water fountains, where it was cold water for white people, and it was bad-tasting, lukewarm water out of the fountain for 'colored' people. So that was blatant discrimination, and then some laws were passed, and things started changing. And growing up in the South, the only way we would have changed was for *laws* to occur, we were *forced* to change. And when that happened, our behavior started changing. The other part of it is that I grew up bigoted. When Martin Luther King died, I remember thinking it was kind of sad, but my family overall thought he was a troublemaker . . . But I changed dramatically by being immersed into a system that would not tolerate prejudice. And I think that if we were immersed in a system that would not tolerate discrimination on a legal basis, behaviors would be changing. Because people see couples just like themselves, they just happen to be same-sex.

Ted's view of the relationship between law and social change stands in direct opposition to the views of people like Sandra Drewitt and Natalie Konstantos, who argued that cultural acceptance of gays and lesbians must come before changes in marriage law. Ted believes that marriage is a higher priority than other issues because of its potential to transform social attitudes and behavior toward gays and lesbians.[9]

In addition to inquiring about the importance of marriage as an issue for the gay movement, I also asked study participants how they would feel about alternative forms of legal recognition for same-sex couples, such as domestic partnership. (The term civil union had not been coined at the time of these interviews.) Virtually everyone replied that domestic partnership was a first step, but it was not sufficient. Study participants said they would welcome some kind of domestic partnership option, but consistently used phrases like "stepping stone" and "temporary solution" to describe their views of this alternative. Only equal marriage was acceptable as the long-term goal, even if it was not achievable in the near-term. I then asked how they would feel about some kind of alternative legal vehicle for gay couples that was legally identical to marriage in every way except it had a different name. Just over half said this would be acceptable, but about one-third did not. The remainder said a separate name would actually be preferable, because it would avoid some of the cultural baggage associated with marriage. Ethan Levinson, for example, commented that "marriage in and of itself may need some changing in a social sense as well . . . so part of me would say, no, let's call it something else, and then maybe a new institution can develop that will encompass these issues." Dwight Winfrey was more emphatic in his preference for a different name. He felt the term "marriage" was not appropriate for his relationship with his partner Paul, yet he did want all the same rights and benefits provided by legal marriage. Dwight commented:

I would like to see, not a marriage law but a domestic partner type law, because I still have trouble with the word marriage because of the connotations of husband and wife. That works for mother and dad, and grandma and grandpa, but for Paul and Dwight it doesn't. There's no husband, there's no wife type relationship. We've got to have a terminology . . . I can see legalizing the relationship as a marriage supposedly does, but I cannot see calling it a marriage per se.

But those who objected to the idea of marriage by another name were skeptical that anything with a different name could ever really be equal to marriage. Several study participants made explicit reference to "separate but equal" facilities for blacks under Jim Crow, the system of legal racial segregation in the American South from the late nineteenth to the mid-twentieth century. These references to the history of Jim Crow were meant to suggest that separate is inherently unequal (as the courts eventually ruled in the case of racial segregation). Becky Rodgers voiced similar concerns when she remarked:

> The reason it would be nice to have the same term, because then there would be no difference. There wouldn't be any kind of "it's less than marriage," or anything like that. As long as it wasn't considered something "less than" . . . I have a feeling, though, if there was a different name, a different term, it would be.

For Becky, and for those who drew the comparison to racial segregation in America's past, the idea of a parallel system of rights and benefits using different terminology fails to deliver on the goal of full equality.

Although a large minority of the study sample felt strongly about retaining the term marriage for legally recognized same-sex relationships, most study participants were willing to compromise on terminology in order to gain full legal recognition for their relationships. These study participants took a pragmatic approach to the issue, realizing that for many straight opponents of same-sex marriage the appropriation of the term marriage for same-sex relationships is a sticking point. "That wouldn't bother me so much," said Anna Roth in response to the idea of marriage by another name. "I'd give the straight people that, if they have an issue with the word marriage, they want that to be their goddamn word, let them have it, I don't care!" Brenda Davis reacted to the idea of a different name in a similar fashion. "That's fine," Brenda said. "Hey, that would be great! I don't care what they call it, as long as it's not derogatory, and even if it is, I don't care. As long as it has the same rights and was acknowledged, call it what you will."

Most study participants thought they would legally marry if it became possible. A few said they would want to examine all the legal and financial ramifications before deciding (and some realized they would pay higher income taxes under the current tax code), but most were quite confident that the benefits of being married would outweigh the costs. Most of the ritual participants were quick to note that they would not use legally marrying as an occasion for another public celebration, but rather would approach the legal step as a formality. And several of the study participants who had not yet had a public ritual but were considering it indicated that the option of legal marriage might motivate them to go forward with planning a ritual.

In considering what the participants in this study had to say about the importance of the marriage issue and the acceptability of marriage alternatives such as marriage by another name, it is important to remember the context in which these couples were interviewed. I conducted the interviews in the years immediately preceding a flurry of significant developments related to legal recognition of same-sex marriage, including the implementation of civil unions in Vermont in 2000, the arrival of legal same-sex marriage in parts of Canada in summer 2003, and the issuance of marriage licenses to same-sex couples in Massachusetts in spring 2004. All of these events have been accompanied by increased media focus on same-sex marriage and increased social movement activity both for and against legal recognition of same-sex couples. It is possible, indeed plausible, that study participants might view the question of legal marriage somewhat differently in the aftermath of these dramatic legal and political developments. For example, some gays and lesbians may assign a higher priority to the marriage issue in the wake of the successes in Vermont and Massachusetts (and the backlash those victories have inspired). The reality of civil unions in Vermont might lead some who previously rejected the idea of "marriage by another name" to reconsider it as a pragmatic or achievable solution, whereas the achievement of marriage itself in Massachusetts might lead others to abandon the view that marriage by another name is sufficient or fair. Thus the specific proportions of study participants holding various views is less important than the general observation that gay and lesbian couples have a range of opinions and aspirations concerning the importance of the marriage issue relative to other gay issues and the acceptability of various forms of legal recognition for same-sex relationships.[10]

People's biography and social location may influence how they view the question of legal recognition for same-sex relationships. I have already noted some differences within the study sample between those who choose to enact marriage culturally through a public commitment ritual and those who do not. In particular, women appear more likely to participate in a public ritual than men, and the ritual participants in this study had somewhat lower socioeconomic status, were more likely to live in the suburbs and had less interest in politics compared to ritual nonparticipants. Are these differences in the cultural embrace of marriage paralleled by differences in how study participants view legal marriage? In my study sample, gender does not seem to make a difference in views on legal marriage, and socioeconomic status does not influence support for legal marriage in the way we might expect, but there does seem to be a difference between the ritual participants and nonparticipants in terms of the importance they attach to the question of legal recognition.

Although ritual participants and nonparticipants did not differ substantially in terms of the reasons they gave for supporting legal same-sex marriage, there was a notable difference in the priority they assigned to the issue of legal recognition, with ritual participants more likely to see legal marriage as a high priority than nonparticipants. Recall that about half of the study participants overall said marriage should be a top priority for the gay rights movement. Among the study participants who had participated in a public commitment ritual, however, nearly two-thirds thought marriage should be a top priority (putting no other specific issues ahead of it), whereas less than one-third of the study participants who had not participated in a ritual ranked marriage as a top priority. And almost half of nonparticipants felt marriage was not a very important issue, compared to less than a third of ritual participants who gave legal marriage low priority.

There are at least two possible explanations for why ritual participants view legal marriage as a more important issue than do people who have not held a public ritual. First, people who care strongly about the issue of marriage may be more inclined to enact marriage culturally by participating in a public commitment ritual. In other words, the ritual participants may be both more invested in marriage as a cultural model and more concerned about attaining the legal right to marry; they have a general pro-marriage stance that encompasses both the cultural and the legal dimensions of marriage. The second possibility is an explanation grounded in the effects of personal experience. The experience of participation in a public commitment ritual may create or enhance some people's desire for access to legal marriage. The cultural enactment of marriage through public ritual might increase one's sense of identity as a married person and identification with the institution of marriage, and the importance attached to legal marriage may represent an interest in fully realizing this new identity. These explanations are not mutually exclusive: it may be the case that people who feel more positively or strongly about marriage are drawn to the cultural enactment of marriage through ritual, *and* the ritual experience itself may increase the desire for legal recognition.

In Chapter 2 I characterized public commitment rituals as a form of middle-ground political resistance to gays' and lesbians' exclusion from full social citizenship. If the actual experience of participating in a commitment ritual does partially account for ritual participants giving higher priority to the goal of legal marriage than nonparticipants, their experience nicely illustrates how these middle-ground forms of resistance can not only reflect but produce resistant consciousness, as the Comaroffs (1991) argue. I asked most study participants whether their views on same-sex marriage had changed over time. Most of the ritual participants did report some change in their views, generally in a pro-marriage direction, and they described various factors motivating the change. Some said they had not really thought about same-sex marriage until they got involved in a serious relationship; others cited coming out or getting older as life-course developments that increased their support for same-sex marriage. And several did specifically mention their own commitment ceremonies as the source of their increased interest in legal marriage. Jacob Berger, for example, said: "I guess I've just done more thinking about it since we had our ceremony, and I feel much more strongly now that it should be legal and we should get the same rights and privileges as straight people, and I feel very strongly about it since we've gotten married." But most ritual participants who said their support for legal marriage had increased over time did not tie this change specifically to their own commitment ceremony, so it is unclear how much of a role the ritual played in their support for legal recognition.

While ritual participation appeared to be associated with giving legal marriage higher priority as an issue, there was no clear relationship between gender and people's views on legal same-sex marriage. The lack of gender differences in views on legal marriage is interesting given that gender seems to have an important influence on cultural practices related to marriage. As described in Chapter 2, women appear to have a greater interest in enacting marriage culturally through public rituals, and they seem more inclined to construct these rituals as gendered cultural objects, but there were no clear gender differences in terms of the reasons study participants gave for supporting legal marriage or the priority they attached to the marriage issue. Since women were more likely to participate in public rituals, and since participants in public rituals on average gave higher priority to legal marriage, the lack of an overall gender difference in the priority given to legal marriage requires some explanation. It is accounted for by the fact that several men who had not had a public ritual rated legal marriage a high priority, whereas none of the women who had not done a public ritual saw marriage as a top concern. The sample is too small to draw firm conclusions, but this finding suggests that the relationship between cultural enactment of marriage and strength of support for legal marriage might work differently for women and men, in the sense that men are more likely than women to rank legal marriage a high priority even if they have not themselves enacted marriage culturally through public ritual. This is consistent with the tone of my interview conversations with the study participants who had not held a public commitment ritual. Several of the men in this group spoke passionately and at some length about the need for legal marriage and the benefits it would bring to same-sex couples and to the gay and lesbian community more generally. By contrast, most of the women who had not had a public ritual offered more lukewarm support for legal marriage, acknowledging that it was necessary as a matter of fairness, that its benefits were desirable, or even that it would bring valuable social legitimacy to same-sex relationships, but also citing concerns about the history of the institution of marriage and the relative unimportance of marriage compared to other concerns facing gays and lesbians or society more broadly.

Given the concerns raised by critics of legal marriage within the gay and lesbian community that legal marriage holds the biggest economic and symbolic payoff for wealthier gays and lesbians, one might expect people of higher socioeconomic status to voice stronger support for the goal of legal marriage. Marriage critics within the gay and lesbian community have argued that wealthier and more educated gays and lesbians will benefit most from marriage because these are the people who have assets to protect through marriage and they are also the people who are closest to mainstream social assimilation. I reported in the last chapter that ritual participants were more likely to be working-class than non-participants, partially refuting the oft-stated assumption that the gays and lesbians who are most interested in marriage are those who are the most well-off in economic terms. If well-off gays were the most interested in legal marriage because they are most likely to reap its benefits, we might expect them to attach greater importance to the issue than other study participants, but this is not the case. In fact, only about a quarter of the upper-middle-class study participants rated the marriage issue a top priority, compared to half of study participants overall. In addition, if wealthier gays were most interested in the concrete legal and financial benefits of marriage, they might be expected to mention these benefits more often in explaining their support for legal same-sex marriage. But this group did not mention the legal and economic benefits of marriage more often than other study participants: about three-quarters of upper-middle-class study participants mentioned these reasons, roughly the same proportion as among the study participants overall. Wealthier gays and lesbians did appear more interested in the social legitimacy effects of legal marriage, however, with two-thirds of them mentioning such benefits compared to half of the sample overall, providing tentative support for the idea that wealthier gays and lesbians are more likely to be drawn to legal marriage for its power to render them socially normal.

Culture as legality, law as cultural resource

I now return to my earlier findings on the cultural enactment of marriage by same-sex couples to make two related arguments. First, comparing my findings on the meaning of public commitment rituals to the typical functions of marriage-related law described earlier in this chapter, I argue that couples' cultural enactments of marriage through ritual represent enactments of legality outside official law. Second, I argue that my findings on couples' views on legal recognition of same-sex marriage forcefully illustrate the unique power of law as a cultural resource, a power that can be approximated but not replaced by extra-legal forms of cultural practice.

The cultural enactment of legality

Same-sex couples produce what Ewick and Silbey (1998) call "legality" through various marriage-related cultural practices, most prominently through choice of language and through the use of public rituals to enact their commitment. Broader than official law (the law made and enforced by the state), the concept of legality refers to "the meanings, sources of authority, and cultural practices that are commonly recognized as legal, regardless of who employs them or for what ends. In this rendering, people may invoke and enact legality in ways neither approved nor acknowledged by the law" (Ewick and Silbey 1998, 22). My argument is that some of the practices of same-sex couples who embrace marriage as a cultural model of relationship should be understood as enactments of legality outside the bounds of official law. These practices are a way to compensate for (and perhaps challenge) the couples' exclusion from law. Specifically, couples are enacting a form of legality when they use cultural practices to assert the reality or officialness of their commitment and to enhance the permanence of their relationship by making exit from the relationship more difficult.

In Chapter 2 I described some of the terminological choices made by same-sex couples to refer to their partners and their committed relationships, and I observed that these are only loosely correlated with the practice of public commitment rituals. Although ritual participants are somewhat more likely to refer to their partners as "husband," "wife" or "spouse," and to define their status as "married" in most social contexts, some couples who had not held public rituals adopt these terms as well. Since alternate terms such as "partner" and "committed" are available to same-sex couples (even if they are sometimes ambiguous or awkward to use), the choice of terms that overlap with legally defined identities and relationships most likely represents one way of enacting a sort of legality through everyday cultural practice. By calling their partners "spouses," their relationships "marriages" and their partners' families "in-laws," some same-sex couples import the terminology of legal marriage into their relationships as a way to establish the reality and seriousness of these commitments.

But more significant and deliberate than these everyday linguistic choices is the use of public rituals to define, celebrate and strengthen committed relationships. In Chapter 2 I recounted how study participants describe using these rituals to establish the reality of their committed relationship and their identity as partners, to enhance the stability and permanence of the commitment, and to illustrate its fundamental similarity to heterosexual marriage relationships. These goals, I argue, parallel the legal functions of marriage in some important respects. As noted above, laws related to marriage serve several functions: recognizing and fostering the emotional attachment of partners, treating the partners as an economic unit and regulating parenting relationships. Although very few ritual participants in my sample claimed that they pursued ritual as a means of defining themselves as a parenting unit, the other legal functions of marriage laws do appear to have close parallels in the goals of couples who enact marriage through public ritual. Official law gives reality to marriage relationships and attempts to foster their stability by honoring the emotional attachments of partners, treating couples as a stable economic unit, and raising barriers to the dissolution of that unit. Without the resource of official law to accomplish these goals, some same-sex couples turn to ritual enactments of their commitment and thereby use cultural practice to enact a form of legality outside the boundaries of official law.

The study participants themselves, of course, do not consciously conceive of themselves as "enacting legality" through their participation in public commitment rituals, but the parallel between the meanings they attach to their ritual practice and the identifiable functions of marriage laws is quite striking. In addition, terms and concepts that suggest notions of legality do seep into their own descriptions of the rituals' meanings and functions, and some study participants spoke explicitly about their rituals as a sort of compensation for the absence of official legal recognition.

Many ritual participants talked about their ceremony as a way of formalizing their commitment or making it more "official." Carol Moore told me that her ceremony with her partner Judith made their relationship "a more formal commitment," and Judith suggested that the language of their ketubah (Jewish wedding contract) was "a little bit more kind of formal and legal." James Logan described his ceremony with his partner Frank as a "formalization of the relationship." Describing the motivation behind her commitment ritual, Janis Sobirov said she and her partner Cindy wanted to have "this formal ceremony where everyone could witness to it," and added that the ritual made their commitment "more formalized." Likewise, Sarah Robbins felt her relationship with her partner Abby was more "official" because their friends witnessed it; it became "more official that we were a couple."

The notions of "formal" and "official" imply standing, endorsement, transition to a higher or more important status as the result of adherence to proper rules or procedures or of the involvement of appropriate and powerful third parties. For some ritual participants, religious authority plays this role of granting formal or official status to their commitment. Sue Bruno, who was united to her partner Claire in a ceremony offici-ated by a Metropolitan Community Church minister, stated: "The church made it real for me." The role of the church in her conception of such unions is so significant that she suggested that same-sex couples who have purely secular commitment ceremonies are just "play-acting." And clergy may actively participate in constructing religious authority as a viable and even superior alternative to the authority of state law. The rabbi who married Judith and Carol, for example, pronounced them married "by a higher authority than the state of Illinois." (He also felt compelled, however, to promise to march down to city hall and sign their marriage license when same-sex marriage becomes legal.) Other clergy enhance the sense of formality or official endorsement by providing same-sex couples with certificates at the end of their ceremonies, and some participants seem to attach a legalistic meaning to this documen-tation. For example, in the middle of discussing legal recognition for gays and lesbians, Andrew Minnelli mentioned the certificate provided by Dignity, the gay Catholic group in which he and his partner Tim had their ceremony. Other study participants who were lifelong Catholics said it was important to them to find a Catholic priest willing to officiate at their ceremony.

The ketubah, or Jewish wedding contract, crafted by Jacob Berger and his partner Joe Neufeld clearly represents an attempt to construct lega-lity through religious practice in the absence of state legal recognition. The ketubah, which the couple drafted with the help of a lawyer friend, states: "We have entered into this agreement with the knowledge and intent of having our relationship as between each other and with respect to third parties treated in all respects as a marriage. Any law of the State of Illinois or of the United States of America which is applicable to marriage or which affects married persons . . . shall be construed or reformulated by any reviewing court in such a way as to apply to this relationship to the maximum extent possible." In recognition of the possibility of legal challenges to the reality of the couple's commitment, the ketubah goes on to state: "Should our relationship ever be challenged by any person in any forum whatsoever, this document shall serve as clear and convincing evidence of the nature of our relationship and of the rights, privileges, and obligations which are appurtenant thereto." This example again highlights the role of religion as a competing source of legality, since ketubahs represent binding contracts under Jewish law. Jacob and Joe's ketubah represents one of the most forceful and dramatic of many efforts by couples to construct legality through cultural and religious practice. Their ketubah explicitly defines their relationship as a marriage deserving of state recognition and challenges state authorities to treat their covenant as a legal union.

In addition to using ritual to establish their relationships as real and "official," some couples also use ritual to enact marriage in the belief that the ritual establishes a new normative order, a new code for behavior and interaction, within their relationships. Specifically, some respondents described the ritual as a commitment to behave differently when times get hard, and the public nature of the ritual was crucial to this aspect for some people. Earlier I drew on Howard Becker's (1966) metaphor of the "side bet" to explain how some couples view the publicness of commitment rituals as a form of insurance for their relationships. Some of the ritual participants believed that the public declaration of commitment in front of assembled witnesses (itself a term with a legal connotation) made relationship survival more likely. For example, I quoted Kim Pierson in Chapter 2 discussing her belief that her ceremony with her partner Brenda signified that "when things get tough I wouldn't just get up and walk out," partly because "we stood up in front of everybody and said we were going to work on this and try to make it last." Likewise Ethan Levinson and Peter Tyler described a shift in their relationship after their ritual, "a sense of being more responsible for each other" that they attributed to the public expression of their commitment. They also said they had both looked back to their ceremony as a source of staying power during difficult times. For some ritual participants, the public act of committing to their partner adds a layer of obligation and constraint that they did not feel in their relationship before.

In addition to making exit from the relationship more difficult, rituals were sometimes described as marking a transition from behaving as two individuals to behaving as a unit. Ricky Suarez described his ceremony with Allen as a transition point from acting as two individuals to acting as a couple and considering each other's interests and feelings at all times:

"We do pretty much everything together now, and . . . everything is no longer like, well, *I'm* going to get this and do this, it's like we've got to talk about it before we do it." Similarly, Carol Moore stated: "I think our friends see us as what married must be like, meaning you have to consider the other person when you're married, you're not just by yourself anymore. It doesn't mean you can't move about by yourself, but just that you have another person to consider." Carol also described how the decision to have a public ritual had helped her and Judith to coalesce around certain major life goals, such as raising children, which in the past had seemed nebulous and unresolved. In all of these cases, respondents are describing what they regard as behavior-changing impacts of the ritual enactment of marriage: working harder at keeping the relationship together, considering the other person's needs and interests, approaching resolution of important life decisions as a couple. These are not merely changes in their perception of the meaning of the relationship, but normative changes in conduct.[11]

Some study participants explicitly framed their rituals as compensating for the lack of access to legal marriage. When I asked Natalie Konstantos to explain the motivation behind her union ceremony, she remarked: "We couldn't do it legally; the only thing we could do is do it emotionally." James Logan told me that the certificate furnished by their Methodist minister, along with other physical artifacts connected to his ceremony, provides tangible evidence of their relationship, "although it's not a legal document." For other participants, this compensatory function of the ritual is so successful that it produces an internal sense of being legally married. Heather Pryor told me she did not feel the need for the government to grant legal recognition of her marriage; the ceremony was enough to make it real. "I really feel, maybe this is just me, but I don't need the government to say that I'm married," Heather said. "I feel perfectly married now." And Andrew Minnelli said his ceremony made him feel "legally married" despite the lack of state recognition.

In short, by using cultural practices (often including religious symbolism and authority), many same-sex couples manage to construct a sense of legality for their relationships outside the purview of state law. Public rituals provide an opportunity to establish the reality, seriousness and even the officialness of same-sex commitments, and at the same time to bind the couple together more closely by raising the costs of relationship dissolution and by encouraging the couple to think of themselves as an interdependent unit. But the cultural practice of commitment rituals in no way represents a perfect substitute for state-sanctioned marriage for these couples. Most obviously, cultural enactments of marriage bring none of the concrete legal and financial benefits of legal marriage, and study participants mentioned those benefits more often than any other reason in explaining their desire for legal recognition.[12] Legal marriage also holds the promise of significant symbolic benefits, at least in the opinion of some study participants. These symbolic benefits do not figure in Chambers' schema of the functions of marriage law, because they are not "legal" functions in a narrow sense of the term. But the perceived symbolic benefits of legal marriage represent an important cultural function of legal marriage. For many study participants, including both those who had held a ritual and those who had not, official law produces a reality, legitimacy and cultural integration that cultural practices such as commitment rituals cannot fully replicate or replace. The rituals enact legality, but always and only in the shadow of official law.

Law as a cultural resource

My interview findings on how people in same-sex couples talk about legal same-sex marriage indicate the powerful symbolic capacities of official law for subordinated social actors. In the specific case of same-sex marriage, law's symbolic effects operate on two levels. For some study participants, legal recognition of same-sex relationships by the state holds symbolic significance in its own right. Others may not view state recognition as intrinsically valuable but anticipate positive ripple effects on mainstream society's beliefs and attitudes.

A number of study participants made statements that indicated that state recognition of same-sex relationships held intrinsic symbolic value. These study participants felt that having their relationships seen and acknowledged by the state was inherently valuable. Phrases like "in the eyes of the state" emerged repeatedly in their discussions of the benefits of legal recognition, suggesting that a politics of official regard underlies some study participants' interest in legal marriage. Carol Moore, for example, said that she would favor legal recognition even though it might lead to higher taxes and other liabilities for same-sex couples, "because it would say that our relationship is just as valid in the eyes of the state and the government as anyone else's." Brenda Davis framed the value of official state recognition in more personal terms, remarking: "I would crusade for us to be married in the eyes of the government, because I think that not only politically would it increase our rights, it individually heals people."

Comments like these call to mind political theorist Nancy Fraser's useful distinction between socioeconomic and cultural forms of injustice. According to Fraser (1997), socioeconomic injustice "is rooted in the political-economic structure of society" and can take the form of exploitation, economic marginalization or material deprivation, whereas cultural injustice "is rooted in social patterns of representation, inter- pretation, and communication" and can take the form of cultural dom- ination, nonrecognition and disrespect (13–14).[13] Fraser describes nonrecognition as "being rendered invisible by means of the authorita- tive representational, communicative, and interpretative practices of one's culture" (14). When members of same-sex couples express a desire for their relationship to be *seen* "in the eyes of the state," they are seeking a remedy for the cultural injustice of nonrecognition. When gays and lesbians express this desire without connecting it to any causal story about state recognition impacting social attitudes and behaviors, it re- flects their perception of the state as a powerful (or, to use Fraser's term, "authoritative") cultural actor. For some, the recognition of the state has intrinsic value and meaning.

But most study participants who perceived symbolic benefits flowing from state recognition of same-sex marriage assumed a causal relation- ship between official law and broader social beliefs and attitudes. These study participants expected state recognition of same-sex relationships to change mainstream attitudes toward gays and lesbians, and some study participants felt this benefit was more significant than any of the more practical legal and economic benefits tied to marriage. Janis Sobirov told me that marriage was one of the most important issues for the gay rights movement, because of the power of legal recognition to reshape attitudes toward gays:

I think a lot of people have this perception that all gay and lesbian people run around and jump into everybody's bed, and my goodness, we all don't have that kind of energy! Much less, we all don't want that, we don't want to be running around like that. And people still have these negative stereotypes, and I think if we were recognized in that way, some of the people in our society who have kind of negative theories toward us would start to say, "Hey, you know those people who live down the street, they just had this union" or whatever, and maybe their perceptions toward us would start to change.

Ted Grasskamp seemed even more certain of the causal linkage be- tween laws and attitudes when he drew on his personal history of growing up in the segregated South to compare the potential impact of legal same- sex marriage to the effects of civil rights laws on attitudes and behaviors. Recall Ted's assertion that "some laws were passed, and things started changing" and his view that "the only way we would have changed was for laws to occur, we were forced to change." Ted acknowledged a change in himself as a result of the civil rights laws and anticipated that "behaviors would be changing" if the marriage laws were revised to include same-sex couples. For people like Janis and Ted, law is a cultural resource because it holds the power to transform the meanings and value that society attaches to gay identities and relationships. The state's choice to undo the harm of nonrecognition embedded in the denial of same-sex marriage would lead to a broader social revaluation of gay and lesbian identities and relationships.

Not all study participants shared this confidence that legal change would produce attitudinal change favorable to gay and lesbian relationships. As I noted earlier, some study participants felt that attitude change must precede legal change. Some even feared that implementing legal change before attitudes had changed would produce a backlash against gays and lesbians (and the national political reaction to the arrival of legal same-sex marriage in Massachusetts provides some evidence for this view). Heather Pryor was skeptical about law's ability to increase social acceptance of gay people and relationships. "People will say, 'Oh, that's just some legal bullshit,' frankly," she remarked. "I don't think that's the way you can change people's minds." Barry Sargent said he feared the gay rights movement had moved too quickly on the marriage issue, making future success more difficult. "We tried to do too much too soon," he complained, noting that the movement should have "waited until more of middle-America was ready to hear it."

In short, many study participants commented positively on law's cultural effects, or what has been variously called the "cultural power of law" (Merry 1995, 11), law's "expressive function" (Sunstein 1987, 2,021) or its "symbolic power" (Bourdieu 1987, 838). Although some study participants explicitly rejected the idea that law could or should enhance the legitimacy of their intimate commitments, roughly half of all study participants mentioned the legitimacy, status and respect that would flow from legal recognition as a primary benefit of legal same-sex marriage. And while some study participants were skeptical about law's power to change attitudes, more were hopeful or even confident that legal change would produce changes in perceptions, attitudes and behaviors toward gays and lesbians. In this sense, many study participants viewed law as a unique and important cultural resource, one that could not be fully replicated or replaced through other forms of cultural practice such as ritual or language choice.

The legal and cultural aspects of same-sex marriage are closely intertwined in the lives of many same-sex couples. Public same-sex rituals may be a joyful celebration of love and commitment, but in the absence of recognition under state law, they are often something more as well:

efforts to construct and communicate legality for relationships outside official law. Same-sex couples' desires for legal recognition represent an understandable interest in gaining access to the myriad tangible benefits and protections of legal marriage, but they are often something more as well: many perceive the law to have a special cultural power, rendering gays and lesbians full social and cultural citizens as well as full rights-bearing legal actors.[14] Both the cultural enactment of marriage and the desire for state recognition point to marriage's importance to some as a source of social identity that can be realized only through the validating gaze of actors outside the couple dyad, whether friends, family or the state itself.

The cultural practices of same-sex marriage demonstrate how people engage in practices that both reflect and produce legality without necessarily describing or recognizing those practices as in any sense "legal." With rare exception, the couples in this study did not attach specifically legal meanings to their participation in public commitment rituals. But my argument is that their practices represent an effort to construct a kind of legality in the absence of official law, often using religion as an alternative source of legal authority. Couples use public rituals to assign quasi-legal identities and statuses to themselves, their relationships and their families, and to establish a heightened normative order within their relationships, most importantly by making exit from the relationship more difficult. The public nature of these events draws its importance from the need for witnesses to this enactment of marriage: in lieu of the third-party witnessing and legitimation of the state, family and friends are called upon to play this role.

Among the couples who do not use public rituals to mark their commitment, there are some people who might be called "legal literalists." These are the people who reject ritual precisely because it lacks the force of official law. Jenny Pyrdol, for example, explained her lack of interest in a public ritual by stating: "It means *nothing* legally, which is what marriage is." Legal literalists like Jenny believe that there is no option to enact legality through cultural practice, because their understanding of the meaning of marriage is so tightly linked to official law. Jenny's words stand in sharp contrast to those of Andrew Minnelli, who so firmly trusted the transformative power of his ritual that he described feeling "legally married" to his partner Tim afterwards. One might infer that the legal literalists like Jenny attach more importance to official law than do the ritual participants, but such a conclusion would ignore the fact that the ritual participants expressed relatively greater interest in legal recognition of same-sex marriage than the nonparticipants. Enacting legality outside the parameters of official law represents neither the rejection of official law nor the denial of its significance. Instead, legality may be a source of meaning that is more salient for some people and therefore cuts across more domains of their lives, leading them to pursue legality culturally and also to more highly value the legality available through state recognition.

Gays and lesbians who enact marriage through ritual attribute law-like consequences to their actions. But the cultural enactment of marriage occurs in the shadow of official law, not only borrowing its terms and functions but always competing with it and being measured against it. Regardless of whether they have participated in commitment rituals, members of committed same-sex couples generally support legal recognition for same-sex relationships through marriage or some similar legal mechanism. Some of this support is driven by practical considerations, including the range of legal and financial benefits that legal marriage would bring. Some of these practical benefits can be obtained only from the state, and some can be replicated outside of the institution of legal marriage only with considerable expense and effort. But study participants rarely cited these practical benefits without also framing legal marriage as a matter of equality or legitimacy. At a minimum, the symbolic benefits of legal same-sex marriage consist of a grudging recognition from straight society that committed same-sex relationships exist. But most people who cited the symbolic benefits of legal same-sex marriage framed them more positively. These individuals looked to the law to perform an essentially cultural task, communicating to the broader society that gay and lesbian couples are "normal," "the same," "just like you," deserving of recognition and respect for the commitment they have made.

The source of law's cultural power, at least for some, is its assumed ability to produce cultural equality through pronouncements of legal equality. This belief may seem naive given the many historical instances in which formal legal equality has not translated into cultural equality for subordinated groups, but the persistence of such a belief in the face of contradictory evidence attests to the central place of the law in the cultural imaginations of many contemporary social actors. Efforts by some to enact legality outside the bounds of official law both reflect and reproduce this cultural power of law.

5 Sin or civil right? Debating marriage in the states

> In our system of government, civil rights violations are remedied by courts, not because we issue "Holy Writ" or because we are "the only repository of wisdom" . . . It is because the courts "must ultimately define and defend individual rights against government in terms independent of consensus or majority will."
>
> – *Baker v. State of Vermont*, opinion of Justice Denise Johnson

> God's Law, Not Man's Law.
> – Sign at Vermont public hearing on same-sex marriage, January 25, 2000

Previous chapters provided a close look at same-sex marriage from the perspective of ordinary same-sex couples, considering how these couples think about marriage as a legal and political issue and sometimes enact marriage through various cultural practices. This chapter widens our perspective to examine recent public debates over the policy question of legal recognition of same-sex marriage. How, if at all, should the state recognize intimate same-sex commitments?[1] I scrutinize the public debates in two pivotal states: Hawaii and Vermont. These were the first states in the nation to wrestle with the policy question of same-sex marriage over an extended period of time. Hawaii was the first state to come close to granting legal recognition for same-sex marriage, and also the first (along with Alaska) to pass a state constitutional amendment to prevent such recognition. Vermont's experience closely parallels Hawaii's in some key respects but diverges from the Hawaii case in terms of how policymakers ultimately resolved the issue.

Examining the debates over same-sex marriage at the state level is useful for two reasons. First, the voices of ordinary citizens have more opportunity to be heard in state-level debates than in the ongoing national debate, which is largely dominated by spokespersons for national groups on both sides and filtered through the prism of national media outlets. Second, the policy issue of recognition for same-sex relationships is likely to be fought out primarily at the state level in the years ahead, with opponents seeking to pass additional state constitutional amendments

152

to bar same-sex marriage (and sometimes other forms of recognition as well), and proponents pursuing their cause in state courts and legislatures. Marriage law has traditionally been the province of the states, so it is fitting that states have been and will continue to be the key battleground in contests over same-sex marriage.

Here I draw on journalistic accounts of the discourses of activists for and against same-sex marriage as well as my own analyses of the discourses of average citizens to describe the main arguments advanced in the public debates over same-sex marriage. While the advocates of legal recognition for same-sex couples gravitate to discourses of rights and equality, their opponents reject the framing of same-sex marriage as a rights question and shift the debate to the terrain of morality, tradition and democracy. When these public debates are juxtaposed to the perspectives of same-sex couples described in previous chapters, it becomes clear that the public debates offer a partial and somewhat distorted image of the stakes in these battles. While my research suggests that many gay and lesbian couples would accept, and some would even prefer, the creation of an alternative legal structure to recognize same-sex relationships, this nuance is lost in the public debates. The two sides in the public debates are highly polarized and the debate reduces to marriage vs. no marriage. The cultural critiques of marriage offered by some members of same-sex couples lack any representation in these debates. Also absent from the public debates is a strong positive argument for same-sex marriage as a moral or social good. The opponents of legal recognition do not hesitate to cast their arguments in the language of morality and social impacts, but when the supporters of marriage venture beyond rights discourses they generally confine themselves to what I will call procedural arguments (arguments that the courts must protect minorities and that church and state must be kept separate) or general appeals for tolerance. There is also virtually no acknowledgment by public advocates of same-sex marriage that many same-sex couples desire legal marriage not only for its rights and benefits but also for social and cultural recognition. In these respects, the public arguments for same-sex marriage fail to capture the lived reality of same-sex couples and their aspirations for legal recognition.

Hawaii: the battle is joined

The battle over same-sex marriage in Hawaii began in late 1990 when three same-sex couples filed applications for marriage licenses and the state health department denied the applications on the grounds that the couples were same-sex. In early 1991, the couples sued the state over the denial of licenses, but their case was dismissed at the circuit court level. In its 1993 ruling in *Baehr v. Lewin*, the Hawaii Supreme Court vacated the circuit court dismissal and sent the case back for a trial, finding the denial of marriage licenses to same-sex couples a potential violation of the Hawaii state constitution. Specifically, the high court ruled that the marriage ban might deny members of same-sex couples a basic civil right because of their gender and thus might represent state-sanctioned sex discrimination, violating the equal rights amendment of the Hawaii constitution. (The logic of this finding of possible sex discrimination is as follows: if a man is allowed to marry a woman but a woman is not allowed to marry a woman solely because of her sex, the woman is being discriminated against based on her sex; if she were a male she could marry a woman. Likewise a man faces sex discrimination when he is prohibited from marrying a man but a woman has the right to marry a man.) The court ordered the state to show that the marriage law's sex-based classification was justified by compelling governmental interests.

Although the initial high court ruling was not the final say on the issue of legal same-sex marriage (because the state still had the opportunity at trial to show a compelling interest in restricting legal marriage to opposite-sex couples), it had an immediate political impact. Within a year, the Hawaii Legislature passed a law declaring that Hawaii's marriage law applied only to opposite-sex couples. This appeared to be only a symbolic gesture at the time, since a court finding of the marriage ban as unconstitutional would presumably invalidate such a statute. The citizens of Hawaii, and eventually the entire country, became aware of the possibility that same-sex marriage might in fact become legal in part of the United States for the first time in history. The national gay rights movement took notice. Lambda Legal, the preeminent legal advocacy group in the movement, joined the case. The Hawaii attorney general's office began plotting its own legal strategies to demonstrate a compelling state interest in barring same-sex couples from marriage. And the US Congress made a preemptive strike with the 1996 Defense of Marriage Act, which states that only opposite-sex marriages are recognized by federal law and that individual states are not compelled to grant recognition to same-sex marriages performed in other states.

When the Hawaii case (now called *Baehr v. Miike*) went to trial in the fall of 1996, the state attempted to show a compelling governmental interest in blocking same-sex marriage by arguing that legal same-sex marriage would be harmful to children's development. The state presented four expert witnesses to establish that children develop best when they are raised in intact families headed by their biological mothers and fathers. But the state's own experts only partially supported this core argument. Two of these expert witnesses conceded that gays and lesbians are capable of being good parents, and one witness stated that he believed children being raised by same-sex couples would be better off if the state granted legal recognition of same-sex marriage. The plaintiffs also presented testimony from four expert witnesses, who rebutted the notion that children's development would be harmed by legal same-sex marriage. These witnesses presented research evidence demonstrating same-sex couples' ability to form lasting relationships and the lack of ill effects on children raised by same-sex couples, and they stressed that the important factor affecting children's development is the quality of parent–child relationships, not the family structure or the sexual orientation of the parents.

Circuit Court Judge Kevin Chang issued his ruling in favor of the plaintiffs in December 1996. Chang found that the state had failed to present a compelling governmental interest in denying marriage rights to same-sex couples. His opinion noted the diversity of family forms present in contemporary society and affirmed that the quality of parent–child relationships, rather than the specific family structure, is most important to children's development. The judge found that the state had failed to establish any causal relationship between same-sex marriage and harm to children's development, and indicated that children raised by same-sex couples would likely be positively affected by legal recognition of same-sex marriage. He ordered the state to cease its denial of marriage licenses to same-sex couples, but stayed his ruling pending the state's appeal to the Hawaii Supreme Court.

Chang's ruling provoked a flurry of public debate and legislative activity in Hawaii. Over time, polls consistently indicated that the majority of Hawaii residents opposed legal same-sex marriage, with opposition hovering in the 60–70 percent range (see "Voters Strongly Oppose" 1997; Yuen 1998). In response to public outcry over the ruling, state legislators passed a bill to put a constitutional amendment opposing same-sex marriage on the ballot in the next statewide election, in November 1998. The proposed amendment stated simply: "The Legislature shall have the power to reserve marriage to opposite-sex couples." The legislature also passed a second bill, the Reciprocal Beneficiaries Act (RBA), to grant some but not all of the rights and protections of legal marriage to any two persons who were legally prohibited from marrying and chose to designate each other as their reciprocal beneficiaries.[2]

As the vote on the constitutional amendment approached, public debate over the issue of legal same-sex marriage intensified and activists on both sides of the issue launched campaigns to persuade voters. The leading organization supporting the constitutional amendment was Save Traditional Marriage '98 (STM), a nominally secular group that received heavy support from both the Roman Catholic Church and the Church of Latter Day Saints (the Mormons). Other groups backing the amendment included the Alliance for Traditional Marriage, the Hawaii Family Forum (affiliated with the right-wing Christian group Focus on the Family), Hawaii's Future Today (a coalition of business leaders) and the Hawaii Christian Coalition. The leading group opposing the constitutional amendment was an umbrella organization called Protect Our Constitution (POC). The POC coalition received extensive organizational and financial support from the Human Rights Campaign, the country's largest gay rights group. POC also received endorsements from prominent local organizations including the League of Women Voters, Marriage Project Hawaii, the Japanese American Citizens League, the American Civil Liberties Union of Hawaii and numerous religious groups.

Both sides in the amendment battle launched well-funded and well-organized efforts to influence the electorate.[3] Protect Our Constitution made a tactical decision, reflected in its very name, to frame the issue as a question of preserving and protecting the state constitution in order to safeguard the rights and liberties of all Hawaii citizens. POC asserted that the amendment would take away the rights of one minority group, possibly leading to similar action against other groups in the future, and drew explicit comparisons to the historical oppression of other minorities. Above all, POC stressed that the amendment was *not* about saving marriage, it was about civil rights. In fact, the POC literature and advertisements said almost nothing about the idea of "gay rights" or same-sex marriage. Supporters of the constitutional amendment, by contrast, put forward a clear and consistent message that the goal of the amendment was to preserve "traditional" marriage. They pointed out that a "right" to same-sex marriage did not exist in Hawaii or anywhere else in the country, and all they were seeking was to preserve the status quo. They emphasized that they were firm supporters of civil rights, but argued that this issue had nothing to do with rights. They also challenged their opponents' rhetoric about "protecting" the constitution by pointing out that the constitution belonged to the people and the amendment process was designed to allow people to express their will and preserve the intent of the constitution's framers.[4]

The amendment battle heated up roughly two months before the election, when both sides began running print, radio and television advertisements. The POC ads against the amendment featured an array of prominent local citizens and stuck to the basic script of avoiding discussion of same-sex marriage while speaking generally of protecting the rights of all citizens. Print and television ads featuring the head of the Japanese American Citizens League drew explicit comparisons between the proposed amendment and the internment of Japanese-Americans during World War II. A separate television ad featured Rodney Powell, a veteran of the civil rights struggles of the 1960s, who stated: "In the early 1960s, I fought alongside Dr. Martin Luther King for civil rights in the Deep South. Today in Hawaii, instead of attack dogs and water hoses, those same groups are using negative advertising." Powell pointed out that if his civil rights had been put to a vote in the 1960s, "they wouldn't exist today." A TV ad featuring a retired two-star army general made the point that one need not be in favor of same-sex marriage to vote against the amendment and its discriminatory effects. Another TV ad, featuring the head of the League of Women Voters of Hawaii, claimed that "not once in the history of the United States has a state legislature amended the constitution to deprive a single group of citizens of a right the courts say is already theirs." This same ad asked ominously, "If they succeed, who is next?"[5] A few POC ads took a softer approach, appealing to Hawaii's tradition of tolerance and respect for differences and invoking "the spirit of aloha."

On the pro-amendment side, the Hawaii Family Forum ran radio and TV spots that claimed to "clarify" for voters the meaning of the ballot measure. These ads stated that a "yes" vote was a vote in support of marriage between one man and one woman, whereas a "no" vote expressed support for "homosexual marriages." The ads run by Save Traditional Marriage (STM) explicitly rejected the rights framing and accused the amendment's opponents of trying to trick or confuse voters by distracting them from the real issue, which was the definition of marriage. One STM print ad stated: "Same-sex marriage isn't a civil rights issue. Common sense tells us marriage is between one man and one woman. Simple, isn't it?" This same ad went on to accuse "radical gays" of "hiding behind civil rights" and trying to "confuse the issue" because they knew they had a losing issue in same-sex marriage. The STM ads consistently portrayed traditional (heterosexual) families as both valuable and vulnerable.[6] The most provocative ad supporting the amendment, sponsored by a group calling itself Pro-Family Hawaii, implied that if same-sex marriages were not stopped, people would next be seeking the right to marry their dogs and their children.

The amendment ultimately passed by a wide margin, with 69 percent in favor and 31 percent opposed. With the amendment in place, the Hawaii Supreme Court ruled that the plaintiffs in the same-sex marriage lawsuit no longer had a case (*Baehr v. Miike* 1999). The law that the Hawaii legislature had passed back in 1994, defining marriage as between one man and one woman, was now in force.

Activists supporting same-sex marriage had sought to frame the issue as a matter of basic civil rights, not only for same-sex couples but for all Hawaii residents. They downplayed the issue of gay rights and tried to appeal to voters' conscience and self-interest by invoking the general concepts of civil rights and tolerance. Activists opposing same-sex marriage explicitly rejected this framing by insisting that the issue was not civil rights but protection of marriage. They countered opponents' arguments about the need to "protect" the constitution by casting the issue as a question of democracy and protection of traditional morality.

Public debate in the letters columns

Ordinary citizens participated in the public debate over same-sex marriage in Hawaii in various ways, including public hearings held by various legislative bodies and letters to the editor appearing in local newspapers (Goldberg-Hiller 2002). I analyzed a sample of letters to the editor on same-sex marriage that appeared during two critical periods in the Hawaii marriage debates (Hull 2001). The first period was the immediate aftermath of the circuit court ruling in favor of the same-sex couples in December 1996. The second period was the period leading up to and immediately following the vote on the constitutional amendment to block same-sex marriage in November 1998. I collected and coded a total of 233 letters appearing in Honolulu's daily newspapers during these two periods to assess the concerns and arguments put forward by ordinary citizens regarding the possibility of legal same-sex marriage in Hawaii.[7] I analyzed these letters to determine their overall position on the same-sex marriage issue and to identify specific themes or discourses that appeared in their arguments for or against same-sex marriage.[8] The analytical approach was inductive, meaning that I did not start out with preconceived categories of argument to be counted, but looked for patterns of argument in the letters and developed categories based on a careful reading of the entire set of letters.

The published letters skewed toward support for legal same-sex marriage, with 60 percent (140 letters) in favor and 40 percent (93 letters) opposed. Clearly, the letters published in the aftermath of the circuit court decision and near the time of the amendment vote were not representative of the views of Hawaii residents or voters, since numerous opinion polls found the majority of Hawaii citizens opposed to same-sex marriage and the results of the 1998 vote on the amendment reflected even greater opposition to same-sex marriage than the poll data.

Table 5.1. *Major themes in letters supporting same-sex marriage (Hawaii), n = 140*

Theme	No. of letters	% of letters
Rights, equality, justice, non-discrimination	69	49
Tolerance, anti-bigotry, anti-prejudice	45	32
Critique of tactics of opponents of same-sex marriage	28	20
Comparison of denial of same-sex marriage to other oppressions	27	19
Protection of minorities/limits to popular rule	22	16
Separation of church and state	16	11

Given that both the *Advertiser* and the *Star-Bulletin* had editorial positions in favor of same-sex marriage, the views of the editors likely influenced the selection of letters for publication. More interesting than the percentage breakdown in positions for and against same-sex marriage, though, is the range of discourses deployed by letter-writers to explain their positions on same-sex marriage and influence the evolving public debate.

Letters supporting same-sex marriage I identified six major themes or arguments in the letters supporting same-sex marriage, themes that appeared in more than 10 percent of these letters (see Table 5.1). The most frequent argument was that legal recognition for same-sex marriage is necessary as a matter of rights and equality under the law, with about half of the supportive letters invoking discourses of rights and equality. Other major themes among these letters included the importance of tolerance and the need to combat hate and bigotry, critiques of the tactics of the opponents of same-sex marriage, comparing the plight of gays and lesbians to other forms of oppression, the role of the courts in protecting minorities, and the need for a separation of church and state.[9]

The prevalence of the rights and equality argument makes sense, given the context of these letters. In the first period (December 1996 – February 1997), letter-writers were responding to the circuit court ruling, which framed the denial of same-sex marriage as infringing on same-sex couples' constitutional rights. Fifty-nine percent of the letters in this period included the rights and equality theme. A Hawaii resident writing in response to the ruling emphasized that gays and lesbians were not seeking special rights or benefits, but merely equal rights and equal protection under the law:

Heterosexuals like myself must come to realize that same-gender couples have not been seeking "special rights," but rather, equal rights. Our state Constitution guarantees equal rights and equal protection for all. By not recognizing same-gender marriage, the state has created a "special rights" situation for us heterosexuals. (*Star-Bulletin* 12/16/96)

Most of the letters sounding the rights and equality theme spoke in general terms about "civil rights," "equal rights" or simply "rights." Smaller numbers used terms such as "legal rights" "right to marry" or "gay rights," and a few avoided the actual word "rights" altogether but invoked related notions of justice, equality and non-discrimination.

The rights and equality theme appeared somewhat less often in the latter period (September – November 1998), around the time of the vote on the constitutional amendment. It showed up in 41 percent of the letters supporting same-sex marriage in this latter period. Rights arguments were central to the organized campaign to defeat the constitutional amendment, so the continuing appearance of the rights and equality theme in the letters of this period may partly reflect the discourses of activists favoring same-sex marriage. One letter-writer asserted his opposition to the constitutional amendment as follows:

As a husband and a father, a heterosexual and a Christian, I plan to vote "no" next month, both to protect the Constitution from being politicized by whatever is currently the hot "tradition" issue for some special-interest group, and to keep our government from infringing on the civil rights of any of our citizens. (*Star-Bulletin* 10/14/98)

While the rights and equality theme declined in frequency in the letters columns between the period of the circuit court ruling and the vote on the constitutional amendment, the theme of tolerance and anti-bigotry gained ground. Less than a quarter of the letters included the tolerance theme in the first period, after the court ruling, but this theme was used roughly as often as the rights and equality theme in the second period, around the amendment vote. The tolerance theme included both exhortations to positive behavior toward gays and lesbians (most often urging tolerance, appreciation of diversity, respect and even love) and condemnations of negative attitudes and behaviors (most often labeled as hate, bigotry, intolerance, prejudice or ignorance). One example of this theme from a letter published just before the amendment vote incorporates both the positive message of acceptance and the condemnation of prejudice:

Gay people are not the shadowy figures of evil that the religious right and its campaign of hate and fear would have us believe. Gay people are around us every day, in our families, our schools, our churches, and in our workplaces and businesses . . . It is time to reject the hysterical fears that come from the hate orchestrated by the religious right and its political agenda. Instead, it is time to teach our children about love, acceptance, and the value of diversity in our community. (*Star-Bulletin* 10/28/98)

Several letters employing the tolerance theme specifically mentioned the importance of the "spirit of aloha" in the Hawaiian context,[10] echoing some of the advertising by Protect Our Constitution. A letter appearing a few days after the amendment vote lamented:

Rather than voting to live aloha, we have voted to live with shame. A profound sorrow overwhelms me. Hawaii, what have we done? Giving the Legislature the power to change our Constitution for the purpose of discriminating against a select group? (*Star-Bulletin* 11/6/98)

The letters invoking tolerance and aloha spirit sought to make the case that opponents of same-sex marriage were out of step with Hawaii's traditions and ethos.

Critiques of the opponents of same-sex marriage appeared frequently, especially after the warring ads between the two camps began to fill the newspapers and airwaves. In particular, many letter-writers accused the amendment supporters of fomenting intolerance, fear and hatred toward gays and lesbians, and sometimes took exception to the content of their ads or the tactics they employed in their efforts to get out the vote. (As I will describe shortly, critiques of the tactics of supporters of same-sex marriage were also a frequent theme in the letters opposing same-sex marriage.)

A number of letter-writers supporting same-sex marriage compared opposition to same-sex marriage to other forms of oppression past and present. Specific examples included comparisons to the plight of African-Americans, Japanese-Americans during World War II, Jews and women. Several letters specifically mentioned the history of legal prohibitions against interracial marriage in the United States, a potentially persuasive comparison for residents of a state with a high rate of interracial marriage. Some of these comparisons echoed the comparisons made in the Protect Our Constitution ad campaign, but these sorts of comparisons also appeared in letters published before the ad wars began, suggesting that Hawaii's tradition of tolerance and sensitivity to oppression in various forms also played a role in producing this discourse.

Some letters supporting same-sex marriage made procedural arguments about the functioning of the different branches of government, pointing out that it is the role of courts to protect rights and decide questions of justice regardless of majority opinion. One such letter asserted:

The judiciary is not required to rule according to public opinion. Ours is a government of laws, not of popular excitements. Our Supreme Court, and that of the United States, are in place to assure, among other things, that the rights of minority citizens are protected in our democratic republic. (*Star-Bulletin* 9/23/98)

Some letters also highlighted a different issue concerning the proper functioning of the democratic system, namely the separation of church and state. This argument was often made in direct response to religious arguments against same-sex marriage. For example, one letter-writer offered this perspective on the constitutional amendment:

People may not condone same-sex marriage due to their religious convictions. However, in good conscience, a person can vote "no" out of an equally compelling conviction that the separation of church and state must be upheld. Support the separation of church and state by voting "no." (*Star-Bulletin* 9/9/98)

These kinds of procedural arguments, about the proper role of the courts and the need to keep church and state separate, were countered by the opponents of same-sex marriage, who offered their own procedural arguments about the importance of majority rule in a democracy and the people's right to amend their own constitution.

Letters opposing same-sex marriage I identified six major themes (appearing in at least 10 percent of the letters) in the letters opposing same-sex marriage (see Table 5.2). The two most frequent themes were the need for the will of the majority to prevail on the issue of same-sex marriage and objections to the tactics of supporters of same-sex marriage. Numerous letter-writers also argued that, contrary to the claims of same-sex rights advocates, same-sex marriage is not a civil rights issue. Other frequent themes included the idea that homosexuality is a choice, the immorality of homosexuality and same-sex marriage, and the assertion that marriage by definition is the union of one man and one woman.[11]

Table 5.2. *Major themes in letters opposing same-sex marriage (Hawaii), n = 93*

Theme	No. of letters	% of letters
Will of the majority should prevail, court has overreached	26	28
Critique of tactics of advocates of same-sex marriage	26	28
Explicit rejection of the rights framework applied to this issue	22	24
Homosexuality is a choice, a behavior, a life style	14	15
Morality and God's will	13	14
Definition of marriage, support for "traditional marriage"	10	11

While supporters of same-sex marriage most often sounded themes of rights and tolerance in their letters, opponents offered arguments based on popular will and morality. Many of these letters emphasized that same-sex marriage, so widely opposed by average citizens, should not be forced by the courts or other elites. Some letter-writers expressed a palpable sense of frustration and unfairness that same-sex marriage might be foisted upon the Hawaii population by judicial decree despite widespread opposition. One letter-writer, objecting to the *Star-Bulletin*'s editorial position in favor of same-sex marriage, exhorted fellow readers: "Come on, people, let's show the elite – including this newspaper – who really is in charge" (*Star-Bulletin* 12/10/96). Another letter stated simply: "Why is the minority infringing on the majority? In a democratic society, the majority rules" (*Star-Bulletin* 12/11/96). Closely tied to this theme of the will of the majority was an explicit rejection of the idea that same-sex marriage was a question of rights. Here the parallel with the campaign of the Save Traditional Marriage organization is quite evident, since STM's ads consistently asserted that the amendment vote was not about rights but was really about the future of marriage. But letters rejecting the rights argument appeared in the earlier period, right after the court ruling, just as often as in the latter period, around the amendment vote, so the STM ad campaign does not entirely account for the resentment some letter-writers expressed toward the rights argument.

One letter rejected the rights argument by stating: "They can call it a civil-rights issue, discrimination, or want to propose a domestic partnership bill. It is still same-sex marriage, a chosen lifestyle" (*Star-Bulletin* 12/11/96). Another letter argued that same-sex marriage was not a rights issue because same-sex couples simply do not fit the requirements of the marriage institution:

Marriage between a man and a woman is an institution . . . It is not a civil rights issue because no one stops them from loving, living, and having sex with anyone they choose . . . Because marriage customarily, traditionally, and universally requires a man and woman, it is not a gender bias issue. It is a gender requirement issue. (*Star-Bulletin* 9/23/98)

This letter combined dismissal of the rights argument with an invocation of the definitional argument against same-sex marriage, which asserts that same-sex marriage cannot be allowed because marriage is, by definition, the union of one man and one woman. Some of the letters using the definitional argument linked it to specific religious beliefs or to discourses of naturalness. For example, one letter protested: "Homosexual marriages are oxymoronic – for a marriage is a union of maleness and femaleness, and cannot by nature be made other than it is" (*Star-Bulletin*

12/6/96). Another stated: "Same-sex marriage is God's business. He instituted the sanctity of marriage between a male and a female, period" (*Star-Bulletin* 12/11/96).

Other letters used arguments grounded in religion or morality without specifically making the definitional argument. A letter supporting the amendment stated: "This is not about hating or mistreating gay people. Christians are commanded to love their neighbor as themselves. But we cannot compromise right from wrong, not when it comes from a command from God" (*Star-Bulletin* 10/5/98). Another letter objected to clergy who had spoken out against the amendment, faulting them for failing to show sinners the path to salvation: "If these ministers really loved these sinners, they would rebuke them, show them the error of their ways, bring them to confession and snatch them from the jaws of hell" (*Star-Bulletin* 10/12/98).

Several letters rejected the rights argument by suggesting that homosexuality differed from other forms of minority status because it is a "choice," a "behavior" or a "life style." Some letters mentioned that homosexuality could not be an immutable trait or status (like race or gender), since some people had lived as homosexuals but then renounced the "life style." One letter argued that even if there is some biological basis to homosexuality, it is still a behavioral choice:

Same-sex marriage is ultimately about the principle of whether civil rights can be based on a behavior choice. Even if the theoretical physical link that causes homosexual desires exists, it is still up to individuals to choose their behavior. Not all people who inherit this link or have homosexual thoughts will become lifelong homosexuals . . . legalizing same-sex marriage would be the same as granting civil rights based on behavior. (*Star-Bulletin* 1/27/97)

As some of these examples illustrate, many letters weave together several themes or arguments in the course of stating their position on same-sex marriage. The immorality of homosexuality, for example, or the assertion that it is a choice, becomes part of the argument against framing same-sex marriage as a question of civil rights.

Finally, in addition to the theme of the will of the majority, the most common theme in letters opposing same-sex marriage was the critique of the tactics of those who supported same-sex marriage (or at least opposed the idea of amending the state constitution to block it). Many of these letters echoed the claims of the STM ads, namely that opponents of the constitutional amendment were "hiding" behind civil rights or were intentionally "confusing" the issue for voters. One letter complained: "I didn't believe proponents of same-sex marriage would fool anyone by hiding behind the guise of protecting our Constitution until the League of Women Voters came out in support of gay marriage" (*Star-Bulletin* 9/7/98).[12] Another objected to a controversial television ad linking same-sex marriage to abortion rights:

This evening I was outraged to see the TV commercial attempting to align homosexual "rights" and the issue of abortion . . . I see no slippery slope beyond the issue at hand – simply an honest and meaningful effort to keep marriage within the bounds of moral decency. Shame on those who deceive through fear and misinformation. (*Star-Bulletin* 10/14/98)

Other letters took issue with the characterization of support for the amendment as a form of hate or bigotry. Some opponents of same-sex marriage seemed to feel that same-sex marriage was being forced upon them despite their moral objections and resented being characterized as bigots for taking what they depicted as a morally imperative stance.

The same-sex marriage debate in Hawaii produced passionate and motivated activists on both sides of the issue. The voices of ordinary citizens, finding expression in the letters columns of the local newspapers, echoed and amplified many of the themes and arguments sounded by activist groups. Those who favored legal recognition of same-sex marriage most often framed the issue as a matter of rights, equality and justice, while some also invoked discourses of tolerance and anti-bigotry or compared the denial of same-sex marriage to the oppressions of other minority groups. The opponents of same-sex marriage often explicitly rejected the rights argument and based their own position on a moral condemnation of homosexuality and a definitional argument about the essential nature of marriage. Opponents insisted that majority will should prevail in a democratic system, whereas supporters defended the role of the courts in protecting vulnerable minorities. And both sides leveled harsh critiques against the strategies and tactics of their opponents in the marriage battle. When the marriage war shifted to a new battleground in Vermont a few short years later, the terms of debate would undergo subtle shifts but not radical change. As in Hawaii, the supporters and opponents of legal recognition of same-sex marriage would continue to debate the issue in ways that revealed fundamentally different approaches to thinking about the role of the state in recognizing intimate relationships.

Vermont: similar debate, different outcome

Just like in Hawaii, it was two lesbian couples and one gay male couple who joined together to sue the state for the right to marry in Vermont. The origins of the Vermont lawsuit date back to the formation of the Vermont Freedom to Marry Task Force in 1995, an activist organization that sought to educate Vermonters on the marriage issue and identify plaintiff couples for a lawsuit challenging the exclusion of same-sex couples from marriage (Moats 2004, 100). By the summer of 1997, the lawyers planning the case had lined up their couples, sent them to local town clerks to apply for marriage licenses which were promptly denied, and filed a lawsuit against the state. The case was dismissed at the superior court level in late 1997 and the couples immediately appealed to the Vermont Supreme Court.

In their appeal, the lawyers for the couples offered multiple arguments for same-sex couples' right to marry. First, they argued that the existing marriage statutes should be read to include same-sex couples. Second, they argued that if the existing marriage laws do not include same-sex couples, they are unconstitutional. The appellants' brief laid out several specific arguments for finding the marriage statutes unconstitutional. The brief argued that the exclusion of same-sex couples from the marriage statutes violated the Common Benefits Clause of the state constitution, which states that "government is, or ought to be, instituted for the common benefit, protection, and security of the people, nation, or community, and not for the particular emolument or advantage of any single person, family, or set of persons, who are a part only of that community." The lawyers for the couples maintained that the state had failed to demonstrate a valid reason for excluding same-sex couples from the benefits and protections of marriage. Their brief also argued that the exclusion of same-sex couples from marriage warrants "heightened scrutiny," meaning that the state must go beyond showing any valid purpose for the exclusion and demonstrate a compelling governmental interest. The attorneys offered several grounds for applying heightened scrutiny in this case, arguing that the marriage statutes discriminate on the basis of gender and sexual orientation, and that same-sex couples are being denied a fundamental right. They concluded their brief by asserting that "the right to marry the person we love, the person with whom we want to share our lives, is one of the most fundamental of all our human and civil rights," and noting that the only thing standing in the way of the appellant couples was "prejudice and intolerance."[13]

The lawyers for the state, by contrast, argued that Vermont's marriage statutes clearly excluded same-sex couples and that this exclusion was justified by legitimate state interests. The state cited six specific interests to justify the exclusion: strengthening the link between procreation and childrearing; protecting the institution of marriage from destabilizing changes; promoting marriage as a means of uniting men and women; supporting childrearing settings that include both male and female role models; making Vermont's marriage law consistent with the laws of other states; and minimizing the use of sperm donors and surrogacy contracts to avoid disputes over child custody and visitation. (All of these justifications except the first – furthering the connection of procreation and childrearing – had been rejected by the lower court.) The state also argued against the claim that heightened scrutiny should be applied to the exclusion of same-sex couples from marriage. The lawyers for the state concluded their brief by arguing that the policy question of state recognition for same-sex couples must be resolved by legislative rather than judicial means, noting that "the Court must interpret and apply the law, but it has no role in reformulating public policy."

On December 20, 1999, the Vermont Supreme Court issued its decision in *Baker v. State of Vermont*, finding that the Vermont marriage statutes violated the Common Benefits Clause of the state constitution and ordering the state legislature to devise a remedy either by revising the marriage statutes or by creating a parallel legal structure to deliver the rights and benefits of marriage to same-sex couples. Specifically, the court stated:

We hold that the State is constitutionally required to extend to same-sex couples the common benefits and protections that flow from marriage under Vermont law. Whether this ultimately takes the form of inclusion within the marriage laws themselves or a parallel "domestic partnership" system or some equivalent statutory alternative, rests with the Legislature. Whatever system is chosen, however, must conform with the constitutional imperative to afford all Vermonters the common benefit, protection, and security of the law.

The court rejected the argument that the existing marriage statutes should be read to include same-sex couples. The court also rejected the argument that the exclusion of same-sex couples from marriage required heightened scrutiny.

The Vermont ruling departed from the Hawaii script in at least two important respects. First, the constitutional basis for the decision was different. In *Baehr v. Lewin*, the Hawaii Supreme Court had ruled that the denial of marriage licenses to same-sex couples appeared to violate the Hawaii constitution's equal rights amendment by discriminating on the basis of sex. In the Vermont ruling, by contrast, the court did not rely on the sex discrimination argument, but on the Vermont constitution's Common Benefits Clause. (This finding foreshadowed the 2003 ruling in the Massachusetts case, *Goodridge v. Department of Public Health*, in which the Supreme Judicial Court of Massachusetts relied on a similar clause in the Massachusetts constitution to find a right to marriage for same-sex couples.) Second, the Vermont ruling departed from Hawaii's example by inviting the legislature into the process of crafting a remedy. Whereas in Hawaii the legislature had participated in a reactive fashion by putting in motion the constitutional amendment process to supersede an anticipated court ruling making same-sex marriage the law of the land, in Vermont the legislature was charged with making the final decision on how to rectify the unconstitutional deprivation of same-sex couples' rights.

The Vermont majority opinion was written by Chief Justice Jeffrey Amestoy and signed by three of the associate justices.[14] The fourth associate justice, Denise Johnson, wrote a concurring and dissenting opinion, expressing agreement with the majority's finding that the denial of marriage to same-sex couples was unconstitutional, but accusing the majority of abdicating its responsibility to provide immediate relief to the plaintiffs by granting them full marriage rights.

In his majority opinion, Amestoy made it clear that the majority had the negative example of Hawaii in mind when choosing the less direct route of involving the legislature. In response to Johnson's claim that the majority offered the plaintiff couples only a "truncated remedy," Amestoy wrote that "our opinion provides greater recognition of – and protection for – same sex relationships than has been recognized by any court of final jurisdiction in this country *with the instructive exception of the Hawaii Supreme Court*" (emphasis added). Amestoy then specifically cited both the *Baehr v. Lewin* ruling and the Hawaii constitutional amendment blocking same-sex marriage, implying that a court ruling imposing same-sex marriage without legislative involvement could ultimately be overturned by a popular backlash, as had happened in Hawaii. Clearly, the majority in *Baker v. State* hoped that involving the state legislature in devising a policy solution would avoid the kind of outcome seen in Hawaii.

With the *Baker* ruling, same-sex marriage immediately became the hottest issue in Vermont state politics and the biggest item on the legislature's agenda. The citizen group Take It to the People, which had filed a brief arguing against same-sex marriage rights with the Supreme Court, held a press conference on the State House steps the day after the *Baker* ruling was issued, urging legislators to take action to protect traditional marriage (Moats 2004, 153). Phone calls on the issue poured into the offices of the governor and the Supreme Court. State lawmakers tackled the issue the next month, starting with hearings held by the House Judiciary Committee.

The judiciary committee hearings extended over a period of several weeks and included testimony from a wide range of experts and advocates. The first to address the committee were Susan Murray and Beth

Robinson, the lawyers for the three same-sex couples who had appealed to the Supreme Court. (Their legal team also included activist attorney Mary Bonauto of Boston's Gay and Lesbian Advocates and Defenders.) Murray and Robinson urged the committee to avoid setting up a "separate but equal" domestic partnership system for same-sex couples. Several other lawyers and law professors also testified on legal aspects of the issue. The committee also took testimony from experts on the history of marriage, the possible fiscal impacts of various responses to the *Baker* ruling, Hawaii's experience with same-sex marriage, religious perspectives on marriage and homosexuality, laws recognizing same-sex relationships in other countries and the history of laws barring interracial marriage in the United States.

In addition to these committee hearings featuring expert witnesses, the House Judiciary Committee teamed with its Senate counterpart to hold two public hearings at the State House on January 25 and February 1, 2000. These hearings were meant to give ordinary Vermonters the opportunity to participate in the debate about how the legislature should respond to the *Baker* decision. Roughly 1,500 people made their way to the State House for the first hearing despite a severe snowstorm, and the committee heard the testimony of 115 randomly selected witnesses, each allowed two minutes to speak. A comparable crowd turned out a week later for the second hearing and an additional 110 citizens testified before the committee. Below I examine the public testimony from the February 1 hearing to assess how the voices of ordinary citizens helped shape the public debate over same-sex marriage in Vermont.

About a week after the February 1 public hearing, the House Judiciary Committee met to decide how to proceed. A majority of committee members coalesced around the option of creating a domestic partnership system, although a few thought same-sex marriage was the better option. None of the committee members took a position opposing both marriage and domestic partnership. The broader House of Representatives was not as united on the issue, however. One representative was pushing an alternative reciprocal beneficiaries bill that would make a limited set of benefits available to a broader range of relationships, including non-sexual relationships. A small group of conservative House members drafted a resolution calling for the impeachment of the Supreme Court justices, and others wanted to pass a resolution urging the Senate to start the process of amending the state constitution to block same-sex marriage.

Responding to some of the testimony at the public hearings that took issue with the term domestic partnership, the Judiciary Committee came up with the term civil unions and hammered out the details of the new status. Civil union licenses would be issued by town clerks and certified in an official ceremony by judges, justices of the peace or clergy. All existing Vermont statutes that made any reference to marriage would now be read to include civil unions as the equivalent of marriages. Committee members hoped that the civil unions bill would prove a workable political compromise that both fulfilled the court's mandate in *Baker* and garnered enough votes to get through the legislature. The committee passed the bill 10–1 on March 1 and sent it to the full House. Five days later, Vermont citizens had another opportunity to express their views on the issue on Town Meeting Day, a Vermont political tradition. More than fifty municipalities voted on non-binding resolutions on same-sex marriage or domestic partnership. None of these resolutions came out in favor of legal same-sex marriage for Vermont. Most of the resolutions on domestic partnership also produced majority opposition, with 38 cities voting against implementing a domestic partnership system and 11 voting in favor (Moats 2004, 205).

When the bill came up for a vote in the full House, legislators engaged in a day of impassioned debate. Representative Bill Lippert was the only openly gay member of the Vermont Legislature and a member of the committee that had crafted the civil unions bill. Lippert spoke forcefully in favor of the bill, citing his own experiences as a gay man and the challenges facing all gay and lesbian couples who lack legal recognition. Lippert condemned the prejudice of those who opposed same-sex marriage and sought to block the civil unions legislation. He told his fellow legislators: "There's something strange about sitting in the midst of a deliberative body that is trying to decide whether I and my fellow gay and lesbian Vermonters should get our rights now; should we wait a little longer; should we ask all the people whether or not we deserve to have those rights?" (quoted in Moats 2004, 217). Lippert concluded his remarks by exhorting his colleagues to seize an "historic opportunity":

Let us move forward, putting into law a bill that will set aside traditional marriage in order to meet the needs of those who somehow feel threatened, but will find a way through this thicket and will grant rights, will give a message to our community that it is time to take another piece of the hatred and the discrimination and the prejudice and remove it, and at the same time give an affirmation to our community about what it means to have full inclusivity, to embrace our neighbors, to affirm committed, loving relationships and to affirm our common humanity. (quoted in Moats 2004, 218)

The next day, the bill passed in the House 76–69 on its final reading.

The legislation then moved to the state Senate, where the judiciary committee held additional hearings to gather testimony from expert witnesses and citizens. Opponents of legal recognition for same-sex couples now had a specific target for their actions. Representative Nancy Sheltra, one of the fiercest opponents of the legislation in the House, organized a "Jericho march" in which opponents circled the State House seven times to express their opposition to the bill. Sheltra told the marchers it was time to "turn Vermont around" and reclaim the state for "godly purposes." "One hundred years ago," Sheltra remarked, "the Christian community, the moral people, they were the ones that controlled the media, controlled the government, and they controlled the schools. Hey, we were a great nation then, folks, weren't we? What's happening now?" (quoted in Moats 2004, 232). Despite the vocal and organized opposition, the Senate Judiciary Committee passed a civil unions bill in April and the full Senate approved it on a mostly party-line vote. On April 25, 2000, the House voted 79–68 to accept the Senate's version of the bill, and Governor Howard Dean signed the bill the next day.

Vermont's civil unions law took effect in July 2000. Since its implementation, over 7,000 civil unions have been formed, mostly by non-Vermonters. Passage of the law spawned a grassroots "Take Back Vermont" movement, which urged state residents to defeat the re-election efforts of legislators who had voted for civil unions. In the fall 2000 elections, Governor Dean faced a Republican challenger who made Dean's support of civil unions a campaign issue, but Dean narrowly won re-election with 50.4 percent of the vote. Sixteen House incumbents who had supported civil unions were defeated. Republicans took control of the House and Democrats retained their majority in the more liberal Senate by the narrowest possible margin. After the 2000 elections, the House passed a bill to replace civil unions with a less extensive reciprocal beneficiaries system, but the bill died in the Senate. By the 2002 state elections, the civil unions issue had largely faded from the Vermont political scene and several legislators who had won their seats in 2000 by running as anti-civil union candidates were turned out of office.

Vermonters bear witness

To examine how ordinary Vermont citizens talked about the same-sex marriage issue and attempted to influence the actions of the legislature in the wake of the *Baker* decision, I analyzed a transcript of the February 1 public hearing co-sponsored by the House and Senate Judiciary Committees and held in the Vermont State House in the state capital of Montpelier. The transcript includes the testimony of 89 witnesses testifying over a period of several hours.[15] The committees selected witnesses randomly from lists of those opposing or favoring same-sex marriage and alternated between the two camps, with testimony held to a firm two-minute time limit. In analyzing this testimony, I used the themes from the Hawaii letters to the editor as a starting point but also searched the testimony for themes or arguments that did not feature prominently in the Hawaii letters.

Many of the themes and arguments that appeared in the letters to the editor in Hawaii a few years earlier also featured in the testimony of Vermont residents speaking for and against legal recognition for same-sex couples. Among supporters of legal recognition, discourses of rights and equality were quite prominent in the testimony, even more prominent than in the Hawaii letters supporting same-sex marriage. Supporters also invoked the values of tolerance and diversity, decried prejudice against gays and lesbians, and asserted the propriety of the courts protecting the rights of an unpopular minority. Vermont witnesses opposing legal recognition for same-sex couples relied most heavily on moral and religious arguments, but also frequently invoked the definitional argument (that marriage by definition is the union of a man and a woman) and the democracy argument (that the will of the majority should prevail). One new twist in the Vermont testimony was more explicit discussion of the impacts of same-sex marriage on children, with both sides referring to the effects on children to support their case. In Hawaii, impacts on children were the core of the state's argument against same-sex marriage at trial, and children sometimes became part of the broader public debate, as when the group Save Traditional Marriage ran a TV ad showing a young child reading a book about same-sex weddings and exhorting viewers to think about the (presumably negative) effects of same-sex marriage on kids. But arguments about children did not constitute a major theme in the letters columns in Hawaii, whereas ordinary Vermont citizens testifying before the legislature more often raised the issue of children.

Because the Vermont judiciary committees decided to structure the February 1 hearing to give equal time to both supporters and opponents of legal recognition, the hearing does not provide a gauge of overall public opinion on the issue. However, hearing witnesses were randomly selected from the list of those who had signed up to testify, making their testimony somewhat more representative of general public opinion than the letters to the editor in Hawaii (which editors selected for publication based on unknown criteria).[16]

The hearing made it clear that opinions on the issue were quite polarized. The putative purpose of the hearing was to allow citizens to advise the legislature on how to respond to the *Baker* decision, which required some action by the legislature and explicitly suggested the possibility of creating some kind of alternative legal status for same-sex couples, such as domestic partnerships. Yet none of the witnesses at the February 1 hearing spoke in favor of a specific compromise solution such as domestic partnership, and many of the witnesses on both sides of the issue spoke against such an approach.[17] More than one-third of the witnesses supporting legal recognition stated that *only* same-sex marriage, not domestic partnerships or a similar scheme, was an acceptable policy outcome. These witnesses often objected that domestic partnership would not bring full equality for same-sex couples, in either legal or symbolic terms. Several specifically noted that "separate but equal" is a discredited approach. On the other side, almost a quarter of the opponents of legal recognition explicitly stated their opposition to *both* marriage and domestic partnership alternatives. Most of these witnesses did not explain why they viewed domestic partnership as an unacceptable alternative to granting marriage rights; they simply dismissed both marriage and domestic partnership in the same breath. One witness did refer to domestic partnership as a "legal Pandora's box," implying concern about the complexity of instituting such a system and possible unintended consequences. Another witness predicted that hundreds of same-sex couples would relocate to Vermont to take advantage of domestic partnership status. But the rest of the witnesses simply stated opposition to domestic partnership and did not offer ideas about how the legislature could comply with *Baker* if it granted neither marriage nor partnership status.

Testimony supporting same-sex marriage I identified eight themes that appeared in the testimony of at least 10 percent of the Vermont witnesses supportive of legal recognition for same-sex couples (see Table 5.3). Discourses of rights, equality and justice dominated, with more

Table 5.3. *Major themes in testimony supporting same-sex marriage (Vermont)*, n = 44

Theme	No. of witnesses	% of witnesses
Rights, equality, justice, non-discrimination	35	80
Tolerance, anti-bigotry, anti-prejudice	12	27
Impacts on children	12	27
Protection of minorities/limits to popular rule	10	23
Separation of church and state	8	18
Comparison of denial of same-sex marriage to other oppressions	8	18
Personal impacts of lack of same-sex marriage	6	14
Vermont tradition of equality and diversity	5	11

than three-quarters of these witnesses invoking the rights and equality theme (compared to roughly half of the supportive letter-writers in the Hawaii marriage debates). After the rights and equality theme, the most common themes in the testimony of supporters included calls for tolerance and condemnation of bigotry or prejudice, and concern about the impacts on children of denying legal recognition to same-sex couples. About a quarter of the supportive witnesses voiced each of these themes. Nearly a quarter of these witnesses discussed the need to protect minorities and limit popular rule, while about a fifth testified about the need for separation of church and state and a fifth compared the denial of same-sex marriage recognition to other forms of oppression. Some witnesses attempted to personalize or localize the marriage issue in their testimony, with six witnesses (14 percent) describing the personal impact of their lack of access to legal marriage and five witnesses (11 percent) invoking Vermont's tradition of equality and diversity as a reason to extend marriage to same-sex partners.[18]

Most of the witnesses who invoked the rights and equality theme made specific reference to rights, although their choice of wording varied. Most commonly, these witnesses talked about marriage rights or the right to marry, equal (or same) rights or civil rights. Some spoke more generally of rights, without any qualifying adjectives, and a few spoke of human rights, legal rights, or gay and lesbian rights. Several witnesses emphasized the importance they attached to the rights in question and insisted on the idea of equal treatment for all citizens. One witness, for example, told the legislators: "I would like to urge you to resist the calls to allow this crucial civil rights issue to be decided by a popularity contest . . . At bottom, democracy involves treating citizens equally." Another witness quoted Abraham Lincoln on the importance of protecting minority rights, and then asserted the centrality of the right to marriage:

Certainly, if such a right exists that is vital, the right to marry is very vital. Do you know what the right entails? The rights of survivorship, the rights of inheritance, the rights of being able to dispose of one's loved one at the time of death and the right to be present in the hospital. These rights are vital and must be protected.

Some witnesses attempted to personalize the rights theme by referring to their own situation or that of family members. For example, a woman in a heterosexual marriage decried the injustice of denying to same-sex couples a right that she enjoys: "I find it incredibly unfair and unjust that I have the right to marry, while gay and lesbian couples cannot marry. Many of them are in relationships equally strong as my husband's and mine, and a lot of them have been married, or together, longer than [we have.]" A man in a heterosexual marriage testified about his gay son, noting that his son "does not enjoy the civil and legal rights that [my wife] and I do, although he has a caring, long-term relationship with another man." And several gay and lesbian witnesses spoke of the issue of rights in the first person. One woman testified that she was attending the hearing with her female partner of fourteen years, with whom she is raising two children. She explained that she and her partner were not seeking approval for their relationship but simply recognition of their rights:

We . . . didn't come here tonight to ask anyone to bless our union, to legitimize it, or even to respect it. We, our friends and our families already do that. I believe that tonight's discussion and the legislative debates that follow it should be, quite simply, about civil rights. The Vermont Supreme Court has decided that under this state's constitution, all Vermonters are entitled to the same rights under the law. That includes gay men and lesbians. Our rights are not up for discussion.

This witness not only invoked the rights and equality theme but explicitly contrasted rights to legitimacy and respect, forms of social recognition that other citizens might not wish to bestow on same-sex relationships.

Some witnesses framed marriage as a rights issue but focused their remarks on the broad goal of equality. One witness, for example, told the legislators:

My dreams are simple. I want to establish a long and lasting love. A love that will nourish my future children. A love that will provide comfort for my family in turbulent times and a love that will be recognized by the state that I live in as entitled to all the rights of marriage. I know that social reform is not easy and is often not backed by popular support. As elected officials, it would take great courage for you to take a stand for equality, civil rights and social justice. Pete Seeger once said that change takes the courage of those who refuse to stand silently by. I urge you to refuse to stand silently by. As you hear stories of those being refused the rights of marriage, as you hear your governor say he'd be more comfortable with domestic partnership, as you hear people in this room tonight advocating for inequality, refuse to stand silently by. Remember as you prepare to draft legislation, that inequality is not abstract. It affects all of our lives in a very real and painful way.

This witness combined the specific themes of rights, equality and justice into a general plea for equal treatment and recognition by the state. She urged legislators to have the courage to wipe out the inequality that "affects all our lives in a very real and painful way." In this way, the witness reframed the rights and equality argument as a claim about the positive benefit of recognizing rights for all of society, not only gays and lesbians.

Some witnesses also invoked the importance of equality specifically to argue that "separate but equal" arrangements cannot really be equal. These witnesses were clearly responding to the possibility of the establishment of some kind of domestic partnership scheme as an alternative to marriage. One witness remarked: "In Vermont, non-discrimination in our laws and institutions is established public policy and so-called 'different but equal' laws would be contrary to the protocol. Therefore, any attempt to pass different but equal partnership legislation must be seen as a bad faith effort because it is inherently discriminatory in nature." Another witness posed the rhetorical question: "I ask you, if you pass domestic partnership instead of gay marriage, are you providing equal access to civil rights to all Vermonters?" In short, witnesses supporting legal recognition invoked the notion of equality both to buttress their rights arguments and to argue against a compromise legislative solution such as domestic partnership.

The rights and equality theme was by far the most frequent discourse in the testimony of same-sex marriage supporters, but other themes also figured prominently in the testimony of supporters. Two themes that appeared in the testimony of more than a quarter of these witnesses were the theme of tolerance and anti-bigotry and the theme of the (positive) impacts of same-sex marriage on children. The tolerance theme in many respects paralleled the calls for tolerance in the letters to the editor in Hawaii. At the Vermont hearing, a dozen witnesses framed their support for legal recognition in the language of tolerance and anti-prejudice. Consistent with the pattern in the Hawaii letters, the use of the tolerance theme was expressed both positively and negatively. One woman, voicing her support for legal recognition for herself and her female partner, offered the following reflection: "Love is expansive, welcoming, the foundation for tolerance. Love reveals confidence, not insecurity." Another witness remarked, "If we can abandon the fear and confusion of how, what we've been taught, we will be able to prove to ourselves and future generations that we, as a people, are inherently tolerant." This witness expressed a belief that tolerance was an intrinsic quality of Vermonters, perhaps temporarily clouded over by "fear and confusion" that resulted from what people had been taught about homosexuality. Several other witnesses also attributed the opposition to same-sex marriage to fear of the unknown, of people who are different, of change, or even of not being re-elected. But other witnesses made stronger statements about the failures of tolerance and acceptance among those opposed to same-sex marriage, charging them with prejudice, bigotry and even hatred. For example, one witness told the legislators that they had "a historically important opportunity, not only to grant the rights and responsibilities of civil marriage to all voters, but to address head-on the prejudice involved and the hatred towards homosexuals that exists in society." Another witness observed that "Vermont is truly at a cross-roads, and the old road of hatred and discrimination must not be an option." And yet another witness warned, "Until our state recognizes that all human beings, regardless of their sexual orientation, deserve the assurances of our Constitution, our children will continue to evolve in a climate of state-sponsored prejudice."

Many of the witnesses backing legal recognition shared this concern about the effects on children of denying marriage to same-sex couples. Arguments about the impacts of state policy on children tied with the tolerance and anti-prejudice theme as the second most common theme in the testimony of these witnesses. Several witnesses talked about children from a personal perspective, either as a gay or lesbian parent or as a heterosexual parent. One woman talked about her 15-month-old daughter Katie, whom she and her female partner were in the process of adopting. She expressed gratitude for the right to adopt as a same-sex couple but also concern that lack of marriage left her family in a vulnerable position:

I implore this legislature to think of our children and protect them. Marriage is not only something that protects the legal rights of couples entering into the legal agreement, but also protects our child. Someday my child will be asked in school if her parents are married. Don't let her say, "No, they have a domestic partnership," something that she will not be able to understand and explain. Let her say, "Yes, my mommies are married." In this way Katie is not different, but equal, part of a larger community. She too will live in a home filled with love and two married parents. Protect our children. Do the right thing. Legalize same-sex marriage.

This parent expressed three distinct concerns about the impact of lack of marriage rights on her own daughter. First, her child lacked full legal protection within their family without marriage. This frames marriage as a legal issue that impacts both adults and children. Second, this mother expressed concern that her daughter will not understand a marriage substitute such as domestic partnership. And third, she suggested that having parents who could not marry would mark her daughter as different, and therefore not "equal" and "part of a larger community." This parent's testimony mixes practical legal concerns with broader concerns about children's social inclusion and their ability to understand and explain their parents' relationship.

Other witnesses, gay and straight, voiced many of these same concerns. Another lesbian parent remarked, "I am worried about what will happen to the children of this state, if they are not taught that they need to value both community and diversity. I fear that the children of same-sex couples, like my children, will grow up and know that their families are stigmatized." A heterosexual parent testified that she had gotten to know same-sex parents through her children's daycare and school. "What I learned recently is that gay and lesbian couples are no different than my husband and I," she commented. "They struggle with how to get their young children to nap, they worry about their children's safety and education, and they value living in the state of Vermont as my husband and I do." Another parent, talking about the future marriage options for his own children, stated, "I wish my children will have the right to civilly marry whomever they love, regardless of race, ethnic origin or gender."

Other major themes in the testimony supporting legal recognition addressed the procedural questions of the role of the courts and popular majorities in a democratic society and the separation of church and state, echoing arguments seen in the debates in the letter columns in Hawaii. Several witnesses supporting legal recognition for same-sex relationships emphasized the need to protect the rights of unpopular minorities in a democratic system. These witnesses often acknowledged that same-sex marriage would not win support in a popular vote, and stressed the role of the courts and the constitution in recognizing and preserving the rights of marginalized groups. One woman who attended the hearing with her female partner told the legislators: "The Vermont Supreme Court has decided that under this state's constitution, all Vermonters are entitled to the same rights under the law. That includes gay men and lesbians. Our rights are not up for discussion. Many people would like to see this issue put to some general vote by Vermont citizens, but that is not how the rights of minorities are guaranteed." Another witness who self-identified as lesbian remarked, "I support gay marriage and I oppose any constitutional change that would discriminate against me or any group of people from a right given to everyone else. Because we are a minority, do you really expect that same-sex marriage will be the popular vote?" Some of the witnesses specifically appealed to the legislators to have the courage to resist popular pressure and uphold justice. For example, one witness stated: "Vermonters have nothing to fear from same-sex marriage. Please don't be tempted into doing only what you think is popular. Do what you think is just and right."

Comparing the plight of same-sex couples to other minority groups who faced oppression or exclusion was another major theme in the testimony of witnesses favoring legal recognition, and this strategy of comparison was often used to fortify arguments about protecting minority rights from majority opinion. One witness compared the current opposition to same-sex marriage to historical opposition to interracial marriage, noting:

Rejection of same-sex marriage comes from the fear of the unknown, a fear of the different. This is similar to the rejections to multiracial marriages only two decades ago. In this parallel struggle for civil rights the lawmakers had to be one step ahead of the people and pave the way for more tolerance. After the races were more legally recognized as equal, our society could begin to follow.

This witness uses the comparison to anti-miscegenation laws to suggest that the legislature has a duty to be "one step ahead of the people" and to "pave the way for more tolerance." Legislators should not wait for public opinion to change but should use their lawmaking power to shape and lead public views. Other witnesses also invoked the comparison to interracial marriage, along with other historical instances of unequal treatment, to urge the legislators to disregard public opinion and uphold court-recognized rights. For example, some mentioned the country's history of slavery and racial segregation as well as the disenfranchisement of women as examples of oppressive policies that had wide popular support. One female witness brought photographs and the immigration papers of her grandparents, and told the legislators that "my decent, gentle grandparents escaped a government where they were considered inferior and immoral, and two generations later I understand that you cannot legislate compassion and understanding, but you do have it in your power now to light the way." Without explicitly drawing the connection, this witness implied that excluding same-sex couples from marriage sent a message that they were inferior citizens, and she implored the legislators to use their power to "light the way."

Besides the theme of protecting minority rights, the other major theme addressing the workings of democracy was the separation of church and state. As in Hawaii, these witnesses were typically responding to moral or religious arguments made by the opponents of same-sex marriage. Some witnesses explicitly referenced the constitutional doctrine of separation of church and state. For example, one witness stated: "We are talking here about civil marriage, nothing to do with religion. Render unto God that which is God's and unto Caesar that which is Caesar's, and one of the founding ideas of this country is separation of church and state." Another witness remarked, "We live in a wonderful country that was wisely founded on the separation of church and state. With that in mind, what the Bible says is irrelevant to the law." Others stated the issue more generally, arguing that moral or religious views are not a valid basis for laws in a secular democracy. One witness identified himself as an atheist and stated:

I am not required to consider your morality weighing on me. I have my own morality. I don't happen to think that mine is any worse. I am sure that there are plenty of people who are not atheists who think that their morality is just as good as yours. The state is not supposed to be in the business of giving people their morality. It's to pass laws based on what is good for the community. Until you have same-sex marriages and find out that they are bad for the community, that we are getting more injury from it than not, you don't have the basis for a political decision regardless of whether you go back to somebody's morality. And as long as you use morality you are going to oppress someone.

Without specifically invoking the separation of church and state, this witness argued against using the particular morality of religious believers as a basis for law. Instead, he suggested that laws should be based on "what is good for the community" and implied that there was no way to determine a priori that same-sex marriages were "bad for the community," other than by resort to moral beliefs that are not universally shared. Another witness observed that the arguments against same-sex marriage "are all rooted in religious tradition. What we have is that these arguments turn out to be basically religious tradition, religious morals and religious natural law. I submit that religious values are not a valid basis for deciding this issue."

Finally, some of the witnesses supporting legal recognition sought to personalize or localize the issue, by testifying about the negative personal impacts of lack of marriage or by linking support for same-sex marriage to cherished Vermont values and traditions. Several witnesses shared personal stories about the obstacles they faced in being recognized as a partner within the health care system. One woman described how her partner was diagnosed with cancer and her partner's physician refused to meet with them as a couple to discuss her diagnosis and treatment options. Another woman described how hospital staff prevented her from being with her partner after surgery, despite the fact that she had established health care power of attorney and would be the medical decision-maker in case of an emergency. A third woman recounted that when she was injured and unconscious after a car accident, her partner was not allowed to make decisions about her medical care because they had not established power of attorney. A girl being raised by a female couple expressed her feelings about her parents' inability to marry:

I didn't know that my moms couldn't get married until I heard one mom say it is still not legal to get married. At first I thought they didn't have time or something. [Laughter from audience.] It didn't occur to me that they couldn't. I was sad inside for them. I was also angry with people who kept them from marriage. If they could get married we could be a real family, not like we aren't, but . . . but it would make me feel like I have a special kind of family. It would make me feel special and good if my moms could get married. I don't and probably never will understand why they can't.

For this young witness, the personal impact of lack of marriage rights was sadness and anger at being prevented from having "a real family" or "a special kind of family." Other witnesses sought to frame same-sex marriage as a local issue by invoking Vermont's special status as a civil rights leader among the states. Several pointed to the fact that Vermont was the first state to outlaw slavery, and some spoke of Vermont's reputation for honoring diversity and individual freedoms. One witness invoked Vermont's history and reputation by stating: "As Vermonters we have a longstanding tradition of both listening to and valuing the freedom of the individual while protecting equality."

Testimony opposing same-sex marriage I identified seven major themes (used by at least 10 percent of the witnesses) in the testimony of witnesses opposing legal recognition for same-sex relationships (see Table 5.4). The most prevalent theme was the invocation of morality or reference to God's will, used by two-thirds of these witnesses. Other themes invoked by more than half of the witnesses opposed to legal recognition were the definition of marriage as male and female (or simply "traditional marriage") and the procedural argument that the will of the majority should prevail in a democratic system. Smaller numbers of witnesses predicted that legal recognition for same-sex relationships would bring the destruction of society, cited the negative impacts of same-sex marriage on children, argued that homosexuality and same-sex marriage are unnatural, and asserted that their own opposition to legal recognition did not represent bigotry or homophobia.

Table 5.4. *Major themes in testimony opposing same-sex marriage (Vermont),* n = 45

Theme	No. of witnesses	% of witnesses
Morality and God's will	30	67
Definition of marriage, support for "traditional marriage"	24	53
Will of the majority should prevail, court has overreached	23	51
Same-sex marriage will bring destruction of society	13	29
Impacts on children	8	18
Unnaturalness of homosexuality and same-sex marriage	7	16
Opposition is *not* based on homophobia or bigotry	6	13

To some extent, these themes overlap with the themes found in the Hawaii letters opposed to same-sex marriage. The three most prominent themes in the testimony of Vermonters opposing legal recognition of same-sex couples – morality, the definition of marriage and the will of the majority – were also major themes in the debates in the letters columns in Hawaii. But several major themes in the Vermont testimony were not as prominent in the Hawaii debates (for example, the destruction of society and the negative impacts on children), and some of the major themes from the Hawaii letters did not have the same prominence in the Vermont testimony (for example, homosexuality is a choice and same-sex marriage is not a rights issue).

Two out of three opposition witnesses in Vermont invoked morality or God's will to support their position, sometimes quoting specific Bible passages to make their point. Some of these witnesses focused on the immorality of homosexuality in general. For example, one witness stated, "God's words state clearly that homosexuality is a sin, and to twist the words of the Bible to say anything else is wrong." Another witness observed, "For thousands of years civilization had condemned homosexual conduct. Those of us here in the opposition do not have a fixation on this particular behavior. We are not homophobes. We would be equally offended by attempts to legitimize incest, rape and adultery or child molestation." And a third witness compared the immorality of homosexuality to alcoholism and drug addiction:

I've seen people hurt by the immorality that they live in. The fact that they live in this immorality causes people to die. People die everyday who don't get to see it. Doing all that, God doesn't hate people. God doesn't hate homosexuals, he loves them. I am a Christian. I've seen when I can help people. I've seen people die and I've seen people get saved. And in that, there, I've seen people's lives change dramatically. Alcoholics become clean, like that on the spot. Drug addicts, I've seen drug overdoses and I've seen people who use dope, you know, do drugs, become saved. Immorality leads to destruction. Homosexuality is immorality.

Most witnesses invoking the theme of morality and God's will went beyond general statements about the immorality of homosexuality to assert more specifically that same-sex marriage was immoral or contrary to God's plan for marriage. One witness, for instance, told the legislators that same-sex marriage is "a violation of a God-given morality which governs all human behavior and law," and went on to predict: "A decision for same-sex marriage will result in a curse for our state, our families, our children and youth. A decision against same-sex marriage will result in God's blessing on our state, families, children and youth." Another witness told the lawmakers, "What I do know is that you or I didn't define marriage in the beginning. Can we dare redefine it now?

God made it clear that marriage is only to be between a man and a woman." These witnesses expressed a belief that the secular institution of marriage could never be separated from its religious and moral foundations. They viewed marriage as an institution created by God and reflecting God's will for human relationships.

Many of the witnesses who based their opposition to legal recognition on moral or religious grounds anticipated the possible objection of the need for separation of church and state and attempted to rebut this point in their testimony. One witness argued that law cannot be separated from morality because morality serves as the foundation for laws:

Some would argue that law is a separate entity from morality. Law involves government and morality involves behavior. This is not a case, this is not the case. Murder and rape are violations against both law and morality. Law is a reflection of the morals of a society. Law cannot be separate from morality. Morality is a reflection of the inner conscience of divine law. All people have an inner conscience of right and wrong. It is God-given and reflects God's moral character. The establishment of a marriage between a male and a female is more than a governmental law, it is a reflection of God's moral character and will. All societies and civilizations have responded to their God-given inner conscience and have created some form of marriage contract or agreement between a man and a woman. No society or civilization has ever legalized same-sex marriage.

Several witnesses addressed the church–state separation issue by arguing that there was ample historical evidence to suggest the importance of morality to the framers of Vermont's constitution. One witness remarked, "Our founding fathers formed this constitution on the basis of biblical values and its commands. Traditional marriage and the family have been the cornerstone of our society and those of the world since time began." Two other witnesses referenced a specific passage in the Vermont constitution (Chapter II, section 68) which states in part: "Laws for the encouragement of virtue and the prevention of vice and immorality ought to be constantly kept in force, and duly executed." This clause was taken as firm evidence that moral considerations had a legitimate place in the process of creating and enforcing state laws, including laws limiting marriage to opposite-sex couples. Citing this clause, one witness remarked: "So the question boils down to this: do same-sex relationships constitute immoral behavior? That is the crux of the debate. God forbid that our state has been driven so far from its origins that we leave God out of the debate of morality. God's word is clear. Same-sex relationships are indeed immoral." Another witness also cited the constitutional clause and then expanded his comments to argue that the founding fathers of both Vermont and the nation recognized a place for morality in the law:

I appeal to the legislature that morality is an issue and can be used for a conclusion of this matter. Our forefathers who wrote the Constitution of the United States of America quoted scripture time and again. How can it not be relevant? Thomas Jefferson called the Bible the cornerstone of American liberty. Patrick Henry said our country should be founded on the Gospel of Jesus Christ. James Madison said, "I would stake our future on the ability to follow the Ten Commandments." George Washington said that we can't have national morality apart from religious principles. Now in the twenty-first century suddenly these men, men of integrity, our forefathers, are being challenged by a group of people who claim that the argument for same-sex marriage is based on a theme of enlightenment and in tune with modern thinking.

These witnesses clearly recognized the potential objections to using religion and morality as a basis for law, but argued that these concerns were overstated or inapplicable in the case of same-sex marriage.

Some of the witnesses who framed the question in moral terms also appealed to the definitional argument against same-sex marriage or expressed their support for preserving "traditional marriage," while others invoked the definitional argument or the notion of traditional marriage without casting these arguments in religious or moral terms. For example, one witness asserted that the definition of marriage as a male–female union transcended specific religions and cultures:

Many of the arguments in favor of same-sex marriage have been emotional in nature last week [at the first public hearing]. "I pay my taxes, I work hard, therefore you should change society's traditional definition of marriage for me." But these do not justify changing the very definition and nature of marriage as agreed to by virtually every culture, every religion, even non-religion in the case of the Communists, throughout all recorded history.

Another witness objected that the definition of marriage was already a settled matter in Vermont law, stating: "The institution of marriage has long been established by the state of Vermont as a matter of law . . . What I ask is why we are trying [to use] the institution of the husband and wife, of marriage, to make way for privileges or equal rights for other individuals?" Others witnesses expressed surprise or frustration that the definition of marriage was even open to question, citing dictionary definitions, state and federal laws, or "God's word" to support their view that marriage must mean a male–female union. One witness commented sarcastically, "Even a child knows that marriage is between a man and a woman." Other witnesses made the definitional argument less directly, by voicing their support for "traditional marriage" with straightforward declarations such as "I do have to say that I am in support of traditional marriage: one man, one woman." Another witness told the legislators: "I'm here in hopes of enlisting your support for a constitutional amendment keeping Vermont's marriages traditional, that is, between one man and one woman. Four hundred years of marriage between one man and one woman is quite a legal precedent."

Another theme in the opposition testimony that relates to both the morality theme and the definition theme is the argument from nature. Seven witnesses (16 percent) specifically argued that homosexuality or same-sex marriage is unnatural and therefore undeserving of legal support. This theme of unnaturalness closely overlaps with the theme of morality: all but one of the witnesses who cite unnaturalness in their testimony also cite morality. Sometimes the two themes are tightly linked, as in the case of the witness who stated flatly: "I believe that homosexuality is immoral or unnatural." In other cases, the nature argument appears to supplement the moral argument, as when a witness referred to homosexuality as a "sexual perversion" and noted that it is "intensely obvious that man and woman were made to fit together." This witness then went on to warn that "as man moves further from his Creator he becomes more and more foolish." In this testimony, the unnaturalness of homosexuality is portrayed as an affront to the intentions of the Creator who designed man and woman to "fit together." The theme of unnaturalness also links to the definitional argument, because some witnesses read in nature evidence for the proper definition of marriage. Specifically, witnesses referenced either the anatomical complementarity of males and females, or their procreative capacity, to imply that the definition of marriage is ordained by nature. "In over five thousand years marriage has changed, but only within the context of heterosexuality," one witness observed. "The heterosexual basis for marriage has remained constant. Now, the reason for this is obvious. Heterosexuality is biologically given. It is intrinsic to species survival and to stable societies. We know that by empirical fact. Homosexuality is not."

After morality and the definitional argument, the most frequent theme in the opposition testimony was the assertion that the will of the majority should prevail. Just over half of the opposition witnesses invoked the democratic procedural argument that the majority view should be expressed in law or that the court had overstepped its jurisdiction in finding a right to legal recognition despite majority opposition, echoing a prominent theme from the debates in Hawaii. Several witnesses equated majority rule with democracy, implying or stating outright that the implementation of legal recognition for same-sex couples by court order was anti-democratic. For example, one witness stated: "The right to same-sex marriage has not been granted anywhere else in the world. The majority of Vermonters do not want it here. The rule of the majority act of voting is called democracy. I would like my [rights] and the rights of many other Vermonters to be considered." This witness not only frames court-mandated recognition of same-sex couples as a violation of democracy, but also suggests that minority rights are being created at the expense of the rights of the ignored majority. Other witnesses also voiced this concern that minority rights were being imposed in an unfair or undemocratic fashion. One witness told the lawmakers that "the government is responsible for protecting minorities from injustice and abuse, not responsible for imposing minority values on the majority." Another witness commented, "To legislate marriage between members of the same sex is one of the greatest injustices that government could impose upon its citizens." By focusing on the lack of deference being shown to the majority viewpoint, these witnesses were able to appropriate the language of rights and justice for their own purposes.

Many of the witnesses calling for the expression of majority will directed their ire at the Vermont Supreme Court and urged the legislature to reassert its own authority. One witness declared, "We need to stop judicial tyranny now. Polls clearly show that the people of Vermont don't want either alternative dictated by the Supreme Court. It is time for our elected officials to represent us and not accept the role of subsidiaries to the judiciary, which has usurped your authority." Another witness stated, "Vermont has a government of the people. The state Supreme Court has usurped the power of the people by mandating legislation to a legislative body. The special interest minority has effectively leveraged their power in creating a situation that should not be tolerated by the majority." Several witnesses encouraged the lawmakers to pass a bill to start the process of amending the state constitution to limit marriage to opposite-sex couples and nullify the *Baker* ruling. "I urge the legislators to challenge the decision of the Supreme Court by not acting on their mandate," one witness testified, "but instead be legislators who support a motion to amend our state constitution to forever clearly state that marriage is only the union of one male and one female."

Two of the major themes in the opposition testimony addressed the likely effects of legal recognition of same-sex relationships, on society as a whole or on children specifically. Nearly a third of the opposition witnesses made dire predictions regarding the effect of legal recognition on the state of Vermont or even on the entire nation. Their statements featured dramatic warnings portending instability, breakdown, decline and destruction. One witness stated, "I'm asking you to hold traditional marriage and the future of society safe from the effects of homosexual chaos." Another witness appealed to the record of history to support his prediction of social collapse: "Throughout history we will see that the downfall of every civilization was preceded by homosexuality." A slightly smaller number of witnesses (eight total) addressed their concerns about the impacts of legal recognition more narrowly to focus on children. Some of these witnesses were vague about the anticipated negative effects on children, but others were more specific, for example citing the need for children to be raised by both a mother and a father, or concern that legal recognition for same-sex relationships would embolden adults interested in sexually exploiting children. One witness described how the loosening of sexual morality had led to many undesirable outcomes including divorce, teen pregnancy and sexually transmitted diseases. He argued that children had often been victimized by these unforeseen consequences of departing from traditional sexual morality, and urged legislators to avoid the further erosion of sexual morality that same-sex marriage would represent.

A final theme in the testimony of witnesses opposed to same-sex marriage is the rejection of being characterized as homophobic or bigoted for opposing legal recognition. In Hawaii, many of the letter-writers had made a point of rejecting the framing of same-sex marriage as a rights issue. In Vermont, the opposition witnesses rarely made that exact argument, but instead spoke at a more personal level to deflect unflattering charges about the motivations underlying their position. Sometimes these assertions of non-prejudice were made with a light touch, as in the case of one witness who addressed the audience at the hearing by stating, "I like what some of you have said, and I would like to tell you that just because I insist on a round wheel, that doesn't make me square-phobic." Another opposition witness commented: "I am not homophobic or heterophobic. I am not always correct in my political correctness, but I plan to correct that." But others took a more serious tone, for example professing "compassion and understanding" for gays and lesbians and remarking, "We don't hate them but we do hate their sins." And a couple of witnesses took a more combative tone, arguing that tolerance must have its limits. One witness asked: "Are we to become a society that tolerates everything?"

The contours of the public debates over same-sex marriage in Hawaii and Vermont were broadly similar, although some clear differences existed. Advocates for same-sex marriage in both states relied most heavily on the rights and equality argument, framing legal recognition as a matter of civil rights and equal treatment under the law. This theme was even more frequently deployed by the Vermont hearing witnesses than by the Hawaii letter-writers supporting same-sex marriage, suggesting that by the time the marriage debate reached Vermont in early 2000, rights discourse had solidified its position as the dominant way of arguing for legal same-sex marriage. The tolerance theme also figured prominently in the discourses of citizens supporting same-sex marriage in both states. Some themes supporting same-sex marriage emerged in Vermont that had not been prominent in Hawaii, including the impacts on children (with some Vermont witnesses arguing that denial of legal recognition harmed children with same-sex parents and taught a lesson of prejudice) and the personal impacts of lack of marriage rights for adults. Many of the Vermont witnesses self-identified as members of same-sex couples and spoke concretely about the impacts of being denied access to legal marriage. Opponents of same-sex marriage in both states gravitated to pro-democracy arguments that asserted the sovereignty of majority rule and moral arguments that cast homosexuality or same-sex marriage as a clear violation of God's will. Citizens in both states also invoked definitional arguments against same-sex marriage. Hawaii citizens placed greater emphasis on rejecting the idea that same-sex marriage was a rights issue, and Vermont citizens more often discussed the negative impacts of same-sex marriage on society in general and children in particular.

Comparing the letters to the editor in Hawaii and the testimony of witnesses at the public hearings in Vermont has its limits as a way of assessing the public marriage debates in the two states. Letters and in-person public testimony are two different forms of public communication, and may draw out different kinds of people. For example, even though letters are published over people's name and place of residence, they are arguably a more "anonymous" form of communication than appearing in person before a crowd of onlookers to deliver oral remarks. Also, the letters to the editor were selected for publication by editors with their own unknown criteria, and may reflect editors' judgments about both form and content. By contrast, the witnesses who testified in Vermont were randomly selected and the organizers of the hearing had no control over the style or substance of their remarks, other than imposing the time limit. For these reasons, the value of putting the letters and the testimony side by side lies less in comparing the precise frequency with which various themes or arguments appeared than in noting the overlaps and divergences in these two state-level debates. And the comparison reveals that a few dominant themes, and indeed conversations between themes, emerged in both contexts.

Public debates and the perspective of same-sex couples

Several implicit conversations or sub-debates can be read off of the public debates over same-sex marriage at the state level. These include debates over the nature of the same-sex marriage issue (whether it is a rights issue or not), over the proper functioning of a democratic system of governance, over the moral status of homosexuality and same-sex marriage and the role of moral judgments in public policy, and over the likely impacts of legal recognition for same-sex relationships. In each of these areas, clear differences emerged between the supporters and opponents of legal same-sex marriage.

The legal advocates, social movement activists and ordinary citizens supporting same-sex marriage consistently frame the issue as a question of rights and equality. By contrast, those opposing same-sex marriage either deny the rights framing explicitly (as in the case of many letter-writers in Hawaii) or simply avoid discussion of rights and equality in favor of other ways of discussing the issue (for example, as a moral question). It seems likely that the opponents of same-sex marriage recognize that the concepts of rights and equality have powerful reson-ance in American political culture. To accept the framing of same-sex marriage as a rights issue would require the opponents to make an argument about why it is permissible to withhold rights or legal equality from a particular social group, a difficult task in the context of an ideology of universal rights. By explicitly rejecting the rights framing, or avoiding any discussion of the rights question, the opponents of same-sex marriage seek to undermine the preferred argument of supporters or at least shift the debate to other territory.

The public marriage debates also contain a running conversation about the nature of democracy and proper functioning of various gov-ernmental institutions. The opponents of same-sex marriage argue that democracy requires majority rule and point to evidence of majority opposition to same-sex marriage. The supporters of same-sex marriage counter that the expression of majority preferences in law and policy is not absolute in a democracy; the courts play a vital democratic role in protecting the rights of small or unpopular minorities from the power of the majority. But for opponents of same-sex marriage, the democratic system has been thrown out of whack as judges have overstepped their jurisdiction and gone beyond legal interpretation to policymaking. In both Hawaii and Vermont, opponents of same-sex marriage expressed a palpable frustration with the perceived ability of an overly powerful minority group to subvert the will of the majority and impose its own preferences and values with the active assistance of the judiciary.[19] In their study of several key debates in American political history, Jeffrey Alexander and Philip Smith (1993) argue that democracy vs. anti-democracy is a fundamental binary code that structures all political debates in the United States. Although this is not the only binary opposition structuring the marriage debates, the prominence of these arguments about the need to follow majority opinion versus the need to protect minority rights lends some support to Alexander and Smith's observation.

Another significant conversation within the debates over marriage centers on morality. Opponents of same-sex marriage freely draw on moral arguments and make assertions about God's will or intentions as they critique legal recognition for same-sex couples. These moral arguments range from general pronouncements of the immorality of homosexuality (often buttressed with citation of specific scriptural passages) to more specific arguments about the immorality of same-sex marriage or the need to retain a legal definition of marriage that is grounded in morality or religion. The supporters of same-sex marriage have two main responses to these moral arguments. First, their pleas for tolerance and respect for diversity and their denunciations of bigotry and prejudice can be read as a call for moral pluralism in matters of public policy, although they are not framed in that language. Occasionally the tolerance argument does more overtly invoke moral considerations, as when love and acceptance are framed as moral imperatives. The second response of same-sex marriage supporters is a procedural argument about the need to keep church and state separate. This argument asserts that particular religious doctrines or moral codes that are not universally shared are not a proper foundation for law and public policy. Entirely absent from the public debates over marriage, however, is any attempt to make a substantive argument for same-sex marriage as a moral good.

The final conversation that emerges in the marriage debates is the speculative discussion of the likely impacts of legal same-sex marriage. Opponents of same-sex marriage paint a dire picture of social destruction. In the Vermont debate in particular, the impacts on children became a specific focus of debate. Opponents of same-sex marriage often assert the negative impact for children without specifying the precise nature of the negative effects or the causal chain leading from legal same-sex marriage to these anticipated effects. Advocates of same-sex marriage have a diametrically opposed vision of the impacts on children, suggesting that it is actually the denial of legal recognition for same-sex couples that harms children, both those who are most directly affected because their parents cannot marry and those who suffer the indirect harm of learning a lesson of intolerance and inequality from this instance of state-sponsored discrimination.

When the terms of these public debates over same-sex marriage are juxtaposed with the discourses of ordinary same-sex couples described in previous chapters, it is striking how the public debates omit or distort the views and concerns of average gays and lesbians. I would suggest that there are three forms of omission or distortion that are especially glaring. First, the omission of a substantive moral argument in favor of same-sex marriage means that same-sex marriage is not discussed as a moral good, even though some gays and lesbians think of it in those terms. Second, the public arguments for same-sex marriage usually downplay or ignore the legitimacy effects of legal recognition, even though my research suggests that social legitimacy is a powerful lure for some gays and lesbians who want legal marriage. And third, the public debates are highly polarized, with supporters of legal recognition insisting that it take the form of marriage and opponents rejecting both marriage and alternative forms of recognition like domestic partnership. This polarization gives the impression that the only pro-gay position is the pro-marriage position. The voices of gays and lesbians who are critical of the institution of marriage or prefer an alternative form of recognition are silenced in these debates; likewise, the willingness of many gays and lesbians to accept a compromise policy solution goes unrepresented.

Neither the letter-writers in Hawaii nor the hearing witnesses in Vermont attempted to mount an argument for same-sex marriage as a substantive moral good. Such arguments have been made in other contexts by scholars and commentators writing about same-sex marriage. Law professor William Eskridge (1996) identifies several normative justifications for same-sex marriage, including that marriage will reduce sexual promiscuity and foster greater commitment in gay and lesbian relationships. Journalist Andrew Sullivan (1996, 182–4) argues that marriage would increase the stability of gay and lesbian relationships, that married gays would serve as role models for gay youth, and that marriage would foster closer relations between gays and their parents. Law professor Chai Feldblum (1998) argues that same-sex marriage should be seen as a moral good because marriages provide support and nurturing as well as opportunities for personal growth and transformation, regardless of the gender of the partners. Feldblum asserts that there is "a moral good in the creation of a relational community by two individuals" (491).

In one of the more extensive efforts to craft a moral argument for gay rights and same-sex marriage, law professor Carlos Ball (2003) proposes the framework of "moral liberalism," which posits that all humans share basic needs and capabilities, and that humans are fundamentally relational beings. Living a fully human and autonomous life requires having one's basic needs met and one's capabilities developed, and relationships with others play a vital role in both of these requirements. Ball argues that moral liberalism "requires society to provide the necessary support and conditions that make it possible for individuals to love and care for others in an atmosphere of stability, safety, and continuity" (108). This perspective recasts the question of morality in terms of the state's obligations to its citizens rather than in terms of sexual behavior. Ball concludes: "Our society, by depriving lesbians and gay men of the opportunity to avail themselves of marriage, the principal way in which it seeks to protect and promote basic human needs and capabilities associated with physical and emotional intimacy in long-term relationships, fails to recognize and provide for the full humanity of lesbians and gay men. Such a failure is immoral" (111).

Arguments for same-sex marriage as a moral and social good were also offered by several study participants in their discussion of the reasons for desiring legal recognition. Specifically, these participants suggested that legal marriage would strengthen commitment between same-sex partners, reduce sexual promiscuity (especially among gay men), provide valuable role models for gay teens and elevate the status of committed relationships within the gay community. Although none of the study participants explicitly framed these points as a moral case for same-sex marriage, their observations have clear moral content (relationship commitment and stability is good, monogamy is better than promiscuity) and they are views that rarely if ever found representation in the state-level debates over marriage.[20]

Likewise the public marriage debates in Vermont and Hawaii gave little voice to gay and lesbian couples' aspirations for social recognition and legitimacy. Roughly half of the study participants discussed social legitimacy as a significant intangible benefit of legal marriage. These individuals believed that legal marriage would at least force a grudging recognition of the reality of committed same-sex relationships in mainstream society, and some believed legal marriage would have more far-reaching effects, endowing gays and lesbians with a form of symbolic capital that would fundamentally reshape how heterosexuals perceived gay and lesbian people and relationships. Yet the advocates for same-sex marriage in the public debates almost never discuss or acknowledge this legitimacy effect. There is a weak acknowledgment of sorts embedded in the tolerance discourse, which implores people to demonstrate respect for gays and lesbians despite their difference, and also an indirect reference to the issue of social legitimacy in arguments about the harmful message sent to children when same-sex relationships are not recognized. But rarely do the advocates of same-sex marriage overtly proclaim social legitimacy as a valid or important reason to grant gays and lesbians marriage rights. By contrast, the opponents of same-sex marriage seem highly attuned to the legitimacy effects of legal recognition, especially when they contemplate the impacts on children and they wonder aloud about the bounds of tolerance. Ironically, the public rhetoric of the marriage opponents is more consonant with the views of gay and lesbian couples than is the rhetoric of their public advocates on the matter of social legitimacy, although of course the opponents of legal recognition acknowledge and *fear* this legitimacy effect whereas some gays and lesbians greet it with positive anticipation.

Finally, in both Hawaii and Vermont the public debates over legal recognition quickly polarized into the options of full legal marriage vs. no legal recognition whatsoever for same-sex relationships. This rhetorical polarization did not translate into a total policy victory for either side: in Hawaii, marriage was blocked by constitutional amendment but the legislature provided a limited set of rights and benefits through the reciprocal beneficiaries legislation, and in Vermont the legislature settled on the middle ground of civil unions. Yet it seems significant that the public debates did not include any prominent voices calling for a compromise policy solution that would provide relationship recognition in a form other than marriage. Again, the views of ordinary gays and lesbians are not well represented in these debates. Although several participants in my study expressed a critical stance toward marriage, the only visible pro-gay position in the public debates was the argument for full marriage rights. And although the majority of study participants expressed a willingness to obtain the relationship rights and benefits under a name other than marriage, this position did not have any visibility in the public debates. One possible explanation is that advocates for legal recognition in Hawaii and Vermont may have made a judgment that it was strategically wiser to pursue the best possible policy outcome (full marriage rights), with an awareness that compromise might ultimately be necessary. In both of these states, court rulings had made full legal marriage imaginable if not certain. In any case, the flexibility expressed by the study participants on matters of terminology was nowhere evident among the pro-marriage advocates in the state debates.

The discourses of judges, activists and ordinary citizens in public debates over same-sex marriage shape the discussion of the issue in particular ways. Comparing the public debates in Hawaii and Vermont to the discourses of the ordinary same-sex couples in this study suggests that the public debates offer only a partial and distorted reflection of the perspectives of those whose lives and relationships are most directly impacted by the policy issue in question. As the marriage debate moves on to other states within the United States, many of the dominant themes identified in the Hawaii and Vermont debates are likely to be replayed, amplified and perhaps adjusted to local circumstances. Complete victories in some locations may have harmful short- or long-term repercussions in other jurisdictions. The decisive victory for marriage advocates in the state of Massachusetts provoked a backlash around the country, leading to the passage of numerous state constitutional amendments, some of which prohibit not only marriage but other forms of recognition such as civil unions or domestic partnerships.[21]

The current state of the marriage debates has the feel of a stalemate. As in other highly charged debates, such as over abortion and the death penalty, the two sides seem to be talking past each other. In the marriage debates, the rights claims of same-sex marriage supporters carry little weight with opponents, who view the issue in moral terms. By the same token, the moral and religious arguments of opponents are shrugged off by same-sex marriage supporters as violating the separation of church and state. And the two sides have differing visions of how a constitutional democracy should work, with opponents of same-sex marriage emphasizing the principle of majority rule and supporters heralding the courts' role in protecting minority rights. In my view, the supporters of same-sex marriage should begin to meet the opposition on its own terrain by supplementing the existing rights discourse with a positive moral argument for same-sex marriage. Such an argument would move beyond rights claims and appeals for tolerance, which tend to reinforce the distinction between gays and lesbians and the rest of the citizenry (Jakobsen and Pellgrini 2003). Following Ball's "moral liberalism," this argument should hold the state morally accountable for providing all citizens with the same opportunities to access the social and legal supports which foster human flourishing in relational context.[22] One way to convey the moral stakes of same-sex marriage battles for gays and lesbians is through personal stories, especially those stories that highlight how the lack of access to marriage impedes loving couples from taking care of each other (and in some cases their children). Personal stories might humanize and concretize the real impacts of the lack of relationship and family protections. Such a shift in discourse would pull the discussion of morality out of the realm of abstract concepts and into the lives of real people. It would also shift the discussion of morality from its current narrow (and usually religiously grounded) focus on the morality of particular sexual behaviors to a more expansive set of moral concerns: respect for affective bonds, social support for relations of care, and social and legal recognition of the material and emotional dependencies that form within relationships and families. Most generally, a positive moral argument for same-sex marriage would endorse recognition and support of all human connections that hold meaning for the people involved and do no harm to the rest of society. Such a discursive shift would at least hold the possibility of breaking the current stalemate and moving the marriage debates onto new ground.

6   Conclusion: marriage and beyond

Love, the strongest and deepest element in all life, the harbinger of
hope, of joy, of ecstasy; love, the defier of all laws, of all conventions;
love, the freest, the most powerful moulder of human destiny; how can
such an all-compelling force be synonymous with that poor little State
and Church-begotten weed, marriage?

–Emma Goldman (1910)

The meanings and purposes of marriage are ever-changing. The history
of marriage features a shift from marriage as a property relationship to
marriage as a consensual expression of mutual love. Over the past two
centuries, the gender hierarchy that once characterized marriage, in both
cultural and legal terms, has largely given way to a new model of equality
and negotiated roles in the United States and other Western societies.
The role of sexual expression within marriage has also evolved, from a
focus on its procreative function to recognition of the value of sexual
pleasure in its own right. And most of the social and legal constraints on
the choice of a marriage partner have fallen away, including restrictions
based on class, religion and, most notably, race (Cott 2000). For some,
same-sex marriage appears as the next logical and inevitable step in the
continuing change and evolution of the institution of marriage. For
others, it represents a dangerous undermining of marriage's basic meanings and functions. Marriage today is contested terrain. My research
findings show how law and culture combine to constitute marriage as
a social institution, furnishing the meanings and resources that give
marriage its power in the social world.

In this concluding chapter, I begin by recapping some of the primary
themes and findings from my study, those related to the mutual constitution of marriage by law and culture. These insights provide a spring-
board for diving into the realm of policy deliberation. Both sides in the
policy struggle over legal recognition for same-sex relationships have so
far failed to acknowledge how law and culture work together to invest
marriage with particular meanings for their opponents. Legal same-sex
marriage is the correct long-term policy solution to the current conflict,

but the current political context in the United States calls for a more diverse array of short-term policy steps sensitive to local conditions. In addition, the achievement of legal same-sex marriage should take place in the context of a broader assessment and reform of government policies toward sexual partnerships and other forms of relationship commitment.

Law, culture and marriage

We have seen how marriage serves as a cultural resource for many committed same-sex couples. Couples draw upon language and ritual associated with marriage to express – to each other, to friends and family, and to the broader society – the nature of their relationship. The cultural trappings of marriage – terminology, rituals and symbols – stand as ready-made cultural tools for couples to express their love and their commitment to a lifetime of mutual support. The power of marriage as a cultural resource lies in the fact that its dominant meanings are so widely shared in contemporary Western culture. As Swidler (2001) points out, these meanings closely parallel the romantic love myth: true love as a unique, decisive and permanent bond that overcomes any obstacles. Indeed, the institution of marriage may well account for the persistence of romantic love ideology in the face of competing under-standings of love and commitment. Gays and lesbians live in the same dominant culture as everyone else, so their frequent attraction to the romantic love myth, and the corresponding institution of marriage, is in some respects unsurprising.

But gay and lesbian couples also have some distance from dominant culture, resulting from their experience of social stigma and the need they often feel to assert the validity, and even the reality, of their intimate commitments. Same-sex couples face challenges as couples that rarely confront their heterosexual counterparts. Many of the participants in this study spoke of their need and desire to make their relationships real to their family and friends (and sometimes even to themselves), to assert their fundamental similarity to heterosexual relationships, and to in-crease the stability of their commitments in an environment that is largely indifferent or even hostile to the success of their relationships. In the face of these challenges, marriage serves as a *practical* cultural resource. Adopting marriage as a cultural model of relationship, espe-cially through the performance of public ritual, becomes a means to establish the reality, equality and permanence of same-sex commit-ments. Participants also sometimes spoke of these rituals as providing the opportunity to combat their exclusion from meaningful family or religious traditions. For some gays and lesbians, religion acts as an especially important cultural resource, either because couples themselves view their religious practice as an ongoing source of meaning and community, or because they perceive religious symbolism and authority to have broad cultural currency that is useful in establishing the commitment as a marriage. In all of these ways, the schemas and resources of marriage as a cultural structure become useful and meaningful to same-sex couples, despite (and in all likelihood because of) the couples' exclusion from legal marriage.

We have also seen that not all same-sex couples are equally attracted to the cultural resources of marriage. Some adopt marriage-related terminology but forego wedding-like ritual, others opt for private rather than public rituals (which suggests that the goal of asserting the reality of their commitment to outsiders is not paramount) and still others self-consciously distance themselves from marriage, signaling their skepticism about marriage as a cultural model for same-sex commitment by avoiding use of marriage terminology and other marriage-related practices. Yet marriage holds broad cultural significance as *the* logical and interpretable way to signify commitment to an intimate partner in contemporary culture, so even those gays and lesbians who are least invested in marriage as a cultural form sometimes find themselves drawn into marriage's cultural orbit, as when they fall back on marriage-related terms for their partner or relationship, participate in the public commitment rituals of friends, or negotiate about having a wedding with a partner who expresses greater interest in the marriage model.

I have argued that when same-sex couples adopt the cultural practices of marriage, especially public rituals of commitment, they are engaging in a form of political resistance as well as constructing an alternative form of legality outside of official law. Their cultural practices of marriage are political, not because they have primarily political goals or take the form of collective resistance, but because they hold the potential to shake up existing power relations by shifting the schemas and resources of the institution of marriage to a new set of previously marginalized relationships. We should also read these practices as the enactment of a form of legality outside the official law, an effort to invest same-sex commitments with law-like powers and qualities. The legality that is attempted through the cultural practices of marriage has both an expressive and a normative dimension. Part of what law does is to name people, things and relationships, and in so naming, invest them with a heightened visibility and reality. Bourdieu (1987, 838) observed that law "confers upon the reality which arises out of its classificatory operations the maximum permanence that any social entity has the power to confer upon another." Law also establishes the parameters of expected or permissible conduct tied to specific roles. In establishing a kind of legality outside official law, same-sex couples seek not only to establish their commitments as an objective and permanent reality, but also to link their commitments to normative expectations of conduct within their relationship and to make exit from the relationship more problematic, much as legal recognition by the state might do.[1]

Up to this point, I have presented these as two distinct arguments about what same-sex couples are doing when they "do marriage" culturally: engaging in a form of political resistance and enacting a form of legality outside the boundaries of official law. In Chapter 2, I argued that the public commitment rituals of same-sex couples are political because these couples appropriate the cultural resources of marriage and put them to new uses, namely the validation of intimate same-sex commitments. In this way, same-sex couples deploy the cultural resources of one of society's most powerful and enduring institutions to celebrate and recognize relationships that are highly marginalized. This action represents a transfer of cultural power to relatively powerless actors, and thereby qualifies as political action despite the fact that the couples usually do not frame their behavior in political terms. Viewing these cultural practices as constructions of legality in the absence of official law suggests another dimension to the politics of these rituals. This enacted legality constitutes a proactive response to the state's denial of legal recognition and, as such, an indirect challenge to the state's supremacy as the definer of "legal" relationships. Couples assert the possibility of making an alternative legal or quasi-legal order outside the boundaries of official law. Compensating for the absence of state recognition, couples use culture (especially language and ritual) to create what the state withholds. As with the appropriation of the cultural resources of marriage, this enactment of legality outside the law is not self-consciously political action but should be read as a form of political resistance nonetheless.

The case of same-sex marriage invites us to think about other instances of the creation of legality outside the law. One fascinating example is the emergence of a "code of the street" in impoverished inner-city neighborhoods, described by Elijah Anderson (1999) in his recent ethnography of the Philadelphia ghetto. Anderson observes that ghetto residents, deprived of adequate protection from legitimate law-enforcement agencies, take the law into their own hands. The code of the street, according to Anderson, is "a set of informal rules governing interpersonal public behavior, particularly violence" (33). These rules tell ghetto residents how to carry themselves in public and how to respond to challenges from others. "They regulate the use of violence," notes Anderson, "and so supply a rationale allowing those who are inclined to aggression to precipitate violent encounters in an approved way" (33). In short, the code of the street functions in some impoverished urban communities as an alternative legality, prescribing expected conduct and the consequences of departing from expectations.[2] As with the case of same-sex marriage, this case points to the possibility of socially marginalized actors compensating for the failure of official law to deliver what they need. Because the state fails to regulate violence and protect citizens in the ghetto, these residents enact the code of the street to do the job instead. The case of the ghetto code also suggests that reading these alternative constructions of legality as a form of politics does not necessarily imply viewing them as heroic or successful adaptations to legal and social marginalization. As Anderson so vividly recounts, the alternative legality of the inner-city streets exacts a heavy toll from local residents, who confront the constant threat of violence and even death. Regardless of whether the alternative legalities are viewed positively or negatively, the key point is that conditions of legal deprivation – social identities or settings that are denied the recognition and protection of official law – sometimes foster constructions of alternative forms of legality, and these alternative legalities represent a kind of middle-ground political resistance as well as a pragmatic response to existing social realities. They are moments in which disempowered social actors contest the supremacy of official law by demonstrating the possibilities of legality outside of law.

Despite the evidence that some same-sex couples find ways to construct legality outside of law, official law is far from irrelevant or unimportant to these couples. Rather, this study points to the unique cultural power of official law. In explaining their support for legal recognition for same-sex relationships, study participants cite not only concrete legal and financial benefits and principles of justice and equality, but also the social and cultural legitimacy which some believe only official law can deliver. About half of the study participants mentioned the legitimating effects of legal recognition in explaining their support for legal marriage (or a comparable legal status). And this desire for the cultural legitimacy conferred by law was not confined to the study participants who appeared most invested in marriage as a cultural model, that is, those who had held a public commitment ritual. Gays and lesbians who chose not to celebrate their relationship through public ritual also expressed interest in the cultural validation of the law. Those gays and lesbians who desire the cultural legitimacy of legal recognition believe that equal legal treatment of their relationships will lead to greater social acceptance and support for those commitments, and perhaps for the gay and lesbian community more broadly, further eroding the social stigma that has traditionally attached to gay and lesbian relationships and identities. As I discussed in Chapter 4, the various reasons same-sex partners give for desiring legal recognition can be distinguished for analytical purposes, but in the accounts of the study participants these reasons are often tightly intertwined. For some study participants, receiving the legal benefits and protections of marriage and achieving equality of legal treatment are not only intrinsically valuable goals, but also significant for their impacts on the social and cultural status of same-sex relationships.

The mutual implication of law and culture also colors the public debates over the legal treatment of same-sex relationships, most notably in the arguments of those who oppose legal recognition of gay and lesbian couples. The supporters of legal recognition often try to minimize the linkage between law and culture in the public debates, for example by relying on rights rhetoric and avoiding discussion of the cultural impacts of legal recognition. Supporters also sometimes emphasize the importance of keeping the legal and cultural dimensions of marriage separate, as when they invoke the principle of the separation of church and state in response to the religious arguments of opponents. The opponents of legal recognition, by contrast, often refuse to recognize the need, or even the possibility, of separating the legal and cultural dimensions of marriage. For many who speak out against legal status for same-sex relationships, the mutual implication of law and culture (especially religion) seems obvious and inevitable. Some opponents have a fundamentally different way of thinking about the nature and definition of marriage than the supporters of legal recognition. The essence of marriage is defined by religion and tradition, not by the state. The state, in their view, has an obligation to conform its legal definition of marriage to cultural and religious understandings of marriage. (Most opponents of legal recognition conveniently ignore the fact that religious denominations are not unanimous in their beliefs about marriage.) Furthermore, some opponents of legal recognition both acknowledge and fear the cultural legitimacy conferred by law and the possibility that this form of social validation might be extended to relationships that they view as deviant, inferior or immoral. This understanding of the cultural significance of law leads some opponents of legal same-sex marriage to oppose *any* form of legal recognition for same-sex couples; in their view, legal recognition inevitably translates into cultural legitimacy, regardless of the nomenclature employed.[3]

Thus we observe an ironic parallel between the views of some opponents of legal same-sex marriage and some gays and lesbians who seek legal marriage for its legitimating effects: both groups regard the legal recognition of the state as a cultural force. In other words, both believe the state is saying something when it confers legal status on close relationships, and the state's message holds cultural as well as legal content. These actors believe that the cultural message of state recognition, at its core, is a message of inclusion, acceptance and approval. It is a message that some gay and lesbian couples are hungry to receive, and that some opponents of same-sex marriage are desperate to block.

Much of marriage's power as a social institution derives from the entanglement of its cultural and legal dimensions. The mutual implication of law and culture in the institution of marriage naturalizes and reifies marriage, making it appear to social actors as a permanent, solid and inevitable whole rather than a socially constructed and amendable arrangement. This reification and naturalization of marriage as a legal–cultural whole manifests itself in myriad social practices that intertwine the legal and cultural aspects of marriage, as when religious officials act as agents of the state in performing marriage ceremonies and signing marriage licenses, or when the state plays an active role in efforts to influence cultural beliefs about marriage.[4] The naturalized and reified quality of marriage also serves to naturalize and reify heterosexual privilege, as long as same-sex couples remain excluded from the full marriage package. I would argue that many opponents of legal same-sex marriage view it as a deep threat, not because they object to granting the specific rights and benefits of marriage to same-sex couples but because legal same-sex marriage challenges their view of marriage as a holistic social institution. Same-sex marriage forces recognition of the separability of the legal and cultural elements of marriage by illustrating that the state definition of marriage need not conform to dominant religious and cultural definitions of marriage. Under legal same-sex marriage, the tight intertwining of the legal and cultural dimensions of marriage is likely to unravel, making it more difficult to maintain the belief that marriage has a single, natural, God-given essence. Under legal same-sex marriage, some religions will celebrate and solemnize same-sex marriages and others will not. Some citizens will read the cultural meaning of state recognition as a validation of same-sex commitments, and others will resist such a reading. Under such conditions, the mystified wholeness of marriage will be irretrievably lost.

For many, of course, marriage has already been demystified by the social trends of the past several decades. High rates of divorce, cohabitation and unmarried parenting, combined with declining marriage rates, have rendered marriage one life-style option among many. This demystification has less to do with separating the legal and cultural elements of marriage than with the distance between the ideal of marriage, in both cultural and legal terms, and its lived reality. I suspect that citizens who hold this demystified view of marriage find the prospect of same-sex marriage somewhat less disturbing than do those who cling to an essentialist view of marriage as uniquely constituted by both culture and law (and perhaps ultimately by God). This may partially account for the fact that younger people, who have grown up in an era of high divorce and cohabitation rates, are generally more supportive of legal same-sex marriage.[5]

Some, but not all, gays and lesbians also seem to be invested in a reified vision of marriage as a holistic institution. For certain couples, cultural practices provide a certain amount of access to marriage, such as through public rituals resembling heterosexual weddings, but the partners still desire legal recognition, and often this desire is not driven by practical concerns alone. For these couples, the cultural practice of marriage somewhat compensates for the absence of legal sanction, but attaining the legal component would complete their cultural identity as "married." By contrast, some of the participants in this study who maintained distance from the cultural model of marriage explained their choice with reference to the absence of legal recognition. These individuals questioned the meaning or the realness of cultural enactments of marriage that were not accompanied by legal recognition. So, for both of these groups, the cultural and legal dimensions of marriage are difficult to disentangle. Other gays and lesbians in this study, however, appeared to have a more demystified view of marriage. For example, some wanted legal marriage but had no interest in culturally enacting marriage, and they described their interest in legal recognition only in practical terms, as a means to obtain more benefits and protections for their relationship. Some who had enacted marriage culturally through public ritual insisted that they were only interested in the legal protections of civil marriage and not in any cultural legitimation it might provide. And others reflected a demystified approach to marriage by remarking that they did not feel strongly that legal recognition must take the form of "marriage" per se; an alternative legal status was acceptable, and for some gays and lesbians even preferable.

My research findings demonstrate how law and culture combine to constitute marriage and endow it with meaning for many heterosexuals *and* gays and lesbians. Understanding the interaction of law and culture in maintaining marriage as a social institution, we can better see why some gays and lesbians are pursuing both the cultural and the legal dimensions of marriage, and why they may feel a sense of incompleteness when they enact marriage culturally but cannot obtain legal recognition for their commitments. We can also better understand the perspective of those citizens most deeply opposed to legal same-sex marriage, whose cultural understanding of marriage places the male–female dyad at the center of their definition of marriage, whether as a matter of tradition, nature or religious belief. The current political impasse over the legal treatment of same-sex relationships must be situated in the context of the multiple and conflicting meanings of marriage grounded in both culture and law. In the rest of this chapter, I explore the relevance of my findings for the ongoing debates about state recognition of same-sex commitments. The same-sex marriage debates invite us to step back and consider the purpose of state recognition of all intimate partnerships and the range of possible policy responses to the needs of contemporary families.

Political compromise and practical equality

Despite recent political setbacks in the United States, most notably the passage of state constitutional amendments blocking same-sex marriage, the establishment of comprehensive legal recognition for same-sex relationships has taken on an air of inevitability. Polls show that most Americans favor some form of legal recognition for same-sex couples, either marriage or an alternate status like civil unions, and most Americans now believe that legal same-sex marriage will eventually be established throughout the United States.[6] The establishment of same-sex marriage in Massachusetts, and comprehensive civil unions or domestic partnerships in Vermont, California and Connecticut, makes this kind of significant legal change tangible and imaginable. Recent decisions by the US Supreme Court have laid the groundwork for plausible claims of a constitutional right to same-sex marriage, especially given the prior case law establishing marriage as a fundamental right of citizenship.[7] The ruling in *Romer v. Evans* in 1996 established the precedent that animus toward gays and lesbians is not a valid basis for laws curtailing their rights, and this precedent may be useful in challenging the constitutionality of the state amendments barring same-sex marriage and other forms of legal recognition for same-sex couples. More recently, the 2003 *Lawrence v. Texas* decision, overturning state anti-sodomy laws, asserted that moral disapproval of particular sexual conduct is insufficient grounds for curtailing the liberties of gays and lesbians. In a stinging dissent, Justice Antonin Scalia warned that the ruling undermined any legal justification for denying state recognition of same-sex marriage, and indeed the *Lawrence* decision was cited approvingly in the *Goodridge* ruling by the Massachusetts Supreme Judicial

Court that established the right to same-sex marriage in that state. More generally, the gay rights movement has made rapid progress on a number of issues in both the legal and cultural realms, including discrimination protections, hate-crimes legislation, and more favorable representations of gays and lesbians in the media. These movement gains may not translate directly into public support for legal recognition of same-sex couples, but their cumulative indirect effect in changing perceptions of the status of gays and lesbians in American society should not be underestimated.

Still, the current resistance to legal same-sex marriage is significant, and the tactics deployed by those seeking to block same-sex marriage (such as amending state constitutions) can leave gay and lesbian partners in a markedly weaker legal position than before the marriage issue emerged. In light of the breadth and intensity of opposition to same-sex marriage, as well as the openness of a significant portion of the citizenry to a compromise solution such as civil unions, it seems wise for advocates of gay and lesbian equality to slow down the push for marriage itself in most parts of the country and instead focus their efforts on alternative vehicles of recognition such as domestic partnership or civil unions. This kind of short-term compromise policy solution would deliver significant benefits and protections to same-sex relationships while giving those opposed to same-sex marriage more time to adjust to the idea, and indeed the reality, of legal recognition for same-sex couples.

In drawing this conclusion, I have been deeply influenced by the arguments and evidence presented by law professor William Eskridge in his recent book, *Equality Practice* (2002). Eskridge develops the concept of equality practice to describe a situation in which an aggrieved minority group is accorded substantial equality in response to their rights claims, yet denied full formal equality under the law in deference to majoritarian concerns about the public good. Eskridge frames equality practice as a synthesis of liberal and communitarian thought. It combines liberalism's insistence on rights recognition with communitarianism's emphasis on community values and deliberative democracy. The notion of equality practice is a supremely pragmatic approach to accomplishing significant social change. As Eskridge notes: "The advantage to equality practice – or something like it – is that it recognizes both the need to accommodate new ideas and the inability of human beings and their communities to do so without a long process of education and personal experience" (xv).

The civil unions laws passed in Vermont and Connecticut are prime examples of equality practice. Civil unions deliver substantial equality to same-sex couples in terms of state law, effectively rewriting all statutes implicating marital status to give couples in civil unions the same rights and benefits as married couples. At the time of its passage, the Vermont civil unions law was the farthest any US state had gone toward recognizing the rights of same-sex couples. But civil unions do not deliver full formal equality, for two reasons. First, civil unions are not portable, that is, they are not recognized by other states or the federal government. Thus, although the state's intention is to treat couples in civil unions as equal to married couples in every respect, the substantial equality at the state level is not extended across state lines or to the federal level.[8] Second, civil unions have a different name from marriage, what Eskridge terms "linguistic segregation" (2002, xii), which renders them distinct from marriage in a formal sense.

The equality practice typified by civil unions (as well as by California's comprehensive domestic partnerships) is the best *short-term* strategy for achieving substantially equal legal recognition for same-sex relationships in most areas of the United States. Ideally, the institutions of equality practice (civil unions or domestic partnerships) would be accomplished through legislative channels, as they were in California and Connecticut, thereby reducing public resistance and quieting accusations of judicial activism. However, in some states judicial involvement may be necessary to put equality practice in place, perhaps with the cooperation of the state legislature (as occurred in Vermont). In supporting equality practice as a short-term goal, I am *not* suggesting that gay and lesbian advocates or their constituents should entirely cease making a claim to the right to marry. Rather, I am asserting that gays and lesbians in most states would best serve their own interests by pursuing equality practice as a near-term political strategy.

The overarching rationale for pursuing substantial but not formal equality for same-sex couples at this time is to allow public awareness and understanding of the legal needs of gay and lesbian couples and families to catch up with the limited legal success that has already been accomplished, primarily through the courts. Shortly after the passage of eleven state constitutional amendments barring same-sex marriage in the November 2004 elections, the executive director of the National Gay and Lesbian Task Force conceded that "the legal strategy to win marriage rights is a decade ahead of the political strategies to educate the public and the legislatures" (Broder 2004). The counter-argument to a pragmatic, incrementalist approach to winning partnership rights is that it is only by pushing for full legal marriage that compromise solutions like civil unions ever come into being (Wolfson 2004, 136). That is why short-term political pragmatism and flexibility should be paired with an ongoing commitment to the long-term goal of formal equality. In more progressive states, which have a track record of recognizing gay rights, pushing for marriage is the logical first step. It may bring formal equality, as in Massachusetts, or at least substantial equality, as in Vermont, Connecticut and California. But in other states, equality practice entails a more moderate strategy, seeking civil unions or domestic partnership, or even more modestly, a subset of the individual rights and benefits traditionally associated with marriage. In other words, equality practice calls for sensitivity to local political conditions and a willingness to temporarily refrain from legal strategies that may outpace broader political and public education efforts, and may result in backlash measures that leave gays and lesbians worse off than before the campaign for partnership recognition started.

My own research findings, combined with evidence amassed by other researchers and a clear-eyed assessment of the current political realities in the United States, lead me to support a strategy of practical equality. A majority of the people I interviewed for this study indicated that equal partnership recognition under a name other than marriage would be acceptable, and in some cases even preferable. This finding suggests a willingness to compromise on terminology for the sake of achieving substantial equality. These interviews were conducted before Massachusetts granted legal recognition of same-sex marriage, and also before the spate of state constitutional amendments to block that outcome in other states. It is plausible that recent legal and political developments would produce different interview responses today. On one hand, the achievement of marriage rights in one state might make some members of same-sex couples less willing to accept alternatives to marriage, even if they delivered substantially equal rights and benefits. But on the other hand, the political backlash against the marriage ruling – manifested in the push for constitutional amendments at both the state and federal level – might make some gays and lesbians *more* receptive to the kind of political compromise forged in Vermont and other states.

My analysis of the public debates over same-sex marriage in Hawaii and Vermont, and particularly the voices of average citizens in those debates, provides insight into the sometimes fierce opposition to legal same-sex marriage and adds weight to the argument for a short-term strategy of equality practice. It is the concept of marriage itself, rather than the bundle of rights and benefits attached to marriage, that appears to be at stake for many of the opponents of same-sex marriage. This is most obvious when people make the definitional argument against same-sex marriage, insisting that marriage is "by definition" between one man and one woman. Some of the moral and religious arguments also suggest the significance of the word marriage, as when people argue that marriage is God's creation or that the civil definition of marriage must conform to religious understandings of marriage. Again, these arguments suggest an essentialized understanding of marriage as a holistic institution that cannot be broken down into distinct legal, cultural and religious components. Indeed, the way marriage is discussed by some opponents of same-sex recognition calls to mind Durkheim's ([1912] 1995) classic distinction between sacred and profane. Marriage seems to function as a kind of totem for some heterosexuals, a sacred object that must be protected from defiling contact with the profane (same-sex intimacy). Hence the rhetoric about defending, protecting and preserving marriage, without any real specificity about how same-sex couples would actually harm the institution. Just as religious totems acted as focal points for group solidarity and the affirmation of shared values in so-called primitive religions, so too marriage as totem provides a focus for celebrating and defending the sacredness of heterosexuality as a privileged status and identity, thereby affirming in-group solidarity at the expense of the marginalized Other.[9]

The equality practice of alternative statuses like civil unions and domestic partnerships offers some hope of side-stepping this thorny problem. Alternative statuses like civil unions will not be acceptable to the most diehard opponents of same-sex marriage, who reject substantial equality as well as formal equality. This sort of hard-line opposition finds expression in most of the existing state constitutional amendments, which bar not only same-sex marriage but comparable legal statuses. It was also evident in the Vermont public hearing I analyzed, in which almost a quarter of the witnesses who testified against same-sex marriage also explicitly objected to an alternate status like domestic partnership. But many if not most of the people who object to extending marriage to same-sex couples may be open to creating alternative legal statuses to deliver rights and benefits to same-sex partners. Poll data from late 2004 indicated that more than half of Americans supported either civil unions or marriage for same-sex couples.[10]

The work of other scholars also provides empirical support for pursuing equality practice. Examining the experience of other countries that have extended partnership recognition to same-sex relationships, Eskridge (2002, Chapter 3) finds that these countries arrived at partnership recognition or marriage through a process of incremental and sequential steps. Reforms such as repeal of anti-sodomy laws and, later, passage of anti-discrimination laws protecting sexual minorities precede the move toward partnership recognition, which may take the form of recognition for same-sex cohabitors (for example, France,

Germany, Israel, South Africa), registered domestic partnerships (the Scandinavian countries) or marriage itself (the Netherlands, Belgium, Spain and Canada). Less comprehensive forms of partnership recognition typically precede more comprehensive forms; for example, Sweden and Norway extended limited legal benefits to same-sex cohabitors before instituting more extensive registered domestic partnerships, and the Netherlands implemented registered partnerships before proceeding to full marriage recognition. A similar pattern obtains among individual US states; those that have moved farthest toward partnership recognition (California, Connecticut, Massachusetts and Vermont) first repealed or partially nullified their sodomy laws, passed legislation to include sexual orientation in anti-discrimination and hate-crimes statutes, had domestic partnership ordinances at the municipal level and extended parenting rights to same-sex couples (Eskridge 2002, Table E.1). Massachusetts implemented a statewide domestic partnership system in 1992, more than a decade before recognizing same-sex marriages. These patterns provide strong support for the equality practice strategy, because they suggest that successful establishment of legal same-sex marriage is almost always preceded by other gay rights protections and more modest forms of partnership recognition.

Analyses of ballot initiatives and the success of gay rights initiatives also provide indirect support for the equality practice strategy. A recent analysis of data on gay rights policy outcomes from 1974 to 1994 found that gay rights victories far outnumbered gay rights defeats in the legislative, judicial and executive branches of government, but gay rights fared poorly when put to a popular vote via ballot initiatives, with only one success against twenty-seven defeats (Werum and Winders 2001). This finding parallels the results of a more general study of civil rights ballot initiatives, which found that voters usually vote against civil rights protections, leading the author to conclude that "political minorities do not fare well at the polls" (Gamble 1997, 253). This kind of evidence argues for an equality practice strategy for securing partnership recognition insofar as more aggressive, court-based strategies in less gay-friendly states or at the federal level foster political support for "direct democracy" efforts to impede same-sex marriage, most notably through constitutional amendments.

There are problems with equality practice as a short-term strategy. Perhaps the most significant is the issue of portability. State-level statutes like domestic partnerships or civil unions currently are not recognized by the federal government or by most other states. Because many important marriage benefits are built into federal laws and programs, state-level measures will be constrained from providing substantial equality in the broadest sense. (This problem could be solved by extending federal recognition to state-level statuses, granting them the same legal treatment as marriage for federal purposes, but such a bold change in federal policy – and departure from the spirit of the Defense of Marriage Act – is unlikely in the near future.) Likewise the non-portability between states stands in sharp contrast to the legal treatment of marriage relationships. Another problem is the inherent symbolism of the "linguistic segregation" effected by alternative statuses like civil unions. Such symbolism may entrench heterosexual privilege and further normalize the treatment of gays and lesbians as a separate class of citizens. A third problem with equality practice is that some jurisdictions will probably never grant partnership rights to same-sex couples through this kind of gradualist, voluntary, democratic approach. Indeed, at this writing more than ten states have already precluded not only formal but substantial equality for same-sex couples by way of expansively worded constitutional amendments, leaving thousands of same-sex couples and families with inadequate legal protection and recognition. A final difficulty with the equality practice approach is coordinating the choices and strategies of a broad range of actors, including gay rights groups, cause lawyers and individual same-sex couples. In practical terms, equality practice can only succeed if these various actors align their strategies. Otherwise, in states most hostile to same-sex marriage, the measured strategies of gay rights groups could be undermined by lawyers and plaintiff couples who decide to press for marriage in the courts and wind up provoking political backlash and unfavorable legal decisions.[11]

Despite these serious drawbacks, the benefits of equality practice as a short-term strategy outweigh its costs. It holds the potential to deliver significant benefits and protections to a large number of relationships relatively quickly, with less political backlash than a more aggressive, marriage-or-nothing strategy. It gives the opponents of same-sex marriage the chance to adjust to legal recognition of gay and lesbian partnerships. The portability problem is serious, but because of existing laws the problem would exist under any scenario short of a Supreme Court ruling establishing a federal constitutional right to marriage for same-sex couples or invalidating the federal Defense of Marriage Act. Equality practice does not immediately satisfy the aspirations of same-sex marriage advocates, but it provides a roadmap toward a long-term policy solution that will deliver both substantial and formal equality, according gays and lesbians their full citizenship rights. The path toward such a long-term policy solution must thread its way through the ongoing turmoil over the present and future of the institution of marriage, a turmoil that both encompasses and transcends the specific issue of same-sex marriage.

Long-term policy options: marriage and beyond

As I stated in the opening chapter, the ferocity of the current debates over same-sex marriage only makes sense when viewed in the context of broader anxieties about the recent past, present and future of the institution of marriage. A number of factors feed into these anxieties. The recent demographic trends in rates of divorce, cohabitation, marriage and unmarried parenting are perhaps the most obvious. Another factor is a set of challenges to the legal boundaries or definition of marriage that includes not only claims for a right to same-sex marriage but also advocacy of legalized polygamy and proposals to supplement legal marriage with new non-marital legal statuses that deliver many of the same rights and benefits as marriage.[12] The movement of other Western nations toward legal recognition of both same-sex relationships and non-marital heterosexual relationships also heightens some people's concerns about the future of marriage within the United States. The definition and significance of marriage continue to be contested in the cultural sphere as well; many religious denominations are struggling over how to treat committed same-sex relationships, and popular culture increasingly depicts various departures from the norm of lifelong monogamous heterosexual marriage, like cohabitation or chosen singlehood, as unproblematic or even positive life options. All of these factors – demographic trends, challenges to the existing boundaries of marriage, international developments and cultural contests over the meaning of marriage – converge to create what family historian Stephanie Coontz (2005, 280) calls "a perfect storm" around marriage.

Family scholars are themselves deeply divided over the import of the recent trends and ongoing conflicts over marriage. Sociologist Andrew Cherlin (2004) recently proposed that marriage has been undergoing a process of "deinstitutionalization" over the past century. Prior to the twentieth century, Cherlin notes, marriage was a formal status tightly regulated by law, social norms and religion. In the early and middle twentieth century, American marriage shifted to a companionate model, placing greater emphasis on relationship quality and marriage as a source of personal happiness and meaning. Cherlin argues that the final decades of the century saw another shift, to what he calls "individualized marriage." Under this new model, marriage loses many of the qualities of a social institution and instead becomes tailored to the individual needs and preferences of its participants. Evidence for deinstitutionalization includes the relaxation of social norms about marriage and legal developments such as no-fault divorce and prenuptial agreements that move marriage from status to contract, allowing spouses to dissolve marriages more easily and to define some of the terms of their legal commitment to each other. Paul Amato (2004) observes that family scholars fall into two main camps in their interpretation of these processes of deinstitutionalization. The "marital decline" camp perceives a declining commitment to the institution of marriage (consistent with the notion of a retreat from marriage discussed in Chapter 3), and attributes this change to the rising individualism of American culture. The marital decline scholars warn that deinstitutionalization of marriage is contributing to a host of serious social problems, including poverty, substance abuse, violence, delinquency, poor school performance and declining neighborhoods. The "marital resiliency" camp, by contrast, sees marriage as a strong and ever-evolving institution, and argues that the recent changes in marriage are not deeply problematic. These scholars assert that greater individual freedom in marriage is good, easier divorce liberates people from unhappy marriages, and most children are not permanently damaged by divorce. People in the marital decline camp tend to favor policies that strengthen legal marriage and keep marriage in a privileged position relative to non-marital relationships, whereas the marital resiliency camp recommends social policies that support all family forms, without privileging families headed by married parents.[13]

There is yet a third perspective on marriage, one that sees legal marriage as a fundamentally flawed institution and advocates the abolition of marriage as a legal form.[14] Feminist scholars have been prominent in staking out this position. Law professor Martha Fineman (1995, 2004) argues that the state should direct its policies toward supporting caretaker-dependent relationships (including but not limited to the parent–child relationship), rather than recognizing and subsidizing horizontal relationships between sexual partners. In Fineman's view, this would make state policy more responsive to the lived reality of family life in contemporary society and would correct the longstanding policy of privatizing dependency within the family. Fineman proposes replacing legal marriage with a system of private contracting between sexual/romantic partners. Rather than assuming a set bundle of obligations and protections through marriage as a legal status, partners would make conscious choices about the kinds of responsibilities they will share (and will have the state recognize and enforce as a matter of contract rather than status). Another legal scholar, Martha Ertman, has made this idea of replacing marriage with private contracts more concrete through her proposal to construct a relationship contract system based on the structures of corporate law (Ertman 2001). Under this proposal, partners would choose among several contracting options, depending on the strength of their commitment and their willingness to undertake various legal responsibilities. As envisioned by Fineman and Ertman, these contractualist alternatives to marriage would be available not only to opposite-sex and same-sex couples but to sexual relationships among more than two people.

A different approach to marriage abolition comes from commentators advocating the replacement of marriage with a new legal status such as civil unions. This option has emerged in direct response to the debates over legal recognition for same-sex relationships and received support from a diverse range of actors, including law professor Alan Dershowitz (2003), queer scholar and commentator Alisa Solomon (2004), the editorial board of the *Los Angeles Times* (2004), and state legislators in New York and Massachusetts (see Stacey 2004). The basic idea is to separate the civil and religious dimensions of marriage by renaming the civil component and offering it to same-sex as well as opposite-sex couples. This "civil unions for all" approach has the advantage of delivering full formal equality while at the same time resolving the conflict and confusion about the definition and meaning of marriage by removing marriage from the realm of state action. In this scenario, couples would be free to pursue marriage through cultural or religious practice, and individual religious denominations would define the bounds of marriage according to their own beliefs, but state recognition of intimate relationships would take place independent of religious or cultural enactments of marriage. Conflict over the boundaries of marriage would undoubtedly persist within some religious communities, but such conflicts would no longer be linked to the public-policy question of marriage. This move would highlight and indeed institutionalize the separateness of the civil and religious dimensions of marriage, a separation which today many Americans are unable or unwilling to acknowledge.

Both versions of the marriage abolition proposal – replacement with private contracts and shift to civil unions – have clear virtues. Neither, in my view, represents a satisfactory resolution of the policy issue of same-sex marriage or a promising roadmap for long-term change in family policy more generally. Fineman makes a forceful argument for shifting state support from sexual affiliations to caretaking relationships of all kinds. There is a burgeoning theoretical and empirical literature on the relationship between "care work" and state policies (e.g. Meyer 2000; Folbre 2001; White and Tronto 2004; Swartz 2004), and most of this work argues that the state can and should do more to support a range of caretaker-dependent relationships. But Fineman's proposal to replace marriage with private contracts minimizes the significant "care work" that happens in long-term romantic/sexual relationships. This kind of care may be qualitatively different – on average more reciprocal and symmetrical – than the care work that occurs in other care relationships, but people in long-term relationships experience all kinds of dependencies and care needs and often their partners act as their main caretakers. It is in the state's and society's interest to continue to recognize and support these relationships through some kind of legal status. I am skeptical about the assumptions of foresight, rationality and equality of bargaining power that must be made for a private contracting scheme to make sense. Also, the proposal to shift to private contracts ignores the possibility that taking on a public legal status may have desirable effects on commitment that would be lost in a privatized system.

The proposal of civil unions as a replacement for marriage also has much to recommend it, but suffers a fatal flaw. A system of public civil unions and private marriage would deliver formal and substantial equality to all similarly situated citizens, while disentangling the legal and cultural components of marriage. The advocates of same-sex marriage would achieve their basic goal of full equality, but the solution also respects the views of those who oppose same-sex marriage on the grounds that it violates the meaning or definition of marriage. The latter group would remain free to embrace their own religious or cultural understanding of marriage, and the state would become neutral on the question of the definition or nature of marriage. Gays and lesbians who want legal protections without the cultural baggage of marriage would also find satisfaction. Because the current entanglement of the religious and civil elements of marriage is so problematic, the idea of civil unions for all has intuitive appeal. But it is this same entanglement of civil and religious marriage that dooms this proposal as a matter of practical politics. There may be a handful of US states in which civil unions for all would be politically viable, but such a proposal would tap the same well of heterosexual resistance as same-sex marriage, and for largely the same reason. Many people hold an essentialist view of marriage in which the legal and cultural/religious aspects of marriage naturally and necessarily overlap. And heterosexuals who are most attached to their own privilege (if only subconsciously) would inevitably experience the replacement of marriage with civil unions as a significant loss or violation.

So rather than abolishing marriage, the more realistic long-term policy direction is to expand the boundaries of marriage and supplement marriage with other forms of legal recognition. Legal same-sex marriage is a viable long-term policy goal, despite the current intense opposition, because it is consistent with the core American principle of equal treatment under the law. This long-term solution seems most achievable via the short-term approach of equality practice, which gives the opponents of same-sex marriage the opportunity to learn from state-level experiments with substantially equal treatment of same-sex relationships. Even if the long-term solution ultimately must be accomplished through judicial rather than legislative means, an intervening period of equality practice will assure that most citizens will be ready to accept the outcome.

But same-sex marriage should not be the end point of collective deliberations over how to recognize and support close, committed relationships. Rather, the challenge of grappling with the same-sex marriage issue should act as a stimulus toward rethinking the role of the state in recognizing and supporting all kinds of close relationships, gay and straight, sexual and nonsexual. Perhaps we can start collectively to envision a future in which the state gives people a range of options for relationship recognition and support. This direction is not brand new; it builds on recent innovations like domestic partnerships, reciprocal beneficiaries, civil unions and de facto legal recognition of long-term cohabitating relationships. However, the United States lags behind many other countries in developing a range of responsive policies and statuses to accommodate people's actual needs and relationships. Those in the marital decline camp are likely to resist and critique the creation of new legal statuses offering recognition to a wider range of relationship forms. Alternatives to marriage, some entailing more limited forms of commitment and obligation, can be viewed as a dangerous threat to the attractiveness and even survival of marriage itself. Some will view these alternative statuses as a way to give people the benefits and protections of marriage without its obligations, and will have concerns about the instability of these forms of relationship (and the ensuing impacts on children) compared to marriage.[15]

As new forms of relationship recognition enter the law, some people will in fact opt to use these new statuses in lieu of marriage, for reasons ranging from the practical to the philosophical. But is that really a problem? I see three main advantages to an expanded menu of relationship statuses. First, people will have more flexibility to match their actual relationships and legal needs to state offerings. The dichotomous choice between marriage and non-marriage is rather confining, especially for couples who desire some form of relationship protection but are not prepared for marriage. Young couples with shared assets and no children, for example, may desire a fairly basic relationship status, with fewer obligations and benefits than marriage. Some same-sex couples (including some interviewed in this study) would appreciate access to a legal status that is equal to marriage but has a different name. (Some straight couples surely would prefer this option as well.) A second advantage to an expanded set of relationship options concerns communication. When more statuses are available to potential partners, the selection of a particular status has more signaling power, both between partners and from the partnership to the broader society. Saying "I do" to a limited form of domestic partnership but not a marriage tells both the partner and the wider community what kind of commitment is (and is not) involved. Finally, a third advantage to a broader range of relationship statuses is the chance to include some relationships that currently lack any recognition or protection. People who have important nonsexual relationships, with either relatives or friends, could benefit from legal statuses that grant recognition and certain rights and obligations to those ties. Widowed siblings, for example, might appreciate the option of mutually establishing a legal bond that includes some of the benefits and protections normally accorded to spouses.[16]

This kind of expanded approach to relationship recognition would make public policy more responsive to the lived realities of today's relationships and families. The price would be a decentering and deprivileging of marriage in legal terms, and probably in cultural terms as well. Some believe this is too high a price to pay, because marriage succeeds as a functional social institution only by virtue of its privileged status. But I am more sanguine about the future of marriage under such a scenario. It will remain a culturally resonant institution for many people, in part because of deep religious and family traditions, and it will be a more meaningful legal status when it is freely chosen from a range of options rather than being the only way to access any significant partnership rights and benefits.

As Emma Goldman (1910) astutely observed nearly a century ago, love and marriage are not synonymous. Indeed, for most of human history, they have had little to do with each other. But at the start of the twenty-first century, the institution of marriage remains a powerful cultural force, and its cultural power both draws upon and transcends its legal dimension. Despite the current fragility of real-life marriages and the partial decentering of marriage as a life goal, marriage remains for many Americans, gay and straight, an important model for expressing and enacting intimate commitment. For the sake of the common good, the state must find ways to encourage and support all such commitments, and beyond marriage, family and caretaking commitments of all kinds.

Epilogue

I ran into Brenda Davis in public in the winter of 2001, about two years after interviewing her for this project. Brenda was, in fact, the very first participant to be interviewed for this study. Her partner Kim Pierson, whom I interviewed separately, was the second. After we exchanged greetings, I began to apologize to Brenda for the fact that she had still not received the promised "report to participants" from the study, and I assured her that it was forthcoming. "Oh, *that* marriage is over," she said with a sigh. After about eight years together, Brenda and Kim had separated in fall of 2000.

Circumstances did not permit an in-depth discussion of the breakup at the time of our chance meeting, but a few weeks later I decided to call Brenda to see if she was willing to be re-interviewed. I explained to her that people often asked me whether my study included the perspective of couples who had "married" in a public ceremony and then subsequently "divorced." This was not part of the original research design, but my chance encounter with Brenda provided the opportunity to incorporate at least one study participant's experience of same-sex "divorce." Brenda agreed to the second interview.

A few weeks later Brenda came to my home, and we talked for about an hour in an interview that generated a few chuckles but more tears. I asked Brenda to describe the circumstances of the breakup, in whatever level of detail felt comfortable for her. We also discussed the effect of the relationship's dissolution on her feelings about same-sex marriage, public commitment ceremonies, and the institution of marriage generally.

Kim and Brenda had held a public union ceremony after they had been together about a year and a half. In the first interview, I had asked Brenda what that ceremony meant to her and what motivated them to have one. She had stressed that she used the ceremony to make a "statement" to her family, a statement that this relationship with Kim was different from her past relationships and was forever. She had also mentioned that they had been planning to raise a child together, and this had been an impetus for the ceremony. "I think we were trying really hard to pave the way for a child, for our child to feel like it was becoming part of an extended family," she had commented. Brenda had described how the ceremony had "relaxed" her and given her a sense of security in the relationship ("I no longer questioned anything about the relationship"). Brenda had also explained that the ritual had effected a change in their friends, noting that Kim's co-workers "kept an eye" on her and threatened to tell Brenda if Kim misbehaved. When I asked for any final reflections at the end of the first interview, Brenda observed that it helps to be married when couples go through hard times together. She said she believed marriage makes people stick with their relationships through ups and downs.

In the second interview, Brenda informed me that Kim had begun a two-year affair with a co-worker about eight months after their union ceremony. After the ceremony, Brenda had successfully become pregnant through artificial insemination, putting the couple on their desired path to parenthood. They also purchased a home together in this time period. Unfortunately Brenda miscarried early in the pregnancy, and this event threw her into a serious depression. Around this time Kim began her affair with her colleague Erica.

Brenda did not find out about the affair for two years. Kim finally revealed it to her when Erica's partner found out about it and threatened to let Brenda know if Kim did not. Brenda said she was "devastated for months and months" after finding out. She and Kim went into therapy together for a time, and "separated" within their home for a few months. Throughout this period, Kim "begged" Brenda not to leave her. After the couples therapy, Brenda decided to give the relationship another chance, but in retrospect she believes they never recovered from the affair:

I think in the ensuing few years, we never got it together again. I mean, I think we really cared about each other, but I think on some level the betrayal was way too much for me, and I'm not sure . . . I think the passion was gone. And I think at another level, she had her own narcissistic injury around what she had done, and being shamed by that, that she couldn't really live with it. And I think between both of us chewing on that stuff, I think that we tried to make it, and the marriage just died around us, I think. The passion really left. And even though I was still in love with her, and I think on some level she was still in love with me, I think once the passion left, it was just a matter of time.

A distance developed in their relationship and Brenda felt Kim was no longer able to tolerate that. The relationship continued for a few more years, but Kim began to spend more time away from home, sometimes even spending nights at the homes of friends toward the end. Kim also began making major life decisions without consulting Brenda.

As the relationship continued to deteriorate, Brenda insisted that they return to couples counseling, but it was too late to save the relationship. By Brenda's account, Kim shut down emotionally and refused to take responsibility for dissolving the relationship. Finally, after a month of "tears and crying and horror," Kim moved out of their house. At the time of the second interview, Brenda and Kim remained on speaking terms, and still had a few loose ends to tie up related to their finances, but their interactions had become "businesslike" and "formal."

I asked whether Brenda felt that having had a public union ceremony made any difference in the way their relationship subsequently played out. Did the ceremony create any pressure or motivation to try to stay together? "Yeah, I think it did add to that [pressure]," she replied, "but I think I was also very much, I just loved her, you know I was really in love with her." In retrospect, Brenda feels she should have ended the relationship after finding out about the affair. In part, the ceremony made Brenda believe that Kim would work harder to save the relationship:

[The ceremony] certainly added to the fact that I wanted to work things out, but it also added to the fact that I thought, because we were married, that she would try and work things out in the future, that she really was more committed than she was. It occurs to me now that she had no clue as to what she was doing in this marriage. And I literally don't know why she married me. I mean, at this point in time I don't know what she was thinking, if she could have an affair within the first year of the marriage.

I asked Brenda if I was right in recalling that Kim was the one who first brought up the idea of getting married, and had formally proposed to Brenda. Brenda confirmed this, and remarked: "She said at one point later that she thinks that her whole abandonment issues, her whole . . . she just felt that I would stay if we were married more." I asked whether their ceremony had been explicitly brought up in the course of their discussions about ending the relationship. "Oh, yeah!" Brenda replied. I asked in what way the ceremony came up, and she responded:

In me saying, "You promised me forever in front of people, in a church, and you know, we're married, and don't you think you owe this marriage a little bit more than that?" Oh, yeah. And I think it's also what kept her there a lot longer than she should have stayed. Clearly she was not as married as I was, and I think she was trying very hard to find a way to stay, and probably the marriage, because we had a union ceremony, my guess is the marriage lasted maybe two, three years longer than it should have, unfortunately.

Brenda had not told friends or family about the affair when she first found out about it, so many people were "shocked" when the relationship ended, and sometimes they would specifically mention the ceremony and how in love the couple had appeared. But no one tried to talk Brenda into staying in the relationship after hearing about the affair.

I asked how the breakup had affected Brenda's attitudes and beliefs about same-sex marriage. Somewhat to my surprise, Brenda said she continues to be a strong believer in same-sex marriage as beneficial to gays and lesbians:

> I think they're still very viable, I think we still need to move towards them. I mean, yeah, I mean it felt . . . I still believe that getting married did something different for me, obviously not for . . . I think it did something different for Kim too. I mean, I really think that her level of shame about what she did was so intense that she couldn't love herself because of what she did, and I think had we not been married, it would have been nothing to her, it would have just been, like, on to the next. And I think there was a real growth piece for her in all of that, in a way that wouldn't have been there otherwise. And I think for me the marriage still represents that I was that much in love with her and that I really wanted the world to treat me in that way, and I wouldn't give it, I don't regret having married her for a minute. I mean, I certainly regret the marriage, and clearly I didn't know her very well, but, um, I knew her, I knew what she was showing me. And she didn't know herself very well, she didn't know herself very well so I couldn't have known what she didn't know. But, I don't regret it. And I think they're still very important, and I think even the divorce, and it *is* a divorce, people take much more seriously because of the level of commitment that they know we gave to the marriage. And it honors in some way my pain at this level better than just breaking up would have.

These comments were striking to me, both for the ambivalence they revealed and because the ritual participants I had interviewed never talked about "divorce" or the possibility that their relationships might not survive, and yet Brenda's ritual had served as a resource for her in the context of her divorce, by making people honor the reality of the relationship and therefore honor her pain at its failure.

I also asked whether Brenda could see herself ever participating in another public commitment ritual. She was unsure. She continues to believe such ceremonies are "valid," and said she "would support anybody getting married, at a very deep level." But she said with a chuckle: "I just don't know if I would stand up there in front of all my friends and family and say, 'Here we go again!'"

Brenda said she and Kim did not have any conflicts about how to disentangle themselves financially and legally, despite the fact that they had significant joint investments and had put in place many legal protections for the relationship at the time of their ceremony. She did consult a lawyer once to make sure she had "legally thought through all the ramifications," but that aspect of the breakup had gone very smoothly. So Brenda did not feel that being legally married would have helped the process of breaking up in their case. She was also skeptical that being legally married would have prolonged their relationship:

I think if we had had the kid [being legally married] would have [prolonged the relationship], and that she'd have left me later, she'd have left me when the kid was a teenager. Maybe. Maybe not. Maybe she would have left still when she did. She doesn't stay when she's disconnected. You know, I think we felt married. We felt legally, as legally married as we could. And, I don't know. I mean, I think that if there were any chance that this marriage could have worked, that gave it the chance . . . Being married gave it the chance. And I don't think . . . I mean, she was emotionally gone; I don't think there's any way that . . . if she had to go to court and dissolve this, she would have just done it. I don't think it would have changed anything. I think the kid would have changed something, I'm not sure much, but something.

At the end of the interview, I asked Brenda whether her experience had changed her feelings or views about the value of marriage as an institution. "Not about marriage as an institution," she replied. "I still think that's a good thing." She did feel the end of the relationship had changed her as a person, and she was still sorting through the nature of those changes. But she remained steadfast in her support of the institution of marriage:

I think we need to get married. I mean, I think gays and lesbians need to be married. I'm not sure I really feel good about courts getting involved in it, but I don't feel good about courts at all either, so . . . I feel there needs to be the legal redress. And I think people saw Kim and I as legally married, I mean I think the people that we knew and loved literally saw us as married. Except for maybe Erica!

* * * * *

What insights can be gleaned from Brenda's "post-divorce" perspective? Obviously this is only one person's reaction to a relationship's dissolution, and other participants in same-sex commitment ceremonies might react quite differently. But Kim and Brenda's story, as perceived by Brenda, does provoke some final reflections on the findings of this study.

On the cultural side, Brenda's retrospective account suggests that for some couples these ceremonies are effective means of enhancing commitment and durability in relationships. Brenda believed that the ceremony caused Kim to stick with the relationship rather than just moving on to the next relationship, and caused Brenda herself to feel more confident that both would try to make it last. But in their case, it is unclear that this enhanced "stability" was actually a positive thing. From

Brenda's perspective, at least, they both stayed in the relationship longer than they should have, and the ceremony was one factor in their decision to do so.

On the legal side, Brenda did not feel that there would have been any benefit to being legally married at the time of their breakup. In fact she was grateful that she did not have to incur the costs and the public exposure that would have accompanied a legal divorce. At the level of status and identity, she also felt the official law could add little to their relationship. They already felt "legally married" as a couple, and Brenda believed that the people close to them also perceived them as legally married. At the point of the relationship dissolving, their cultural enactment of legality through ritual had "worked" in the sense that others treated them as a married couple and treated their breakup as equivalent to a divorce. But just as official law cannot guarantee permanence in relationships, the legality produced through cultural practices does not offer any final assurances.

Finally, the second interview with Brenda raises interesting methodological questions. When I interviewed Brenda and Kim at the very start of my research, the revelation of Kim's affair was two years in their past, but neither of the partners made any mention of it in my separate interviews with them. When I asked about crises or turning points in the relationship, neither was willing to discuss this painful and ultimately fateful development in their recent past.

There are many reasons Kim and Brenda would not want to discuss the affair. In the context of an interview about marriage, revealing the affair might seem embarrassing or an admission of failure in their own marriage. They may have been influenced by the "model minority effect" (see Carrington 1999, 178), wanting to portray themselves as happy, stable and fully committed, thereby demonstrating the possibilities for same-sex couples generally. I had known Kim and Brenda for several years as casual acquaintances, and this pre-existing tie may also have influenced their willingness to discuss the affair. It may have enhanced their concerns about my opinion of them, or it may have made them leery of sharing such personal information with me, given our mutual acquaintances. (Guarantees of confidentiality only go so far in allaying these kinds of concerns.) Perhaps they were at a point where they were feeling optimistic about their relationship's future and they did not want to resurrect unpleasant memories. When I pointed out to Brenda that she had not mentioned the affair in the first interview, she simply replied that it was something she did not talk about with anybody.

Kim and Brenda's choice not to tell me about the affair in the initial interviews calls attention to the limits of in-depth interviewing as a research technique and the need to interpret the content of these interviews with caution. Undoubtedly other interview participants also withheld similarly significant information about the past or present of their relationships. This does not invalidate the study's findings, but it underscores the importance of treating interview data as moments of discursive production rather than as straightforward reports about "reality."

The in-depth interview is not simply an occasion for unilateral transmission of information to the researcher. Interviews are social encounters, and the resulting discourses are inevitably shaped by the particular interests and experiences of both interviewer and interviewee. In asking people about their personal and relationship histories, their wedding stories, and their views on legal and political questions, I solicited some "facts," but more importantly I invited people to construct stories or accounts of their own lives and relationships. The primary value of the resulting narratives does not rest in their capacity to convey fixed truths about the past experiences or interior lives of these individuals. Rather, these narratives are interesting for what they reveal about what is sayable and unsayable for people occupying a particular social location in a particular historical moment. How does the existence of marriage as a central social institution structure the ways different people talk about intimacy and commitment? How does the law, with its powers of recognition and exclusion, structure people's discourses about what is real, what is valuable and what is just?

These interview discourses may also hold significance as a form of resistance in and of themselves, rather than merely as accounts of past moments of resistance. Ewick and Silbey (2003) argue that when people tell stories about how they have resisted or contested existing social structures, they extend that resistance through space and time. Thus for the study participants, the interview becomes an opportunity not only to pass along information but to keep past resistances alive through story-telling. For the ritual participants in particular, the telling of the wedding stories may be not only a chance to describe happy memories of a significant past event, but also to replay and extend their efforts to define the reality of their relationship and its place in the social world. For all of the study participants, my hope is that the interview experience empowered them by giving them a space in which to tell the story of their own lives and relationships, with the knowledge that parts of their story would ultimately circulate to a wider audience and thereby contest the marginalization of gay and lesbian lives and loves.

Appendix A: Interview guides

INTERVIEW GUIDE – MEMBERS OF SAME-SEX COUPLES

Note: Topics enclosed in brackets ([]) were discussed only with people who had participated in a public commitment ritual, and topics enclosed in arrowheads (<>) were discussed only with people who had not participated in a public commitment ritual.

Start of interview: explanation of research project, discussion of confidentiality protections and request for permission to tape interview.

BASIC SOCIAL BACKGROUND INFORMATION

- personal/family history (inquire about parents' marriage)
- past and current socioeconomic status (occupation of self/partner; home rent or own)
- education – highest attained
- family history
- age
- racial/ethnic identity
- religious identification
- political orientation
- sexual identity

YOUR "COMING OUT" STORY

- when and how you came to identify as gay/lesbian/bisexual/other
- subjective experience of process
- relationship history
- views on the nature of sexual identity (constructed vs. essentialist)

HISTORY OF YOUR CURRENT COMMITTED RELATIONSHIP

- its beginnings
- its evolution (development stages; levels of commitment; crises) and duration

[THE "WEDDING" STORY

- decision to construct a ritual
- material representations of event (review together)
- components of ritual: program; rings; vows; participants, etc.
- meaning of the event
- personal and social reactions to the event]

ONGOING CONTENT OF THE RELATIONSHIP [AND IMPACT OF RITUAL ON THE RELATIONSHIP]

- perceived impact of ritual on relationship
- division of labor
- management of finances
- legal arrangements to establish protections and mutual understandings
- sexual and emotional fidelity
- status of the relationship within extended families and friendship networks
- terminology for status (e.g. "married") and partner (e.g. "spouse")
- how to answer the question "Are you married?"
- plans for having children or other dependents

<DECISION NOT TO HAVE A PUBLIC RITUAL

- contributing factors (political, philosophical, personal, etc.)
- views on commitment rituals of other same-sex couples
- whether there might be a ritual in future, what factors would influence that decision>

VIEWS ON LEGAL RECOGNITION FOR SAME-SEX MARRIAGE/RELATIONSHIPS

- for or against legal recognition – reasons
- level of priority as movement goal
- acceptability of alternative forms such as domestic partnership
- would you legally marry if it became possible?
- likelihood of legal recognition; timeframe

EVOLUTION OF YOUR VIEWS ON SAME-SEX MARRIAGE

- as cultural practice
- as political goal

REACTION TO OPPOSITION TO SAME-SEX MARRIAGE

- opposition from mainstream society
- opposition from within the gay and lesbian community

RELATIONSHIP TO THE ORGANIZED GAY RIGHTS MOVEMENT

- primary social networks in general (family, co-workers, friends with shared interests, straight vs. gay) – who you spend time with, who you turn to in times of crisis
- involvement in gay/lesbian community (memberships, volunteer activities, attendance at cultural events, giving money, reading gay/lesbian publications)
- attitudes toward gay rights movement, local and national (approval/disapproval, concerns)
- sense of ownership in movement
- personal political participation (ever worked on a campaign? voting habits?)

REQUEST CONTACTS FOR ADDITIONAL INTERVIEWS

INTERVIEW GUIDE – CLERGY PERFORMING SAME-SEX MARRIAGES

Start of interview: explanation of research project, discussion of confidentiality protections and request for permission to tape interview.

BACKGROUND

- Tell me bit about yourself – where you grew up, when you decided to become clergy, what motivated that decision, how you like your work now
- Describe your congregation

PARTICIPATION AT SAME-SEX RITUALS

- Tell me about your experience(s) officiating at same-sex commitment rituals. (Who were the participants, what was the ceremony like, etc.)
- Was it a difficult decision to perform such a ritual?
- What is the context for that decision – how does your religion/denomination view such ceremonies? How do you view them, compared to heterosexual wedding ceremonies?
- What do you think will be the ultimate fate of such rituals in your religion/denomination?

COMPARE/CONTRAST TO HETEROSEXUAL WEDDINGS

- How would you compare these rituals to heterosexual weddings you have performed? Are there any interesting similarities or differences?

COMPARISONS AMONG SAME-SEX RITUALS (FOR THOSE WITH MULTIPLE EXPERIENCES)

- How would you compare the same-sex ceremonies to one another? Any interesting differences or similarities that struck you?
- What do you think same-sex couples are looking for in these rituals?
- (For those with experience with both male and female couples) Did you notice any significant differences in how men and women approach these ceremonies?

REQUEST FOR CONTACTS

- same-sex couples, other clergy or religious groups

Appendix B: Sample characteristics

Gender and participation in public ritual

		Female	Male	Total	
Participated in public ritual?	Yes	30	19	49	(69%)
	No	11	11	22	(31%)
Total		41	30	71	
		(58%)	(42%)		

Race/ethnicity

White, European ancestry	77%	(55)
Latino/Latina	6%	(4)
African-American	8%	(6)
Other (Asian, biracial or multiracial)	8%	(6)

Current socioeconomic status (SES)

Upper middle class	28%	(20)
Middle class	48%	(34)
Lower middle class or working class	24%	(17)

Education

High school graduate	3%	(2)
Associate's degree or some college education	18%	(13)
Bachelor's degree	30%	(21)
Graduate or professional degree	34%	(24)
Unknown	15%	(11)

Any religious affiliation

Yes	62%	(44)
No	38%	(27)

Political views

Democrat/liberal/radical	65%	(46)
Independent/moderate	18%	(13)
Apathetic/apolitical	16%	(11)
Unknown	1%	(1)

Residential location

City	56%	(40)
Suburb	44%	(31)

Study participant's age (years)

Minimum	26	Maximum	66
Mean	41	Median	41

Relationship length (years)

Minimum	0.8	Maximum	36
Mean	8	Median	7

Appendix C: Study participants

Below is a descriptive listing of the same-sex couple study participants. Couples are listed together; if only one member of the couple participated in the study, his or her partner is listed in brackets. All names are pseudonyms, and some other identifying information such as occupation has been slightly altered for some individuals to protect confidentiality.

William Austin and Ken Glascott: William is a 39-year-old architect, and Ken, 38, is an actor. Both men are white and college-educated. They currently live in the city but have plans to move to the suburbs for William's job. William and Ken have been together two and a half years, and had a commitment ceremony after one year.

Jacob Berger [and Joe Neufeld]: Jacob is a 34-year-old small-business owner who describes his race/ethnicity as "white Jew." Jacob and his partner Joe, who have been together twelve years, live in a condo in an upscale gay-friendly neighborhood in the city. They had a large commitment ceremony after nine years together.

George Brodie and Anthony Parisi: George is a 41-year-old dentist and Anthony is a 35-year-old psychologist. Both are white. George and Anthony own a home together in the suburbs. They have been together nine years, and had a commitment ceremony two years into their relationship.

Claire Bruno and Sue Bruno: Claire and Sue have been together for six years. Claire is 41, white, and a social worker. Sue, a 49-year-old therapist, describes her race/ethnicity as part European and part American Indian. The couple had a commitment ceremony after one year together, and Sue took Claire's surname as her legal name at that time. They are active members of the Metropolitan Community Church. Claire and Sue share a rented apartment in the suburbs.

Robbie Caputo and Alex Gellar: Robbie is a 26-year-old white accountant, and Alex is a 27-year-old African-American stockbroker. Robbie and Alex met in college and have been together six years. They recently purchased a home together in a gentrifying neighborhood in the city. The couple has not had a commitment ritual. Alex is a practicing Catholic. Robbie and Alex were interviewed separately.

Larry Clemens and Brian O'Toole: Larry, 51, is a counselor, and Brian, 42, is a professional musician. They met on a blind date and have been together for twelve years. Larry was previously married to a woman and has two grown children. Both men are white. Larry and Brian own a home together in the suburbs. Both are practicing Methodists. They had a commitment ceremony after three years together.

Paul Colvin and Dwight Winfrey: Together for thirty-six years, Paul and Dwight have the longest relationship in the study. Paul, 63, is a book-keeper, and 57-year-old Dwight is a licensed practical nurse. Both are white. Paul and Dwight are currently active in the Metropolitan Community Church. They held a commitment ceremony in a Lutheran church after twenty-five years together, and held a "recommitment ceremony" in an MCC church five years later. They own a home in the suburbs.

Cindy Dahl and Janis Sobirov: Cindy and Janis are a white suburban couple who hope to become parents soon. Cindy, 45, works as a retail clerk. Janis, 28, teaches school. They are active members of the Metropolitan Community Church. Cindy and Janis have been together eight years, and held a commitment ceremony after five years together.

Tim Daniels and Andrew Minnelli: Tim and Andrew have been together two and a half years, and just recently had their ceremony, which they refer to as their wedding. Tim is 37 years old, white, and works in fundraising. Andrew, 48 and white, works several part-time jobs including landscaping and office administration. Tim is Catholic and the couple is involved in Dignity, a group for gay and lesbian Catholics. A Catholic priest officiated at their wedding. Tim and Andrew live in an apartment in the city. They were interviewed separately.

Brenda Davis and Kim Pierson: Brenda is a 44-year-old white professor. Kim, 37, is African-American and works in government administration. When I first interviewed Kim and Brenda, they had been together about six years and lived in a home they had bought together in the city. They had a commitment ceremony one and a half years into their relationship. Kim and Brenda were interviewed separately, and Brenda was re-interviewed about two years later, after they had broken up.

Monique Dillon and Carmen Ruiz: Monique and Carmen, together for two and half years, had a commitment ritual after their first year together. Monique, a 41-year-old security guard, is African-American. Carmen, 42 and unemployed because of disability, is African-American and Puerto Rican. They live in an apartment in a racially mixed neighborhood in the city.

Amanda Dimarco and Christine Pasminski: Amanda is 37 years old, white, and the director of a social service agency. Christine, 38 and white, works as a dentist. They have been together fourteen years and own their home in the suburbs. The had a small public commitment ritual after a year and a half together, back in the mid-1980s. ("We did it before people were doing it," Christine remarked.) Both women identify as Catholic, with considerable ambivalence, and a Catholic priest affiliated with the gay Catholic organization Dignity performed their ceremony.

Sandra Drewitt and Jenny Pyrdol: Sandra is a 41-year-old therapist and Jenny, 55, runs her own graphic design business. Sandra and Jenny are white, Catholic homeowners living in a quiet residential area in the city. They have been together thirteen years and are raising a five-year-old daughter together. They cite becoming parents as a major turning point in their relationship. They had a private "mini-ceremony" when they exchanged rings after their first year together, but neither has any interest in a public commitment ritual.

Paula Dunham and Sally Mitchell: Paula and Sally have been together for 30 years. Paula, 51, teaches high school and is mostly in the closet because of her career. Sally is 66 and retired. Both women are white. Paula is Catholic and Sally is a "card-carrying Methodist." They have attended friends' commitment ceremonies but cannot imagine having one themselves. Sally was married to a man in her early adulthood and has two grown children from the marriage; Paula and Sally are proud grandparents of Sally's daughter's kids. Paula and Sally own their home in the suburbs.

Kevin Forrest and Brad Schuster: Kevin is a 47-year-old white accountant. He was previously married to a woman and has a son from the marriage. Brad, also 47 and white, is a communications executive. Kevin and Brad have been together two years and share a home in the suburbs. Kevin is non-religious and Brad is Catholic. They had a commitment ceremony after one year together, and Brad wanted it to be as close to a Catholic wedding as possible; an Episcopal priest officiated.

Betty Freeman and Mandy Walker: Betty and Mandy, both African-American, have been together three years. Betty, 57, is a city bus driver and Mandy, 41, is a home health care worker. Mandy had two prior marriages to men and has an 11-year-old daughter who lives with the couple. The couple owns their home in a working-class black neighborhood in the city. They had a public commitment ritual after just three months together (but had known each other for twenty years prior to becoming a couple). Mandy is Baptist and Betty belongs to a non-denominational Christian church. A minister friend officiated at their ceremony.

Ted Grasskamp [and Damien Ivers]: Ted is a 46-year-old white registered nurse. Ted and his partner Damien have been together seven years. Up to this point they have maintained separate residences but were in the process of buying a home together when I interviewed Ted. Ted lives in a gay-friendly neighborhood in the city. Ted would like to have a commitment ceremony but Damien is not interested. They exchanged rings privately several years ago as a symbol of their commitment.

Gerry Halloran and Heather Pryor: Gerry and Heather, together seven years, are a white suburban couple. Gerry, 36, is a physical education instructor, and Heather, 43, is a technical writer. They met through volunteer work in the lesbian community. Heather was previously married to a man. Gerry and Heather exchanged rings privately after two years together, and then had a public commitment ceremony two years later.

Bess Hardin and Susan Lemus: Bess is a 37-year-old veterinarian, and Susan, 29, is completing graduate school. The women, both white, live in a suburban home owned by Bess. They have been together four years. They exchanged rings privately after a year together, and neither has any interest in a public commitment ritual. Both Bess and Susan are skeptical about importing the marriage model into gay and lesbian relationships.

Joel Hauser and Christopher O'Neal: Joel is 35, white and an engineer. Christopher, 32 and white, works as a retail manager. Joel and Christopher met in a bar and have been together five years. They live in a condo in the city. A year and a half ago, they did a private ring exchange during a trip to Europe. Neither man has any interest in a public commitment ceremony, although they are not opposed to the idea in principle.

Pam Jackson and Dorothy Purnell: Pam and Dorothy have been together for five years. Pam is a 40-year-old office administrator and self-identifies as biracial. Dorothy, 56, is an African-American school teacher. Dorothy was previously married to a man and has an adult daughter and a grandson. Pam also has a grown daughter and two grandchildren, and her daughter's family currently lives with the couple in a suburban condo owned by Dorothy. Pam and Dorothy were interviewed separately.

Judith Klein and Carol Moore: Judith Klein is a 33-year-old white publishing executive. Carol, 34 and white, is a market researcher. Judith and Carol have been together six years, with a six-month separation in the middle of their relationship. They live in an apartment in the city. Judith is Jewish and Carol has no current religious affiliation. They just recently had their commitment ceremony in a downtown synagogue, co-officiated by a rabbi and a friend Carol considers her spiritual mentor.

Natalie Konstantos and Becky Rodgers: Becky is a 39-year-old white store manager. Natalie is a 50-year-old white social worker. The couple has been together eight years, and had a commitment ceremony after their first year together. Both women self-identify as Catholic, and they modeled their ritual on a Catholic wedding ceremony. They own a home in the suburbs. Natalie was married to a man for over twenty years and has several children. Natalie and Becky were interviewed separately.

Allen Lembas and Ricky Suarez: Allen and Ricky have been together just ten months, and held a small public commitment ceremony after six months together. Allen, 51, is a salesman, and 29-year-old Ricky is a bank teller and full-time student. Allen is white and Ricky is Mexican-American. Allen was previously married to a woman for eight years. Allen and Ricky met through the personal ads. Neither has a current religious affiliation, but they had an MCC minister officiate at their ceremony. They live in Allen's home in the suburbs.

Ethan Levinson and Peter Tyler: Ethan and Peter are white, highly educated professionals who share an apartment in the city. Ethan, 30, is a psychiatrist and Peter is a history professor. They have been together four years. They had a non-religious commitment ceremony a year ago, and asked close friends to officiate. Ethan and Peter are in a rough patch in their relationship right now and appreciate having the memory of their ceremony as a positive support for their commitment.

Anita Lindstrom and Peggy Wong: Anita and Peggy have been together for ten years. At the six-year point, they had a commitment ceremony co-officiated by five ministers. Anita is a 39-year-old white teacher and is pregnant with the couple's first child. Peggy, 34, is an Asian immigrant and works as a nurse. Anita and Peggy are both practicing Presbyterians. They own their home in the suburbs.

James Logan and Frank Pasternak: James is a 36-year-old white corporate manager. Frank is 41, white and a government engineer. They have been together thirteen years. When they first became involved, James was still in a marriage with a woman. He is grateful that he left that marriage when he was still young and childless. Frank and James had a commitment ceremony after seven years together. They live in a condo in a gay-friendly area in the city.

Maria Martinez and Linda Sanchez: Maria is a 40-year-old Mexican-American homemaker. Linda ("Chico") is 43, Mexican-American and a hotel maintenance worker. Maria divorced her husband eight years ago and has three children from the marriage. Maria and Chico are raising the kids together, and also caring for Chico's elderly mother who lives with them. Maria and Chico have been together a little over a year, and just recently had a commitment ceremony; an MCC minister officiated. They own a home in a racially mixed working-class neighborhood in the city.

Silvia Mendez and Marisol Ochoa: Silvia is a 44-year-old biracial retail executive. Marisol, 37 and Latina, works as a fundraiser for a nonprofit agency. Silvia and Marisol met through volunteer involvement in the lesbian Latina community and have been together four years. Neither has much interest in a public commitment ritual. Silvia married a man when she was only 15 and had two children before she was 20. Silvia has a low opinion of the marriage institution, and Marisol has never felt drawn to the marriage model. The couple shares an apartment in the city.

Teresa Morton [and Samantha Wolfe]: Teresa is a 54-year-old white artist who is independently wealthy. Teresa lives in a high-rise in a downtown neighborhood. She and her partner Samantha have been together for seven years and do not currently live together. They tried living together for a couple years, but Teresa prefers to live alone. Teresa feels a commitment ceremony would be a waste of time and money, but she is not opposed to other couples using rituals to define their relationships. She feels very little connection to the gay and lesbian community or movement.

Jeff Muldoon and Gary Weaver: Jeff is a 43-year-old white freelance writer. Gary, 38, is a white Jewish psychotherapist. Jeff and Gary have been together for seven and a half years. They have considered a public commitment ceremony but remain ambivalent. They exchanged rings in a private ritual they created a few years ago, and both feel that may be all they need, although they are considering some kind of event for their tenth anniversary. Jeff and Gary rent an apartment in a heavily gay section of the city. They were interviewed separately.

Howard O'Hara and Barry Sargent: Howard and Barry have been a couple for nine years. Howard, 46, is a former Catholic priest and currently works as a corporate trainer. Barry is a 29-year-old manager. Both men are white. They exchanged rings and vows privately on their fifth anniversary. They are lukewarm about the idea of a public commitment ceremony for various reasons, but they are thinking about doing some kind of ritual for their tenth anniversary. Howard and Barry live in a condo in the city.

Martha Petrillo and Diane Wilson: Martha is a 43-year-old white management consultant. Diane is a 50-year-old white attorney. Diane was married to a man for thirteen years and has two children from the marriage, including a teenage son who lives with Diane and Martha. They have been together for seven years, and had a commitment ceremony after two years together. Neither is religiously affiliated but they had a Methodist minister officiate at the ceremony. They live in a condo in the city.

Sarah Robbins and Abby Souter: Sarah and Abby have been a couple for eleven years. Sarah, 41, is a graphic artist. Abby is 43 and works as an office manager. Both are white. Abby was previously married to a man for seven years. Sarah and Abby had a public commitment ceremony at their home after two years together. Rather than having a single officiant, several close friends played different roles in their ritual. The couple owns their home in a working-class white neighborhood.

Anna Roth and Carrie Woodward: Anna is a 27-year-old teacher, and Carrie, 28, works as a program director in a nonprofit agency. Both are white. They have been a couple for two years and just had their commitment ceremony. Carrie is Unitarian and Anna sometimes goes to church with her but is not a member of the denomination. A lesbian minister from Carrie's congregation officiated at their ceremony. Anna plans to go to graduate school, and the couple would like to start a family in a few years. They live in an apartment in a city neighborhood popular with lesbians.

Annette Royce and Vicky Staples: Annette is 48 years old and self-identifies as multiracial. Vicky is 37 and white. Annette is currently unemployed because of disability, and Vicky is a computer programmer. The couple has been together eleven years, with one separation at the six-year point. They just recently had a commitment ceremony. Both are members of the Metropolitan Community Church. They live in an apartment in the suburbs.

Ralph Scripps [and Jack Zemon]: Ralph is a 42-year-old white research scientist. He and his partner Jack have been together five years and recently became the parents of twin baby boys. Jack proposed to Ralph two years ago, but the process of becoming parents threw their plans for a ceremony off track. Ralph thinks they will have a public commitment ritual once they find time to plan it. Ralph and Jack live in a condo in an upscale gay city neighborhood.

Justin Tanner [and Frederick Weiss]: Justin, 47, is a white administrative assistant. He and his partner Frederick have been together six and a half years. Justin converted to Judaism, Frederick's religion, four years ago. Justin has talked with their rabbi about having a commitment ceremony, but Frederick is currently not interested, mainly because he is not out to many of his relatives, neighbors and co-workers. Justin and Frederick share a home in the suburbs.

Notes

1: MARRIAGE, CULTURE AND LAW

1 Throughout the book I use the terms "same-sex" and "gay and lesbian" interchangeably to identify couples made up of two men or two women. The former term is more precise and accurate, because it makes no assumptions about the sexual identity of members of such couples, who may self-identify as gay, lesbian, homosexual, bisexual, transgender, queer, or other, or who may resist adoption of any fixed label for their sexual identity. I sometimes use the terms "gay and lesbian" or simply "gay" to refer to people in same-sex relationships, because these are the words used by the large majority of people in this study to describe their sexual identity. Specifically, 31 study participants (25 males and 6 females) self-identified as "gay," 31 as "lesbian," 5 (4 males and 1 female) as "homosexual" and one as "bisexual." Three people did not offer a specific term to describe their sexual identity.

2 For an interesting discussion of these religious debates from a European perspective, see Coulmont (2004), and for an ethnographic study of one denomination's internal struggles over homosexuality, see Moon (2004).

3 The Common Benefits Clause, as quoted in *Baker v. State of Vermont*, states: "That government is, or ought to be, instituted for the common benefit, protection, and security of the people, nation, or community, and not for the particular emolument or advantage of any single person, family, or set of persons, who are a part only of that community." In finding that the denial of the benefits and protections of marriage to same-sex couples violated the Clause, the Court wrote: "The extension of the Common Benefits Clause to acknowledge plaintiffs as Vermonters who seek nothing more, nor less, than legal protection and security for their avowed commitment to an intimate and lasting human relationship is simply, when all is said and done, a recognition of our common humanity."

4 California domestic partnership is now virtually identical to civil unions in the level of legal recognition provided. The key differences between the two statuses are that California domestic partners cannot file state income taxes jointly, whereas members of civil unions in Vermont and Connecticut can, and the creation of a domestic partnership does not require a civil ceremony, whereas creation of a civil union does.

5 See Lahey and Alderson (2004) for a concise overview of recent same-sex marriage developments around the world and interviews with same-sex couples

from several countries, and Bourassa and Varnell (2002) for a personal account of one couple's efforts to win marriage rights through the Canadian courts.

6 Although several scholars have effectively argued that the concerns of new social movements are not really unique to late twentieth-century movements (e.g. Calhoun 1993), the idea of a recent shift toward more culturally focused movements has been influential in the social movements field. And this shift has provoked debates among scholars and activists about whether such movements are really doing "politics" and whether this turn toward the cultural is harmful to the larger project of the political left (Gitlin 1995; Kauffman 1990).

7 I use the term "cultural structure" to refer to elements of the social world that have symbolic content, that constrain or direct human action to some degree and that are durable across time. Given Sewell's (1992) formulation that social structures consist of both schemas and resources, it could be argued that all social structures are cultural structures to some degree, that is, all structures have a cultural aspect since schemas endow structures with their meaning(s). I would agree that all social structures have cultural content, and I use the term "cultural structure" simply to highlight the cultural dimensions of particular social structures (in this instance, law). Alexander and Smith (1993, 156) define cultural structures as sets of interrelated symbols that constitute "nonmaterial structure." I do not find this distinction between material and nonmaterial structures useful, because all social structures have both material and nonmaterial elements (for example, the social structure of "law" includes material resources such as courthouses and prisons as well as nonmaterial schemas such as legal doctrines or commonsense beliefs about legal authority).

8 Social scientists who are strongly committed to a positivist approach to social inquiry believe that social science should emulate the physical sciences in attempting to ascertain verifiable facts about an observable external reality. Positivist modes of inquiry emphasize the need for researcher objectivity and minimize the role of interpretation in social scientific research. From this perspective, the effects of the researcher's own social position on the research process must be controlled or eliminated. Thus positivists might sound an alarm about a lesbian researcher who has herself participated in a commitment ritual conducting a study on same-sex marriage. For my part, I am deeply skeptical of the ability of *any* researcher to achieve complete objectivity in a research enterprise that focuses on questions of human meaning. In this kind of interpretive work, I strive to occupy a position of "conscious partiality" (Mies 1983), aware of my own beliefs and interests, sensitive to how they might influence my research approach, and open to the possibility that my own perspective will be transformed by my active engagement in the re-search process. I have also been influenced by feminist perspectives on research methodology, especially the view of research findings as the collaborative prod-uct of the researcher and the researched, and also standpoint theory's notion of the epistemic advantage of the socially disadvantaged (Harding 1996), which holds that researchers who themselves experience social marginalization may have an advantage in understanding and interpreting the experiences of other socially disadvantaged actors.

2: DOING THE RITE THING: CULTURAL PRACTICES OF COMMITMENT

1 Disapproval of homosexuality in the United States has softened somewhat in recent years but remains the majority view. In the General Social Survey conducted by the National Opinion Research Center, respondents are asked whether "sexual relations between two adults of the same sex" are "always wrong, almost always wrong, wrong only sometimes, or not wrong at all." The proportion responding "always wrong" remained near or above 70 percent during the 1970s and 1980s but declined noticeably in the 1990s. In 1998, 56 percent responded that homosexual behavior was "always wrong," compared to 31 percent who said it was "not wrong at all" (Loftus 2001, 767).

2 Civil unions differ from other public commitment rituals because they have a legal component, but the civil unions data are nonetheless relevant to gauging gender differences in interest in public rituals. The civil unions law requires couples to participate in a union ceremony with a state-approved officiant, meaning all civil unions are by definition created out of public commitment rituals. And over 80 percent of the couples who have entered civil unions in Vermont are not state residents (Bayles 2004), meaning most couples enter civil unions for their symbolic value rather than their legal effects, since civil unions are not legally recognized by other states or by the federal government.

3 On the first day that marriage licenses were available to same-sex couples, two-thirds of the same-sex couples who applied for a license were female (Greenberger and Dedman 2004). The pattern held up over time, with roughly two-thirds of the marriage licenses issued to same-sex couples in the first year of legal marriage going to female couples (Bellafante 2005). Of course, the data on gender differences in obtaining Massachusetts marriage licenses are less directly relevant to the issue of gender differences in public commitment rituals, since these licenses bring legal as well as symbolic benefits.

4 There is probably a great amount of overlap in the reasons for the gender differences in participation in non-legal commitment ceremonies and in accessing legal statuses such as civil unions or marriage (where available). Differences in gender socialization, parenting status, and cultural values around monogamy all could contribute to women's higher interest in public commitment rituals as well as their greater use of legal partnership recognition. One additional factor that might explain women's greater use of legal recognition statuses, but is probably irrelevant to their greater interest in public rituals, is the difference in men's and women's economic situations. Women earn less than men, on average, so they may have greater economic incentive to enter legal unions that will provide some financial security and material benefits (Bellafante 2005).

5 Of course, in some instances the standard ceremony materials required modification to suit the specific circumstances of a same-sex ritual. A Reform rabbi explained to me that the main difference between same-sex ceremonies and heterosexual weddings involves language. At the end of the exchange of

rings in the Jewish wedding ritual, the traditional formula for the blessing is: "Behold you are consecrated to me with this ring, according to the law of Moses and Israel." This final phrase must be changed for same-sex ceremonies, according to the rabbi, because technically these rituals are not in conformance with "the law of Moses and Israel," that is, Jewish law. In addition, the rabbi noted that the seven blessings, which follow the betrothal in the Jewish rite, contain numerous references to the bride and groom, so same-sex couples also must alter the gender-specific language in this part of the ceremony.

6 This finding suggests that practices of "drag" or cross-dressing are themselves gendered, in the sense that they carry profoundly different meanings for male and female practitioners. Perhaps this is unsurprising given the broader social context of gender inequality: for men, dressing in female attire holds the risk of a loss of power and status through identification with the female/feminine, whereas for women cross-dressing may represent a (temporary) claim to male power and status. Thus male cross-dressing can be either playful and comical (drag queens) or furtive and shame-inducing ("closet" transvestites), but rarely a serious strategy for improving one's social position. By contrast, history is replete with examples of women who successfully "passed" as men to gain access to the symbolic and material privileges of maleness.

7 There is relatively little social science literature on contemporary US wedding rituals. In his study of dating and marriage practices using 1984 data from the Detroit Area Study, Whyte (1990) compared the wedding practices of three cohorts: those married in 1925–1944 (prewar), those married in 1945–1964 (baby boom) and those married in 1965–1984 (recent). Whyte found some trends toward increasing religiosity and "elaborateness" in the construction of wedding rituals. The use of religious officials as officiants held steady across the three cohorts at 82 percent, but Whyte found an increase in the use of religious settings (churches, synagogues, etc.) as the site of the ritual, from 68 percent in the prewar and baby boom cohorts to 74 percent in the recent cohort. Whyte found indicators of increasing wedding "elaborateness" in terms of increases across cohorts in the median number of wedding guests (from 30 in the prewar cohort to 80 in the recent cohort), the percentage of weddings accompanied by a reception (from 64 percent in the prewar cohort to 88 percent in the recent cohort) and the median number of guests attending receptions (from 50 in the prewar cohort to 150 in the recent cohort). Whyte's data do not include information on the specific content of the rituals, however. A more recent analysis of marriage license data from eighteen states found that the proportion of marriage ceremonies performed by civil rather than religious authorities increased or held steady in most states between 1980 and 2001. In these states, the rate of non-religious civil marriages averaged 40 percent of all marriages in 2001, up from about 30 percent in 1980 (Grossman and Yoo 2003).

8 The meaning of the term "coming out" has shifted over time. It generally refers to the process of coming to accept a gay or lesbian identity and to sharing that identity with others. Chauncey (1994) traces its origins to a campy reference to the high-society ritual of debutantes' introduction to

the society of their peers. In pre-World War II American cities, gay men "came out" by attending "enormous drag balls that were patterned on the debutante and masquerade balls of the dominant culture" and the phrase did not become associated with the idea of coming out of "the closet" until much later (Chauncey 1994, 7). In the post-Stonewall period, gay liberationists suffused the practice of "coming out" with political meaning. "To come out of 'the closet' quintessentially expressed the fusion of the personal and the political that the radicalism of the late 1960s exalted," according to D'Emilio (1983, 235). Most non-historical scholarship on "coming out" is now concentrated in psychology, where there has been an effort to identify the distinct stages in the process of gay identity formation as well as variations in coming-out experiences along dimensions such as gender and race/ethnicity (Troiden 1998; Gonsiorek and Rudolph 1991). The ruling consensus is that coming out as gay or lesbian should be viewed as an ongoing process rather than a one-time event, and a fairly non-linear process at that.

9 The United Fellowship of Metropolitan Community Churches is a Christian denomination with a special outreach to gays, lesbians, bisexuals and transgendered people. The denomination was founded in 1968 by Rev. Troy Perry, a former Pentecostal minister who had been defrocked for his homosexuality. The UFMCC now has approximately 300 churches in eighteen different countries, with total membership exceeding 30,000. The denomination has been active on a range of gay and lesbian issues, including advocacy for legal recognition of same-sex marriage.

10 The cultural and political consequences of making gay and lesbian lives visible vary by context and the end results are sometimes ambiguous. For example, in his study of depictions of sexual minorities on daytime TV talk shows, Joshua Gamson (1998) describes the "tightrope of visibility" confronting sexual minority communities. On one hand, the kind of visibility offered by talk shows offers the chance to familiarize straight audiences with gay and lesbian lives and perhaps increase tolerance and understanding of sexual minorities. On the other hand, the shows are commercial enterprises with an economic interest in sensationalizing people's lives and identities, and sexual minorities do not have complete control over how they are represented on the shows. (The greater tolerance for some may come at the expense of increased stigmatization of others, as when gays and lesbians are featured as normal in contrast to bisexuals and transgender people.) The resulting risk is that sexual minorities will be depicted as freaks in shows meant to highlight their otherness rather than their humanness. Gamson's case illustrates a broader tension within sexual minority communities between those who wish to manage queer visibility to achieve greater social acceptance and those who prefer a more confrontational use of visibility to celebrate difference and challenge the norms and values of the dominant culture. Same-sex commitment rituals generally seem to represent the former approach to visibility, seeking to depict the reality of gay and lesbian lives in a way that emphasizes similarity rather than difference.

11 In the year of Shepard's murder, there were 1,260 hate-crimes incidents motivated by sexual orientation bias reported nationwide, representing 16 percent of all federally reported hate crimes. Many more such crimes

are thought to go unreported due to victims' fear of stigmatization and mistreatment at the hands of law enforcement.

12 It should be noted that these rituals preceded the arrival of legal same-sex marriage in Massachusetts and the spread of civil disobedience elsewhere, which often took the form of ceremonies with dubious legal effect but clear symbolic content. It seems plausible that couples holding commitment ceremonies today might have a more explicitly political understanding of their own action, given recent events and the current political and legal climate. These interviews from the pre-Massachusetts era, then, might help to document how a particular form of cultural practice evolved from being primarily a personal event with political implications to being an event created with a more conscious political purpose.

3: HOW DO I LOVE THEE? QUESTIONING THE MARRIAGE MODEL

1 Ettelbrick has softened her opposition to the goal of legal marriage somewhat since she wrote the piece for *OUT/LOOK*. In more recent writings she argues that marriage rights should be pursued as one piece of a broader approach that extends benefits and protections to various kinds of "functional families," not just those centered around a married couple (Ettelbrick 1996, 2001; Ettelbrick and Shapiro 2004).

2 Warner is curiously silent on the question of parenting and the socialization of future citizens. Parenting and stable long-term sexual couples are obviously two different things, but it is their tight conceptual and empirical linkage that leads many to believe that the state does in fact have an interest in fostering stable, long-term couples.

3 Some but not all marriage advocates are explicit in their rejection of the liberationist strand in gay politics and culture. Jonathan Rauch (2004, 56), for example, states: "Marriage not only blesses our unions; it changes them. It changes us. It closes the book on gay liberation: it liberates us from liberation, if you will. And that is good." By contrast, Michael Warner situates his critique of marriage within a broader critique of current gay and lesbian politics, arguing that the gay and lesbian movement is turning into "an instrument for the normalization of queer life" (1999, 80).

4 A classic statement of gay liberationist thought is Carl Wittman's "Refugees from Amerika: A Gay Manifesto," first published in 1970. "Traditional marriage is a rotten, oppressive institution," Wittman asserted, and "[g]ay people must stop measuring their self-respect by how well they mimic straight marriages." According to gay liberationist philosophy, people's need for love, security and a sense of belonging can be met by a range of close relationships. "The things we want to get away from," Wittman wrote, "are: 1. exclusiveness, propertied attitudes toward each other, a mutual pact against the rest of the world; 2. promises about the future, which we have no right to make and which prevent us from, or make us feel guilty about, growing; 3. inflexible roles, roles which do not reflect us at the moment but are inherited through mimicry and inability to define equalitarian relationships" (Wittman 1972, 161–162).

5 Lower rates of open relationships in my sample may partly reflect the specific focus of my study, i.e., sexually exclusive couples may have been more interested than nonexclusive couples in participating in a study focused on marriage. It is also possible that some male study participants were uncomfortable talking about sexual nonexclusivity with a female researcher.

6 In some other parts of the world, most notably in Scandinavia and in Quebec, Canada, long-term cohabitation has established itself as a socially accepted alternative to marriage, even for couples who become parents (Kiernan 2002; Le Bourdais and Lapierre-Adamcyk 2004).

7 Criteria for coding of socioeconomic status included self-report, occupation, education level, home ownership, and size, appearance and location of the residence (almost all interviews were conducted in the study participants' homes). If the couple's finances were merged, both members were assigned the same code. If separate finances were maintained, the partners were coded individually. Because I did not ask study participants to report their income or net worth, some judgment was necessary in assigning these codes. The general guidelines I used were as follows:

Upper Middle Class: self-report as "upper middle class," "upper class" or similar (e.g. "doing very well"); professional occupation; college or graduate-level education; owner of expensive home (estimated value in excess of $150,000) or renter in high-rent location.

Middle Class: self-report of "middle class" or similar; semi-professional or administrative occupation; college or graduate education; owner of moderately expensive home (estimated value of $100,000–$150,000) or renter in moderate-rent location.

Lower Middle Class/Working Class: self-report of "lower middle class," "working class," or similar (e.g. "struggling"); manual or semi-skilled occupation; less than college education; owner of inexpensive home (estimated value less than $100,000) or renter in lower-rent location.

Obviously few people would precisely meet all the criteria for any one category, so study participants were assigned to the category that most closely matched their characteristics.

8 The sample also contained three people – all from the ritual participant group –who mentioned they had previously participated in a same-sex commitment ritual with a different partner. Two of these prior rituals were public and one was private. I did not specifically ask study participants whether they had participated in such rituals with other partners in the past, so it is possible that other study participants also have such a history but did not mention it during the interview.

9 To gain a sense of study participants' embeddedness in lesbian and gay communities and cultures, I asked a number of specific questions near the end of the interview. These included questions about people's primary social networks (who are the people they are closest to, spend the most time with, would turn to in a crisis), their consumption of gay-specific culture and information (reading gay publications, attending gay cultural events), and their level of involvement with gay organizations and institutions (through volunteering, membership, paid staff work, or financial or other support). Based on their answers, I coded all study participants along two dimensions

of embeddedness in gay communities and cultures, the dimensions of "networks" and "practices." For primary social networks, people were coded according to whether their networks were a) minimally or not at all composed of other gays and lesbians, b) an even mix of gays/lesbians and straights, or c) primarily other gays and lesbians. For practices, I coded study participants according to whether they were a) minimally or not at all involved in gay/lesbian communities and cultures, b) moderately involved, or c) heavily involved.

Although I developed distinct categories for coding purposes, it makes the most sense to think of these two dimensions – networks and practices – as continuums with ideal types at either pole. With regard to social networks, the ideal types would include, at one pole, someone who has no gay or lesbian friends or acquaintances, and at the other pole, someone whose primary social networks are composed exclusively of other gays and lesbians. My sample did not include anyone who represented either of these ideal types, although many study participants clearly were closer to one or the other pole of the continuum. Similarly, the continuum of practices runs from one pole, whose ideal type has no participation in any aspect of gay/lesbian cultures or communities, to the opposite pole, with an ideal type of total immersion in gay/lesbian cultures and communities. Here, too, my sample contained no ideal types but included many people who were closer to one or the other pole of the practices continuum. Taken together, these two dimensions of networks and practices provide a sense of the relative importance of "gayness" – gay people, activities and institutions – in study participants' daily lives.

Various structural constraints might influence people's positions on the networks and practices continuums, including social, geographic, economic and informational constraints. For example, some study participants complained that they simply could not afford tickets to many of the community events that appealed to them, and people in far suburbs also indicated that their distance from the city prevented them from more frequent involvement in gay and lesbian organizations and events. Thus, it would be wrong to assume that people freely choose their positions on these continuums and that their positions can somehow be read as straightforward indicators of their interest in, or commitment to, gay and lesbian communities and cultures. It should also be acknowledged that, in addition to constraints that "push" people away from gay communities and cultures, other factors may "pull" them toward other (non-gay) commitments and involvements. For example, several study participants told me they would like to be more involved in gay and lesbian culture but they were currently quite focused on building their careers or on relationships with biological family members.

10 All study participants were coded for their level of "outness" and their desire for assimilation into mainstream society. For outness, I coded people according to whether they were a) out to few if any friends, co-workers and relatives, b) out to some but not all friends, co-workers and relatives, or c) out to all or almost all friends, co-workers and relatives. Aspiring to assimilation was coded dichotomously, according to the presence of any comments during the interview indicating a desire to assert "normalcy,"

strong critiques of perceived negative elements in gay/lesbian culture and behavior compared to mainstream society, or significant concern over media depictions of gay/lesbian people and lifestyles. Examples of comments that were coded "assimilationist" include Tim Daniels' comment that he felt it was important to call his commitment ceremony a wedding because that "helps to affirm us as being normal," and Gary Weaver's concerns that gay male culture is characterized by "arrested adolescence" and "endless partying." I did not ask specific interview questions designed to gauge the level of study participants' interest in assimilation. It is possible that if such questions had been included in the interview, more study participants would have been identified as aspiring to assimilation.

4: MAKING IT LEGAL: MARRIAGE, LAW AND LEGALITY

1 Hawaii uses the term "reciprocal beneficiaries" instead of "domestic partners." In Hawaii, this status is available to same-sex couples and to other relationships ineligible for marriage (e.g. an unmarried parent and his/her adult child). Vermont also has a reciprocal beneficiary status, enacted as part of the civil unions law, which makes a limited set of benefits available to people related by blood or adoption who are ineligible for marriage.

2 San Francisco pioneered the concept of equal benefits ordinances, passing its law in 1997. Other local governments that have passed equal benefits laws include Berkeley (CA), King County (WA), Los Angeles (CA), Minneapolis (MN), Oakland (CA), San Mateo County (CA), Seattle (WA) and Tumwater (WA). A statewide equal benefits law takes effect in California in 2007 (HRCF 2004, 16). New York City's equal benefits law was struck down by a state appellate court in early 2005 (HRCF 2005, 14).

3 For example, a recent Human Rights Campaign publication called *Answers to Questions About Marriage Equality* contains a section titled "Why Civil Unions Aren't Enough" (HRC n.d.). The report states: "Comparing marriage to civil unions is a bit like comparing diamonds to rhinestones. One is, quite simply, the real deal; the other is not" (HRC n.d., 6). The section then outlines the specific legal differences between marriage and civil unions.

4 This finding echoes the finding of Stiers (1999), who reports that all but one of the ninety gays and lesbians she interviewed favored legal same-sex marriage. Our findings differ, however, with respect to the distribution of reasons given for favoring legal same-sex marriage and also the level of priority the marriage issue should receive from gay rights groups. Stiers found that all of her study participants who favored legal marriage cited the issue of civil rights and equal treatment as a reason, and the majority (73 percent) cited the legal and economic benefits associated with legal marriage, whereas only 7 percent said it would legitimize gay relationships in the eyes of society (Stiers 1999, 165, Table 7.2). In my interviews, study participants also mentioned all of these reasons, but they expressed much greater interest in the impacts that legal same-sex marriage would have in terms of legitimizing same-sex relationships in society. A recent interview-based study of "non-heterosexuals" in Great Britain also found widespread support for the right to marriage, but also considerable anxiety about the dangers of assimilation to a heterosexual

norm; only a minority of the interviewees expressed a personal interest in marrying (Weeks, Heaphy and Donovan 2001, 192–5). This greater ambivalence toward marriage in the British sample may reflect cultural differences between Britain and the United States, as well as differences in the legal and financial benefits available through marriage versus other relationship statuses.

5 Some study participants seemed unaware of the fact that under the current tax code many married couples pay *higher* income taxes than they would if each filed individually as a single person (the so-called marriage penalty). However, there are income tax advantages to being married for some couples.

6 There are two transgender individuals in the study sample, Linda "Chico" Sanchez and Vicky Staples. Chico is anatomically female and discussed no interest in sex reassignment, but thinks of himself as a male and prefers to be addressed as a male. Near the beginning of the interview, when I asked about sexual orientation, Chico said he was "gay all the way . . . I consider myself a male." Chico said the preferred terminology for his relationship with Maria was "husband and wife." However, Chico did not self-identify as "transgender." Vicky Staples is a male-to-female post-operative transsexual. Vicky described her sexual identity as lesbian "with potential for erotic bisexuality." She explained that she does not currently identify as transsexual because she considers her sex change part of her history rather than part of her current identity.

7 Here again, my findings differ somewhat from those of Stiers (1999, 179), who found that most of her study participants who felt marriage should be a priority saw other issues as even more important. This difference might reflect the fact that Stiers' data is from the early 1990s, before events in Hawaii catapulted the same-sex marriage issue into the national spotlight and made legal marriage seem like a realistic short-term goal.

8 As of early 2005, sixteen states and the District of Columbia had anti-discrimination laws that provided comprehensive protection against sexual orientation discrimination (i.e. covering both public and private employers). An additional eleven states had laws covering only public employment. At the local level, 173 cities, counties and local government organizations had comprehensive employment protection (HRCF 2005, 27). Based on comparable data from a year earlier, I estimated that about 45 percent of the US population live in areas with employment protection based on sexual orientation in both the public and private sector (Hull 2005).

9 This disagreement among study participants about the causal relationship between law and social change parallels an ongoing debate among social scientists. On one side are scholars who argue that the historical record does not support the idea that legal reforms produce deep and lasting social change. These scholars sometimes argue that focusing on legal strategies and remedies is actually counterproductive to goals of social change. Important examples of this type of argument include Gerald Rosenberg's *The Hollow Hope* (1991), which argues that major court decisions such as *Brown v. Board of Education* and *Roe v. Wade* did not lead to the social changes they sought to produce, and Stuart Scheingold's *The Politics of Rights* (1974), which suggests that citizens are drawn in by a "myth of rights" promising social justice

and equality that the law cannot in fact deliver. On the other side are scholars who believe that, although the law may be an imperfect tool, legal change (or sometimes merely the pursuit of legal change) can lead to significant transformations in social behaviors and attitudes. A prominent example of this line of work is Michael W. McCann's *Rights at Work* (1994), documenting the positive impact of legal mobilization on the pay equity movement despite limited success in court cases. See Rochon (1998) for a general discussion of the relationship between legal/political and social change.

10 There are very few little data available on views about marriage and other forms of legal recognition held by the gay and lesbian population in the United States. The best recent data source is the exit polls conducted during the 2004 national election. According to Sherrill (n.d.), 51 percent of the voters who self-identified as gay, lesbian or bisexual supported legal same-sex marriage, 31 percent favored civil unions and 17 percent opposed any form of legal recognition for same-sex relationships. (The 17 percent opposed to any legal recognition for same-sex relationships seems high; these may be people who are philosophically opposed to state regulation of any intimate relationships regardless of the sex of the partners.)

11 My argument that same-sex couples forge a new normative order and establish a more formal identity as a couple through their rituals in some ways parallels Berger and Kellner's ([1964] 1977) description of marriage as a "*nomos*-building instrumentality" (5). Berger and Kellner argue that marriage creates a new order or sense of reality for the marriage partners, with consequences for how the partners think about their relationship and how they act:

> As of the marriage, most of each partner's actions must now be projected in conjunction with those of the other. Each partner's definitions of reality must be continually correlated with the definitions of the other. The other is present in nearly all horizons of everyday conduct. Furthermore, the identity of each now takes on a new character, having to be constantly matched with that of the other, indeed being typically perceived by people at large as being symbiotically conjoined with the identity of the other . . . In other words, from the beginning of the marriage each partner has new modes in his meaningful experience of the world in general, of other people, and of himself. By definition, then, marriage constitutes a nomic rupture. In terms of each partner's biography, the event of marriage initiates a new nomic process. (12)

Berger and Kellner wrote this essay in 1964, before premarital cohabitation had become a widespread practice, and so in a time when marriage usually marked a greater transition in the circumstances of daily living for the members of a couple. Nonetheless, it is interesting to observe the parallels between the kinds of changes brought on by (legal) marriage in Berger and Kellner's view, and the kinds of changes desired or experienced by the participants in same-sex commitment rituals. Berger and Kellner's notion of *nomos* is somewhat broader than the notion of legality I am employing, meant to capture how married couples jointly construct a shared reality for themselves, but the concepts do overlap.

12 Same-sex couples have the option of replicating some but not all of the benefits and protections of legal marriage through private contracting, as

discussed earlier in this chapter. Of the 38 couples represented in the study, 23 (61 percent) had put in place some legal protections for their relationship and/or parenting status at the time of the interview. Specific protections instituted by the couples included wills, trusts, living wills, powers of attorney for health care and/or property, guardianship provisions, domestic partnership registration, second-parent adoption of non-biological children and partnership agreements. Some couples had also taken more limited steps to establish themselves as an economic unit and protect against loss in the event of death or disability; such steps included joint tenancy mortgages and other joint ownership of property, and designation of partners as beneficiaries on insurance policies and investments. I classify these as more limited steps because they do not require the same level of initiative. Taking out a mortgage requires the borrower to decide what type of ownership will be used (individual, joint tenancy or tenants in common); likewise insurance policies and investments routinely request owners to designate a beneficiary in the event of death or disability.

13 Fraser is quick to acknowledge that "this distinction between economic injustice and cultural injustice is analytical" (1997, 15). In practice, "economic injustice and cultural injustice are usually interimbricated so as to reinforce each other dialectically" (15). In other words, the harms of misrecognition are often accompanied by, if not productive of, harms of maldistribution and vice versa. This is quite obviously the case with the denial of same-sex marriage recognition, which produces both socioeconomic and cultural harms for same-sex couples.

14 See Phelan (2001) for a thoughtful discussion of the citizenship status of sexual minorities in the United States.

5: SIN OR CIVIL RIGHT? DEBATING MARRIAGE IN THE STATES

1 A parallel set of debates is taking place in various religious denominations nationally and internationally. Many denominations are struggling over what form of religious recognition (if any) to grant to committed same-sex relationships, as well as other questions related to homosexuality, such as whether openly gay men and lesbians will be allowed to serve as clergy. See Moon (2004) for a rich ethnographic study of such struggles within two Methodist congregations in the Chicago area.

2 Specifically, the RBA allowed beneficiaries access to hospital visitation rights, inheritance rights, survivor benefits and initially health insurance coverage. But shortly after the RBA was signed into law, a group of private companies brought a lawsuit to challenge it, prompting the state attorney general to issue an advisory opinion that the health provisions of the act did not apply to public or private employers who self-insured for health coverage, effectively gutting the act's health coverage provisions (Goldberg-Hiller 1999).

3 The two sides were fairly well matched in terms of funding. According to a newspaper report after the election, STM spent $1.31 million on the amendment battle and POC spent $1.59 million ("Same-Sex Issue Cost" 1999, cited in Goldberg-Hiller 2002, 251 n83). An early news story reported that

the majority of STM's funding came from direct donations from the Mormon Church, and over half of POC's money came from individual contributions of $100 or less (Christiansen and Kresnak 1998).

4 In this respect, the Hawaii debates over same-sex marriage paralleled other state-level debates over anti-gay ballot initiatives seeking to block gay rights through constitutional amendments. Levin (1997) argues that the debates over a proposed anti-gay amendment in Idaho in 1994 revealed competing visions of constitutional democracy. "Liberals" conceived of the constitution as creating individual rights and protecting minorities, and they venerated the role of the courts in upholding such protections in the face of majority hostility. "Communitarians," by contrast, argued that the constitution should embody a moral consensus regarding public and private behavior, saw new rights for minorities as an imposition on the community's rights and viewed the role of the courts with skepticism. Thus Levin argues that the idea of the constitution functions as an ambiguous rhetorical symbol in these debates. For further discussion of state and local anti-gay initiatives, see Schacter (1994) and various papers in Witt and McCorkle (1997).

5 The most controversial ad run by POC seemed designed to answer that very question. It featured a local physician describing how some of the groups behind the push for the amendment were also strongly opposed to abortion. The ad suggested that if these groups were successful in passing the marriage amendment, they would next try to use the amendment process to repeal abortion rights in Hawaii. The ad drew widespread criticism, even from some supporters of POC.

6 One controversial TV ad featured a little boy sitting on a couch and reading aloud from the picture book *Daddy's Wedding*, a book meant to explain same-sex relationships to children. The ad focused in on a page of the book that shows two men kissing as the ad's off-screen narrator intoned: "If you have never really thought about how homosexual marriages will impact our society, think about how they will impact our children." Another STM television ad depicted a man and a woman in wedding garb running toward each other on the beach, only to have the man run past the bewildered woman and into the arms of another man.

7 The specific time periods examined were December 1996 through February 1997 and September through November 1998. I included all the letters on same-sex marriage I could find in the *Honolulu Star-Bulletin* and *Honolulu Advertiser* during these two periods. My sample of letters includes 105 letters published in the first period and 128 in the second period. I accessed these letters electronically from both the website of the *Star-Bulletin* and the web-based archives of an internet mailing list (or "listserv") devoted to same-sex marriage. The current web addresses for these data sources are <<http://starbulletin.com>> and <<http://lists.qrd.org/mailman/listinfo/marriage>>. The content of the *Advertiser* is not available online. One regular contributor to the marriage mailing list, a Hawaii resident, attempted to transcribe and post all letters on same-sex marriage from the major Honolulu papers. However, my own cross-checking with the *Star-Bulletin* website confirms that the mailing list does not contain every published letter from the periods of

interest, so my coverage of letters from the *Advertiser* is likely less complete than from the *Star-Bulletin*. In addition, the *Star-Bulletin* website does not include the Sunday edition, so I may be missing a small number of letters that appeared on Sundays and were not posted to the mailing list. My sample includes 181 letters from the *Star-Bulletin* and 52 from the *Advertiser*.

8 As data on public opinion, letters to the editor have some rather obvious limitations (Grey and Brown 1970) but also some important strengths. Only some of the letters received by the newspapers are actually printed, and the selection criteria of the editors are unknown, so the letters printed may not be representative of the letters received. Also, people who write letters to the editor may not be representative of the general public; in fact, some past research has shown them to be wealthier, better educated and more politically active than average (Buell 1975; Volgy et al. 1977). They may also have stronger feelings or more "extreme" views about the issue prompting them to write (Volgy et al. 1977). The letters tend to be brief, or they are edited for length, so the richness of their content is restricted by their form. And, activists on controversial topics often organize letter-writing campaigns intended to bombard the newspapers with a particular viewpoint, sometimes even providing the text of letters for others to sign and send.

Despite these various limitations, the letters to the editor in the Hawaii newspapers have certain advantages as an empirical window onto non-elite public debates on same sex-marriage. They are unobtrusive measures (Webb et al. 1966). As a form of persuasive communication, they usually contain arguments meant to justify positions, rather than just a bare statement of position. This is particularly useful for assessing the kinds of arguments or framings of the issue that circulate and receive validation in the public sphere. And the fact that the letters are likely the product of people with particularly strong views can be an advantage, since these individuals may provide fuller and more complex statements of the justifications offered in support of competing positions. At least two studies of letters to the editor on provocative political issues found that letters can in fact be representative of public opinion when the issue addressed stimulates strong feelings and a large volume of letters (Hill 1981; Sigelman and Walkosz 1992), although a recent study of letters on a controversial anti-gay initiative in Idaho found the letters did not reflect public opinion (McCorkle and Most 1997). In an era of heavy reliance on opinion polls and survey data, letters provide a glimpse of the kinds of arguments presented by everyday people to justify the positions quantified by polls and surveys. As Herbst (1993, 62) states in reviewing historical trends in the expression and measurement of public opinion, "Letters to public officials and editors seem to be one of the few modern exceptions to the pattern of increasing rationalization of expression."

9 Other themes mentioned in support of same-sex marriage, appearing somewhat less frequently, included: the argument that same-sex marriage is a minor issue and the state of Hawaii needs to focus on important problems like its economy and threats to tourism (13 letters); the fact that so-called "traditional" families have plenty of problems of their own, such as divorce and child abuse (9 letters); the idea that same-sex marriage is an expression of love and does not hurt others or detract from heterosexual marriage

(7 letters); the notion that same-sex marriage represents true family values (5 letters); the need to protect the state's constitution (5 letters); the idea that homosexuality is innate, not a choice or a learned behavior (3 letters); critiques of media coverage of the issue (3 letters); and the notion that if one group's rights can be taken away, no one is safe (3 letters).

10 The "Aloha Spirit" is actually defined by statute in Hawaii. The definition reads:

"Aloha Spirit" is the coordination of mind and heart within each person. It brings each person to the self. Each person must think and emote good feelings to others. In the contemplation and presence of the life force, "Aloha," the following unuhi laula loa [free translations] may be used:

"Akahai" meaning kindness, to be expressed with tenderness;
"Lokahi" meaning unity, to be expressed with harmony;
"Oluolu" meaning agreeable, to be expressed with pleasantness;
"Haahaa" meaning humility, to be expressed with modesty;
"Ahonui" meaning patience, to be expressed with perseverance.

These are traits of character that express the charm, warmth, and sincerity of Hawaii's people . . . "Aloha" is more than a word of greeting or farewell. "Aloha" means mutual regard and affection and extends warmth and caring with no obligation in return. "Aloha" is the essence of relationships in which each person is important to every other person for collective existence. (Hawaii Revised Statutes section 5–7.5, quoted in Morris 1996, 119)

11 Other themes that appeared less frequently in the letters opposing same-sex marriage included: concern that same-sex marriage will destroy society (9 letters); people's right to change the constitution or the need to return to the framers' intent (9 letters); family values, ill effects on kids, importance of procreation (8 letters); fear of a negative impact on Hawaii's image and tourism (6 letters); equating gays with disease and death (5 letters); critiques of the media coverage of the issue (5 letters); and rejection of the idea that this issue was comparable to other oppressions (4 letters).

12 This letter-writer conflated opposition to the constitutional amendment with "support of gay marriage," although in fact the League had only taken a position against the amendment without stating a position on the desirability of same-sex marriage.

13 The briefs filed by the appellants and the state were accessed online at <<http://www.vtfreetomarry.org/-fs_lawsuit.html>>.

14 Justice John Dooley wrote a concurring opinion in which he expressed agreement with the majority opinion's central finding (that the marriage statutes violated the Common Benefits Clause of the constitution) and remedy, but took issue with the opinion's reasoning. Dooley asserted that the case should have been treated as a civil rights case triggering heightened scrutiny (i.e. holding the state to a higher standard in terms of justifying its exclusion of same-sex couples from marriage). Dooley argued that it would be consistent with Vermont law and past judicial opinions to treat gays and lesbians as a "suspect class," because they represent a discrete social group with a clear history of disfavored treatment. The majority opinion, however,

opted not to use this type of legal analysis and instead maintained that the court must simply weigh the state's claimed interest in excluding same-sex couples from marriage against the guarantee of equality embedded in the Common Benefits Clause. Specifically, the majority opinion declared that the state must justify its exclusion of same-sex couples by showing that the exclusion bore a "reasonable and just relation to the governmental objective in light of contemporary conditions."

15 I obtained audio recordings of both the January 25 and February 1 public hearings from the Clerk of the House of the Vermont Legislature. The recording quality for the January 25 hearing was so poor that it was not feasible to transcribe that hearing, so I limited my analysis to the latter hearing. A research assistant transcribed the February 1 recording, which included the testimony of 89 witnesses. News reports said roughly a hundred people testified on February 1, and a summary report prepared by the chair of the House Judiciary Committee placed the total at 110 witnesses, so it appears that the testimony of about 10–20 witnesses did not make it onto the audio recording. The hearing transcript was coded and analyzed using ATLAS.ti software for qualitative data analysis.

16 Of course, the Vermont testimony is representative of the views only of those citizens who were willing to travel to the capitol for the hearing and speak before a large public gathering which was broadcast live on television and radio. As with the case of letters to the editor, such a forum for expressing opinion on an issue likely draws people who have strong views one way or the other. Thus, the testimony cannot be taken as completely representative of the views of all Vermont residents.

17 One witness who testified against same-sex marriage and expressed support for a constitutional amendment to define marriage as a male–female union did also tell the legislators, "I would challenge you to provide help for these people that are being denied their legal rights." However, he did not specify how the legislature should go about helping same-sex couples gain rights, or which rights he had in mind.

18 Other themes that occurred less frequently in the testimony of witnesses supporting same-sex marriage included freedom, democracy, and the lack of impact of same-sex marriage on heterosexuals or on society generally. A few witnesses argued that appeals to tradition were a flawed argument for excluding same-sex couples from marriage, and two witnesses suggested that opponents of same-sex marriage used Bible passages selectively. Two witnesses argued that homosexuality is natural, and two argued for same-sex marriage as a way to give recognition and legitimacy to same-sex relationships.

19 See Goldberg-Hiller's (2002) study of the Hawaii case for a detailed discussion of this dynamic, in which minority rights become framed as an excessive imposition or intrusion on the rights and sovereignty of an embattled majority.

20 Moral arguments for same-sex marriage might also entail certain risks or costs. Insofar as these arguments invoke comparisons to heterosexual marriage as a standard or ideal for intimate relationship, they may serve to reinforce heteronormativity and thereby inadvertently contribute to the

ongoing subordination of gays and lesbians. Similar concerns have been raised by Honig (1993) and Babst (1997) in their critical discussions of strategies for overturning sodomy statutes that rely on demonstrating the fundamental sameness of homosexual relationships to heterosexual marriage. Another potentially significant cost to moral arguments in favor of same-sex marriage inheres in their possible impact on gays and lesbians who choose to express their sexuality outside the confines of marriage-like relationships. By arguing that same-sex marriage is good, its proponents may create the impression that other forms of same-sex intimacy are less good. Both Ettelbrick (1992) and Warner (1999) argue that same-sex marriage would create new forms of inequality among gays and lesbians by further stigmatizing same-sex relationships and sex outside the context of marriage. Existing normative arguments for same-sex marriage also seem problematic insofar as they continue to bracket (ironically enough) the fundamental question of the morality of homosexuality itself. Arguing that same-sex marriage will promote relationship stability will not persuade those who completely oppose any manifestation of homosexuality; in fact, it might strengthen their opposition. To the extent that opposition to same-sex marriage is grounded in deeply held convictions that homosexuality itself is morally wrong, convincing normative arguments for same-sex marriage might need to first address this more fundamental question of the moral status of homosexual desires and behaviors. Alternatively, supporters of same-sex marriage could try to convince opponents that their moral views on homosexuality should not form the basis for public policy because they are grounded in religion or because they violate a basic tenet of liberalism by favoring one definition of the good life (heterosexuality) over another.

21 Thirteen state constitutional amendments were passed in the 2004 election cycle following the issuance of marriage licenses to Massachusetts couples. The states that passed amendments in the summer or fall of 2004 are Arkansas, Georgia, Kentucky, Louisiana, Michigan, Mississippi, Missouri, Montana, North Dakota, Ohio, Oklahoma, Oregon and Utah. States that had passed amendments in earlier years are Alaska (1998), Hawaii (1998), Nebraska (2000) and Nevada (2002). The Hawaii amendment technically does not ban same-sex marriage but empowers the state legislature to do so. Kansas passed an amendment in early 2005, bringing the total number of state amendments to eighteen. Eleven of the eighteen state amendments include language to prohibit not only same-sex marriage but other forms of legal recognition such as civil unions or domestic partnerships.

22 I agree with Ball (2003) that marriage is not the *only* way the state can support human flourishing in intimate relationships, and in the next chapter I argue for the desirability of creating a range of state recognitions and supports for close relationships of all kinds.

6: CONCLUSION: MARRIAGE AND BEYOND

1 Given the high divorce rate, this faith in marriage as a way to ensure relationship permanence might appear misplaced. The fact that some gays and lesbians believe that marriage has the power to hold relationships together,

in the face of resounding evidence to the contrary, attests to the mystified quality of marriage in contemporary society.

2   This notion of an alternative legality is hinted at in a curious and ironic bit of street lingo that Anderson relates. Anderson observes that part of the code of the street is doing what you can to get by, without consideration for whether acts are officially legal or illegal. Thus ghetto residents who are most fully committed to "the street" are often active in the illegal drug trade, and on the street this involvement is referred to as "getting legal" (Anderson 1999, 103).

3   Many of the recent legal measures to block same-sex marriage reflect this viewpoint, insofar as they bar not only the recognition of same-sex marriages but also other forms of legal recognition that grant the benefits of marriage, approximate or resemble marriage, or constitute its legal equivalent. Nine of the thirteen state constitutional amendments passed in 2004 blocking same-sex marriage also contain a more expansive prohibition of legal recognition; the specific language varies across the amendments. Years of litigation will undoubtedly be required to sort out the scope of these prohibitions, for example whether they prohibit state governments and university systems from providing same-sex domestic partner benefits to their employees. (A constitutional amendment passed in Nebraska in 2000 also contains a broadly worded ban on relationship recognition for same-sex couples and in early 2005 a federal judge ruled the amendment unconstitutional, but the ruling is subject to appeal.)

4   Two recent examples of the state seeking to influence cultural understandings of marriage are the 1996 welfare reform legislation and the Bush administration's ongoing marriage initiative. The welfare reform law (the Personal Responsibility and Work Opportunity Reconciliation Act of 1996) frames the problem of welfare dependence primarily as a problem of unmarried parenting. The findings section of the law (which is meant to establish the need for welfare reform) begins with the following statements: "(1) Marriage is the foundation of a successful society. (2) Marriage is an essential institution of a successful society which promotes the interests of children" (Public Law 104–193). The stated goals of the 1996 legislation include promotion of marriage and reduction of out-of-wedlock pregnancies. The Bush administration's Healthy Marriage Initiative is headed by the federal Administration for Children and Families, the same agency responsible for administering the welfare program. The marriage initiative provides funding to projects that seek to improve marriage's cultural standing, especially but not only among the low-income population. Proposed activities listed on the initiative's website include public education campaigns and high school education programs extolling "the value of healthy marriages" (<<http://www.acf.dhhs.gov/healthymarriage/about/mission.html>>, accessed on 12/13/04).

5   A December 2003 Gallup poll found that 44 percent of respondents age 18–29 agreed that "[h]omosexual marriage should be recognized by law," compared to 33 percent of 30–49 year olds, 27 percent of 50–64 year olds, and 16 percent of those age 65 or older (Bowman and O'Keefe 2004, 23). Other recent polls have found similar age differences in support for same-sex marriage (Bowman and O'Keefe 2004, 24–27).

6 For example, a CBS News/*New York Times* poll conducted in November 2004 asked: "Which comes closest to your view? Gay couples should be allowed to legally marry. OR, Gay couples should be allowed to form civil unions but not legally marry. OR, There should be no legal recognition of a gay couple's relationship." 21 percent favored legal marriage, 32 percent favored civil unions and 44 percent favored no legal recognition, with 3 percent unsure. (Poll results accessed on 1/3/05 at <<http://www. pollingreport. com/civil.htm>>.) Several earlier polls found similar majority support for either legal marriage or civil unions (see Bowman and O'Keefe 2004, 26–34). A 2004 *Los Angeles Times* poll found that 59 percent of Americans believe that legal same-sex marriage is inevitable (Mehren 2004).

7 The line of US Supreme Court decisions establishing marriage as a fundamental right includes *Loving v. Virginia* (1967), ruling anti-miscegenation statutes an unconstitutional infringement of the freedom to marry; *Zablocki v. Redhail* (1978), invalidating a state law that prohibited remarriage by a person who had unpaid support obligations from a previous marriage; and *Turner v. Safely* (1987), invalidating a state law that barred marriage by most prison inmates. For recent, extended discussions of same-sex marriage and constitutional law, see Gerstmann (2004) and Strasser (1997).

8 Under current legal conditions, Vermont same-sex marriages would have encountered similar portability problems, just as Massachusetts same-sex marriages now do. This lack of portability results from the federal Defense of Marriage Act (DOMA), comparable state-level statutes (the so-called baby-DOMAs), and state constitutional amendments prohibiting recognition of same-sex marriages performed in other states. The Massachusetts marriages may have a long-term advantage over civil unions on the portability question, though, as the federal DOMA, state DOMAs and even state constitutional amendments can be challenged as unconstitutional abridgments of a fundamental right to marry seated in the US Constitution.

9 Mary McIntosh (1968) makes a similar point about the homo–hetero binary in her classic essay on the "homosexual role." McIntosh notes that the labeling of homosexuality as a distinct form of deviant sexuality serves as a form of social control that segregates the deviants from the rest of society: "The creation of a specialized, despised, and punished role of homosexual keeps the bulk of society pure" (183–184). Perhaps marriage serves as a totem not only for the sacredness of heterosexuality, but also and relatedly for the sacredness of a gender system characterized by two distinct, non-overlapping, essentialized, functionally opposite and complementary genders.

10 See the poll results cited in note 6, above.

11 See Rubenstein (1997) for a general discussion of this coordination problem in the realm of gay rights litigation. A concrete example of such coordination problems recently emerged in Florida, where Ellis Rubin, a lawyer not affiliated with any of the major national gay rights groups, began filing lawsuits in both state and federal courts pressing the marriage rights of same-sex couples. (In a bizarre twist, Rubin was also the lawyer for Anita Bryant in her successful effort to repeal a gay rights ordinance in Dade County, Florida in the late 1970s.) Gay rights groups opposed his actions,

citing a hostile legal/political climate and the likelihood of setting unfavorable legal precedents. After initial defeats in federal court, Rubin was eventually persuaded by the gay rights groups to drop the lawsuits (see Silvestrini 2005).

12 Two prominent and much-debated examples of proposals to grant legal recognition to non-marital relationships are a 2002 report by the American Law Institute (ALI) titled *Principles of the Law of Family Dissolution* and a 2001 report by the Law Commission of Canada (LCC) titled *Beyond Conjugality: Recognizing and Supporting Close Personal Adult Relationships*. The ALI report recommended treating cohabiting relationships as de facto legal unions at the time of their dissolution, giving cohabitors the same rights and responsibilities as married spouses with respect to support payments and property distribution (ALI 2002). In Canada, the Modernization of Benefits and Obligations Act, passed in 2000, mandates virtually equal treatment of all cohabiting couples regardless of marital status and covers both opposite-sex and same-sex couples. (Unmarried cohabitors are covered by the law after living together for one year.) The LCC *Beyond Conjugality* report recommended expanding legal recognition of adult relationships even farther, to cover a broader range of close relationships of care and support, including nonsexual and non-cohabiting relationships. The report proposed a registration system that would allow people to register their important adult relationships and to make conscious and informed choices about the rights and responsibilities to accompany that registration. The LCC stopped short of recommending that such a system of partnership registration replace legal marriage, mainly because this move was deemed politically impossible in the current climate (LCC 2001).

13 Major works cited by Amato as representing the marital decline perspective include David Popenoe's *Life Without Father* (1996), Linda Waite and Maggie Gallagher's *The Case for Marriage* (2000) and James Q. Wilson's *The Marriage Problem* (2002). Cited works representing the marital resiliency perspective include Stephanie Coontz's *The Way We Never Were* (1992), Arlene Skolnick's *Embattled Paradise* (1991) and Judith Stacey's *In the Name of the Family* (1996).

14 My categorization of the three perspectives on marriage combines Amato's identification of the two "camps" on marriage (marital decline vs. marital resiliency) with the categories sketched by Shanley (2004), who identifies the following three main positions: conservative (seeking to strengthen marriage and retain its definition as a monogamous heterosexual union); equal status (advocating equality between marriage partners and equal access to marriage for same-sex couples); and contractualist (proposing to abolish legal marriage and replace it with private contracts between partners). Based on my research on the marriage promotion movement in the United States, I view the marital decline perspective as including a diversity of views on the issue of same-sex marriage, and generally favoring equality within marriages (although this may be defined differently by different people). Also, Shanley identifies contractualism as the policy position advocated by marriage abolitionists, but I also see a second viewpoint among abolitionists, advocating for the replacement of marriage with an alternative legal status such as civil unions.

15 In a 2004 report titled *What Next for the Marriage Movement?*, leaders of the marriage promotion movement identified two crises in marriage law that threaten efforts to recreate a "marriage culture." The first crisis is the emergence of "changes intended to blur or eliminate entirely many of the legal distinctions between married and unmarried couples," and the second is the continuing conflict over same-sex marriage. The report is available at <<www.marriagemovement.org>>. At least one prominent gay commentator and supporter of same-sex marriage, Jonathan Rauch, has also taken the position that new relationship statuses have a destructive impact on marriage. Rauch (2004, Chapter 2) argues that people concerned with preserving marriage should get behind same-sex marriage in order to stem the proliferation of "marriage-lite" statuses that compete with marriage.

16 One notable real-world example of this kind of status is the reciprocal beneficiaries status in Vermont, established under the 2000 law creating civil unions. The reciprocal beneficiaries status gives people related by blood or adoption access to a limited set of spousal benefits and responsibilities, mostly related to medical care and arrangements upon the death of one member of the relationship.

Court cases

Baehr v. Lewin, 852 P.2d 44 (1993)

Baehr v. Miike, 994 P.2d 566 (1999)

Baker v. Nelson, 191 N.W.2d 185 (1971)

Baker v. State of Vermont, 744 A.2d 864 (1999)

Bowers v. Hardwick, 478 US 186 (1986)

Brown v. Board of Education, 347 US 483 (1954)

Goodridge v. Dept. of Public Health, 798 N.E.2d 941 (2003)

Jones v. Hallahan, 501 S.W.2d 588 (1973)

Lawrence v. Texas, 539 US 558 (2003)

Loving v. Virginia, 388 US 1 (1967)

Roe v. Wade, 410 US 113 (1973)

Romer v. Evans, 517 US 620 (1996)

Singer v. O'Hara, 522 P.2d 1187 (1974)

Turner v. Safely, 482 US 78 (1987)

Zablocki v. Redhail, 434 US 374 (1978)

References

Adam, Barry. 1987. *The Rise of a Gay and Lesbian Movement*. Boston: Twayne Publishers.

————. 2003. "Relationship Innovation in Male Couples." Paper presented at the American Sociological Association annual meeting, Atlanta, GA, August 2003.

Alexander, Jeffrey C., and Philip Smith. 1993. "The Discourse of American Civil Society: A New Proposal for Cultural Studies." *Theory and Society* 22: 151–207.

ALI: American Law Institute. 2002. *Priniciples of the Law of Family Dissolution: Analysis and Recommendations*. Newark (NJ): LexisNexis.

Amato, Paul R. 2004. "Tension between Institutional and Individual Views of Marriage." *Journal of Marriage and Family* 66: 959–965.

Anderson, Elijah. 1999. *Code of the Street: Decency, Violence, and the Moral Life of the Inner City*. New York: Norton.

Babst, Gordon A. 1997. "Community, Rights Talk, and the Communitarian Dissent in Bowers v. Hardwick." Pp. 139–172 in *Playing with Fire: Queer Politics, Queer Theories*, edited by Shane Phelan. New York and London: Routledge.

Ball, Carlos. 2003. *The Morality of Gay Rights: An Exploration in Political Philosophy*. New York and London: Routledge.

Bayles, Fred. 2004. "Vermont's Gay Civil Unions Mostly Affairs of the Heart." *USA Today*, January 7.

Becker, Howard. 1966. "Notes on the Concept of Commitment." *American Journal of Sociology* 66: 32–40.

Bellafante, Ginia. 2005. "Even in Gay Circles, the Women Want the Ring." *New York Times*, May 8.

Berger, Peter L., and Hansfried Kellner. [1964] 1977. "Marriage and the Construction of Reality." In *Facing Up to Modernity: Excursions in Society, Politics, and Religion*, by Peter L. Berger. New York: Basic Books.

Bernstein, Mary. 1997. "Celebration and Suppression: The Strategic Uses of Identity by the Lesbian and Gay Movement." *American Journal of Sociology* 103: 531–565.

————. 2001. "Gender, Queer Family Policies, and the Limits of Law." In *Queer Families, Queer Politics: Challenging Culture and the State*, edited by Mary Bernstein and Renate Reimann. New York: Columbia University Press.

2002. "Identities and Politics: Toward a Historical Understanding of the Lesbian and Gay Movement." *Social Science History* 26: 531–581.

Blankenhorn, David. 1995. *Fatherless America*. New York: Basic Books.

Blumstein, Philip, and Pepper Schwartz. 1983. *American Couples: Money, Work, Sex*. New York: William Morrow and Company.

Bourassa, Kevin, and Joe Varnell. 2002. *Just Married: Gay Marriage and the Expansion of Human Rights*. Madison: University of Wisconsin Press.

Bourdieu, Pierre. 1977. *Outline of a Theory of Practice*. Translated by Richard Nice. Cambridge: Cambridge University Press.

——— 1987. "The Force of Law: Toward a Sociology of the Juridical Field." *Hastings Law Journal* 38: 805–853.

Bowman, Karlyn, and Bryan O'Keefe, comps. 2004. *Attitudes About Homosexuality and Gay Marriage*. Washington, DC: American Enterprise Institute.

Brady, Lois Smith. 2003. "For Gay Couples, New Rituals at the Altar." *New York Times*, November 23, National Edition, Sec. 9.

Brekhus, Wayne. 2003. *Peacocks, Chameleons, Centaurs: Gay Suburbia and the Grammar of Social Identity*. Chicago: University of Chicago Press.

Broder, John M. 2004. "Groups Debate Slower Strategy on Gay Rights." *New York Times*, December 9.

Buell, Emmett H., Jr. 1975. "Eccentrics or Gladiators? People Who Write About Politics in Letters to the Editor." *Social Science Quarterly* 56: 440–449.

Bumiller, Kristin. 1988. *The Civil Rights Society*. Baltimore: The Johns Hopkins University Press.

Bumpass, Larry, and Hsien-Hen Lu. 2000. "Trends in Cohabitation and Implications for Children's Family Contexts in the United States." *Population Studies* 54: 29–41.

Calhoun, Craig. 1993. "'New Social Movements' of the Early Nineteenth Century." *Social Science History* 17: 385–427.

Card, Claudia. 1996. "Against Marriage and Motherhood." *Hypatia* 11: 1–23.

Carrington, Christopher. 1999. *No Place Like Home: Relationships and Family Life Among Lesbians and Gay Men*. Chicago and London: University of Chicago Press.

Chambers, David L. 1996. "What If? The Legal Consequences of Marriage and the Legal Needs of Lesbian and Gay Male Couples." *Michigan Law Review* 95: 447–491.

Chasin, Alexandra. 2000. *Selling Out: The Gay and Lesbian Movement Goes to Market*. New York: St. Martin's Press.

Chauncey, George. 1994. *Gay New York: Gender, Urban Culture, and the Making of the Gay Male World, 1980–1940*. New York: Basic Books.

——— 2004. *Why Marriage? The History Shaping Today's Debate Over Gay Equality*. New York: Basic Books.

Cherlin, Andrew. 1992. *Marriage, Divorce, Remarriage: Revised and Enlarged Edition*. Cambridge: Harvard University Press.

——— 2004. "The Deinstitutionalization of American Marriage." *Journal of Marriage and Family* 66: 848–861.

Christiansen, Jean, and William Kresnak. 1998. "Mormons Give Big to Fight Same-Sex." *Honolulu Advertiser*, October 24.

CMFCE, IAV and RCFP: Coalition for Marriage, Family and Couples Education (CMFCE), Institute for American Values (IAV), and Religion, Culture, and Family Project (RCFP), University of Chicago Divinity School. 2000. *The Marriage Movement: a Statement of Principles*. New York: Institute for American Values.

Cohen, Philip N., and Suzanne M. Bianchi. 1999. "Marriage, Children, and Women's Employment: What Do We Know?" *Monthly Labor Review* 122: 22–31.

Comaroff, Jean, and John Comaroff. 1991. *Of Revelation and Revolution: Christianity, Colonialism, and Consciousness in South Africa*. Volume I. Chicago: University of Chicago Press.

Congregation for the Doctrine of the Faith. 2003. *Considerations Regarding Proposals to Give Legal Recognition to Unions Between Homosexual Persons*. July 31. Available at <http://www.vatican.va/roman_curia/congregations/cfaith/doc_doc_index.htm>>.

Coontz, Stephanie. 1992. *The Way We Never Were: American Families and the Nostalgia Trap*. New York: Basic Books.

2005. *Marriage, a History: From Obedience to Intimacy or How Love Conqueres Marriage*. New York: Viking.

Cott, Nancy F. 2000. *Public Vows: The History of Marriage and the Nation*. Cambridge: Harvard University Press.

Coulmont, Baptiste. 2004. "Devant Dieu et face au droit? Le mariage religieux des homosexuels aux Etats-Unis." ["Under God and Before the Law? Religious Same-Sex Marriage in the US."] *Critique Internationale* 25: 43–52.

Crawley, Sara L. 2001. "Are Butch and Fem Working-Class and Antifeminist?" *Gender and Society* 15: 175–196.

D'Emilio, John. 1983. *Sexual Politics, Sexual Communities: The Making of a Homosexual Minority in the United States 1940–1970*. Chicago and London: University of Chicago Press.

DaVanzo, Julie, and M. Omar Rahman. 1993. "American Families: Trends and Correlates." *Population Index* 59: 350–386.

Dershowitz, Alan. 2003. "To Fix Gay Dilemma, Government Should Quit the Marriage Business." *Los Angeles Times*, December 3.

Durkheim, Emile. [1912] 1995. *The Elementary Forms of Religious Life*. Translated by Karen E. Fields. New York: Free Press.

Elizabeth, Vivienne. 2000. "Cohabitation, Marriage, and the Unruly Consequences of Difference." *Gender and Society* 14: 87–110.

Engel, David M. 1984. "The Oven Bird's Song: Insiders, Outsiders, and Personal Injuries in an American Community." *Law and Society Review* 18: 551–582.

Engel, David M., and Frank W. Munger. 2003. *Rights of Inclusion: Law and Identity in the Life Stories of Americans with Disabilities*. Chicago: University of Chicago Press.

Epstein, Steven. 1987. "Gay Politics, Ethnic Identity: The Limits of Social Constructionism." *Socialist Review* 93/94: 9–54.

Ertman, Martha. 2001. "Marriage as a Trade: Bridging the Private/Private Distinction." *Harvard Civil Rights – Civil Liberties Law Review* 36: 79–132.

Eskridge, William. 1993. "A History of Same-Sex Marriage." *Virginia Law Review* 79: 1419–1513.

——— 1996. *The Case for Same-Sex Marriage: From Sexual Liberty to Civilized Commitment.* New York: The Free Press.

——— 2002. *Equality Practice: Civil Unions and the Future of Gay Rights.* New York and London: Routledge.

Ettelbrick, Paula L. 1992. "Since When Is Marriage a Path to Liberation?" In *Lesbian and Gay Marriage: Private Commitments, Public Ceremonies,* edited by Suzanne Sherman. Philadelphia: Temple University Press. Reprinted from *OUT/LOOK National Gay and Lesbian Quarterly* 6 (Fall 1989).

——— 1996. "Wedlock Alert: A Comment on Lesbian and Gay Family Recognition." *Journal of Law and Policy* 5: 107–166.

——— 2001. "Domestic Partnership, Civil Unions, or Marriage: One Size Does Not Fit All." *Albany Law Review* 64: 905–914.

Ettelbrick, Paula, and Julie Shapiro. 2004. "Are We on the Path to Liberation Now? Same-Sex Marriage at Home and Abroad." *Seattle Journal for Social Justice* 2: 475–493.

Ewick, Patricia, and Susan S. Silbey. 1992. "Conformity, Contestation, and Resistance: An Account of Legal Consciousness." *New England Law Review* 26: 731–749.

——— 1998. *The Common Place of Law: Stories from Everyday Life.* Chicago and London: University of Chicago Press.

——— 2003. "Narrating Social Structure: Stories of Resistance to Legal Authority." *American Journal of Sociology* 108: 1328–1372.

Faderman, Lillian. 1991. *Odd Girls and Twilight Lovers: A History of Lesbian Life in Twentieth-Century America.* New York: Columbia University Press.

Feeley, Malcolm. 1979. *The Process is the Punishment: Handling Cases in a Lower Criminal Court.* New York: Russell Sage Foundation.

Feldblum, Chai. 1998. "A Progressive Moral Case for Same-Sex Marriage." *Temple Political and Civil Rights Law Review* 7: 485–493.

Fineman, Martha Albertson. 1995. *The Neutered Mother, the Sexual Family and Other Twentieth Century Tragedies.* New York and London: Routledge.

——— 2004. *The Autonomy Myth: A Theory of Dependency.* New York and London: The New Press.

Folbre, Nancy. 2001. *The Invisible Heart: Economics and Family Values.* New York: New Press.

Fraser, Nancy. 1997. *Justice Interruptus: Critical Reflections on the "Postsocialist" Condition.* New York and London: Routledge.

Gamble, Barbara S. 1997. "Putting Civil Rights to a Popular Vote." *American Journal of Political Science* 41: 245–269.

Gamson, Joshua. 1995. "Must Identity Movements Self-Destruct? A Queer Dilemma." *Social Problems* 42: 390–407.

——— 1998. *Freaks Talk Back: Tabloid Talk Shows and Sexual Nonconformity.* Chicago: University of Chicago Press.

Geertz, Clifford. 1973. *The Interpretation of Cultures: Selected Essays.* New York: Basic Books.

——— 1983. *Local Knowledge: Further Essays in Interpretive Anthropology.* New York: Basic Books.

Gerstmann, Evan. 2004. *Same-Sex Marriage and the Constitution*. Cambridge: Cambridge University Press.

Gibson, Christina, Kathryn Edin and Sara McLanahan. 2003. "High Hopes But Even Higher Expectations: The Retreat From Marriage Among Low-Income Couples." Center for Research on Child Wellbeing Working Paper #03-06-FF. Princeton: Center for Research on Child Wellbeing, Princeton University.

Giddens, Anthony. 1992. *The Transformation of Intimacy: Sexuality, Love, and Eroticism in Modern Societies*. Stanford (CA): Stanford University Press.

Gitlin, Todd. 1995. *The Twilight of Common Dreams: Why America is Wracked by Culture Wars*. New York: Metropolitan Books.

Gluckman, Amy, and Betsy Reed. 1997. "The Gay Marketing Moment." Pp. 3–9 in *Homo Economics: Capitalism, Community, and Lesbian and Gay Life*, edited by Amy Gluckman and Betsy Reed. New York and London: Routledge.

Goldberg-Hiller, Jonathan. 1999. "The Status of Status: Domestic Partnership and the Politics of Same-Sex Marriage." *Studies in Law, Politics, and Society* 19: 3–38.

2002. *Limits to Union: Same-Sex Marriage and the Politics of Civil Rights*. Ann Arbor: University of Michigan Press.

Goldman, Emma. 1910. "Marriage and Love." In *Anarchism and Other Essays*. New York: Mother Earth Publishing Association.

Gonsiorek, John C., and James R. Rudolph. 1991. "Homosexual Identity: Coming Out and Other Developmental Events." In *Homosexuality: Research Implications for Public Policy*, edited by John C. Gonsiorek and James D. Weinrich. Newbury Park (CA): Sage Publications.

Graff, E. J. 1996. "Something Old . . . Something New." *Ms.* 6 (May): 92–94.

Greenberger, Scott S., and Bill Dedman. 2004. "Survey Finds Women in Majority." *Boston Globe*, May 18.

Grey, David L., and Trevor R. Brown. 1970. "Letters to the Editor: Hazy Reflections of Public Opinion." *Journalism Quarterly* 47: 450–456, 471.

Grimes, Ronald L. 2000. *Deeply into the Bone: Re-Inventing Rites of Passage*. Berkeley: University of California Press.

Griswold, Wendy. 1987. "A Methodological Framework for the Sociology of Culture." *Sociological Methodology* 17: 1–35.

Grossman, Cathy Lynn, and In-Sung Yoo. 2003. "Civil Marriage on Rise Across USA." *USA Today*, October 7.

Harding, Sandra. 1996. "Standpoint Epistemology (a Feminist Version): How Social Disadvantage Creates Epistemic Advantage." In *Social Theory and Sociology: The Classics and Beyond*, edited by Stephen P. Turner. Cambridge (MA): Blackwell.

Herbst, Susan. 1993. *Numbered Voices: How Opinion Polling Has Shaped American Politics*. Chicago and London: University of Chicago Press.

Herek, Gregory M. 1990. "The Context of Anti-Gay Violence: Notes on Cultural and Psychological Heterosexism." *Journal of Interpersonal Violence* 5: 316–333.

1995. "Psychological Heterosexism in the United States." In *Lesbian, Gay, and Bisexual Identities Over the Lifespan: Psychological Perspectives*, edited by

Anthony R. D'Augelli and Charlotte J. Patterson. New York: Oxford University Press.

Herman, Didi. 1997. *The Antigay Agenda: Orthodox Vision and the Christian Right*. Chicago: University of Chicago Press.

Hill, David. B. 1981. "Letter Opinion on the ERA: A Test of the Newspaper Bias Hypothesis." *Public Opinion Quarterly* 45: 384–392.

Hochschild, Arlie Russell. 1997. *The Time Bind: When Work Becomes Home and Home Becomes Work*. New York: Metropolitan Books.

Hollander, Jocelyn A., and Rachel L. Einwohner. 2004. "Conceptualizing Resistance." *Sociological Forum* 19: 533–554.

Honig, Bonnie. 1993. *Political Theory and the Displacement of Politics*. Ithaca and London: Cornell University Press.

HRC: Human Rights Campaign. n.d. *Answers to Questions About Marriage Equality*. Washington, DC: Human Rights Campaign.

HRCF: Human Rights Campaign Foundation. 2004. *The State of the Workplace 2003*. Washington, DC: Human Rights Campaign Foundation.

2005. *The State of the Workplace 2004*. Washington, DC: Human Rights Campaign Foundation.

Hull, Kathleen E. 2001. "The Political Limits of the Rights Frame: The Case of Same-Sex Marriage in Hawaii." *Sociological Perspectives* 44: 207–232.

2003. "The Cultural Power of Law and the Cultural Enactment of Legality: The Case of Same-Sex Marriage." *Law and Social Inquiry* 28: 629–657.

2005. "Employment Discrimination Based on Sexual Orientation: Dimensions of Difference." In *Handbook on Employment Discrimination Research: Rights and Realities*, edited by Robert L. Nelson and Laura Beth Nielsen. Dordrecht (the Netherlands): Springer.

Hunter, Nan D. 1991. "Marriage, Law, and Gender: A Feminist Inquiry." *Law and Sexuality* 1: 9–30.

Illouz, Eva. 1997. *Consuming the Romantic Utopia: Love and the Cultural Contradictions of Capitalism*. Berkeley: University of California Press.

Ingraham, Chrys. 1999. *White Weddings: Romancing Heterosexuality in Popular Culture*. New York and London: Routledge.

Jakobsen, Janet R., and Ann Pellgrini. 2003. *Love the Sin: Sexual Regulation and the Limits of Religious Tolerance*. New York and London: New York University Press.

Johnston, Hank, and Bert Klandermans, eds. 1995. *Social Movements and Culture*. Minneapolis: University of Minnesota Press.

Kauffman, L. A. 1990. "The Anti-Politics of Identity." *Socialist Review* 20: 67–80.

Kennedy, Elizabeth Lapovsky, and Madeline D. Davis. 1993. *Boots of Leather, Slippers of Gold: The History of a Lesbian Community*. New York: Penguin Books.

Kiernan, Kathleen. 2002. "Cohabitation in Western Europe: Trends, Issues, and Implications." In *Just Living Together: Implications of Cohabitation on Families, Children, and Social Policy*, edited by Alan Booth and Ann C. Crouter. Mahwah (NJ): L. Erlbaum Associates.

Kurdek, Lawrence A. 1988. "Relationship Quality of Gay and Lesbian Cohabiting Couples." *Journal of Homosexuality* 15: 93–118.

1991. "Sexuality in Homosexual and Heterosexual Couples." In *Sexuality in Close Relationships*, edited by Kathleen McKinney and Susan Sprecher. Hillsdale (NJ): Lawrence Erlbaum Associates.

Lahey, Kathleen A., and Kevin Alderson. 2004. *Same-Sex Marriage: The Personal and the Political*. Toronto: Insomniac Press.

Laumann, Edward O., John H. Gagnon, Robert T. Michael and Stuart Michaels. 1994. *The Social Organization of Sexuality: Sexual Practices in the United States*. Chicago and London: University of Chicago Press.

LCC: Law Commission of Canada. 2001. *Beyond Conjugality: Recognizing and Supporting Close Personal Adult Relationships*. [Ottawa]: Law Commission of Canada.

Le Bourdais, Céline, and Evelyne Lapierre-Adamcyk. 2004. "Changes in Conjugal Life in Canada: Is Cohabitation Progressively Replacing Marriage?" *Journal of Marriage and Family* 66: 929–942.

Leff, Lisa. 2004. "San Francisco's Gay Newlyweds Came From 46 States and Included 57 Percent Women." Associated Press, March 18.

Levin, Daniel. 1997. "The Constitution as Rhetorical Symbol in Western Anti-Gay Rights Initiatives: The Case of Idaho." Pp. 33–49 in *Anti-Gay Rights: Assessing Voter Initiatives*, edited by Stephanie L. Witt and Suzanne McCorkle. Westport (CT) and London: Praeger.

Lewin, Ellen. 1998. *Recognizing Ourselves: Ceremonies of Lesbian and Gay Commitment*. New York: Columbia University Press.

Loftus, Jeni. 2001. "America's Liberalization in Attitudes Toward Homosexuality, 1973 to 1998." *American Sociological Review* 66: 762–782.

Los Angeles Times. 2004. Editorial, July 14.

Manning, Wendy D., and Pamela J. Smock. 2002. "First Comes Cohabitation, and Then Comes Marriage? A Research Note." *Journal of Family Issues* 23: 1065–1087.

Marshall, Anna-Maria, and Scott Barclay. 2003. "In Their Own Words: How Ordinary People Construct the Legal World." *Law and Social Inquiry* 28: 617–628.

McAdam, Doug. 1988. "Gender Implications of the Traditional Academic Conception of the Political." In *Changing Our Minds: Feminist Transformations of Knowledge*, edited by Susan Hardy Aiken, Karen Anderson, Myra Dinnerstein, Judy Nolte Lensick and Patricia MacCorquodale. Albany: SUNY Press.

McCann, Michael W. 1994. *Rights at Work: Pay Equity Reform and the Politics of Legal Mobilization*. Chicago: University of Chicago Press.

McCorkle, Suzanne, and Marshall G. Most. 1997. "Fear and Loathing on the Editorial Page: An Analysis of Idaho's Anti-Gay Initiative." Pp. 63–76 in *Anti-Gay Rights: Assessing Voter Initiatives*, edited by Stephanie L. Witt and Suzanne McCorkle. Westport (CT) and London: Praeger.

McIntosh, Mary. 1968. "The Homosexual Role." *Social Problems* 16: 182–192.

McWhirter, David P., and Andrew M. Mattison. 1984. *The Male Couple: How Relationships Develop*. Englewood Cliffs (NJ): Prentice-Hall.

Mehren, Elizabeth. 2004. "Acceptance of Gays Rises Among New Generation." *Los Angeles Times*, April 11.

Merin, Yuval. 2002. *Equality for Same-Sex Couples: The Legal Recognition of Gay Partnerships in Europe and the United States*. Chicago: University of Chicago Press.

Merry, Sally Engle. 1990. *Getting Justice and Getting Even: Legal Consciousness Among Working-Class Americans*. Chicago: University of Chicago Press.

　　1995. "Resistance and the Cultural Power of Law." *Law and Society Review* 29: 11–26.

Meyer, Madonna Harrington. 2000. *Carework: Gender, Labor and the Welfare State*. New York: Routledge.

Mies, Maria. 1983. "Towards a Methodology for Feminist Research." In *Theories of Women's Studies*, edited by Gloria Bowles and Renate D. Klein. London: Routledge and Kegan Paul.

Moats, David. 2004. *Civil Wars: A Battle for Gay Marriage*. Orlando: Harcourt.

Mohr, Richard D. 1994. *A More Perfect Union: Why Straight America Must Stand Up for Gay Rights*. Boston: Beacon Press.

Moon, Dawne. 2004. *God, Sex and Politics: Homosexuality and Everyday Theologies*. Chicago: University of Chicago Press.

Morris, Robert J. 1996. "Configuring the Bo(u)nds of Marriage: The Implications of Hawaiian Culture & Values for the Debate About Homogamy." *Yale Journal of Law and the Humanities* 8: 105–159.

Nielsen, Laura Beth. 2000. "Situating Legal Consciousness: Experiences and Attitudes of Ordinary Citizens About Law and Street Harassment." *Law and Society Review* 34: 1055–1090.

　　2004. *License to Harass: Law, Hierarchy, and Offensive Public Speech*. Princeton: Princeton University Press.

Ortner, Sherry. 1984. "Theory in Anthropology Since the Sixties." *Comparative Studies in History and Society* 26: 126–166.

Otnes, Cele C., and Elizabeth H. Pleck. 2003. *Cinderella Dreams: The Allure of the Lavish Wedding*. Berkeley: University of California Press.

Pascoe, Peggy. 2000. "Sex, Gender, and Same-Sex Marriage." In *Is Academic Feminism Dead?*, edited by The Social Justice Group at the Center for Advanced Feminist Studies, University of Minnesota. New York and London: New York University Press.

Patterson, Davis G., Teresa Ciabattari and Pepper Schwartz. 1999. "The Constraints of Innovation: Commitment and Stability Among Same-Sex Couples." In *Handbook of Interpersonal Commitment and Relationship Stability*, edited by Jeffrey M. Adams and Warren H Jones. New York: Kluwer Academic/Plenum Publishers.

Peplau, Letitia, and Susan Cochran. 1988. "Value Orientations in the Intimate Relationships of Gay Men." In *Gay Relationships*, edited by John DeCecco. New York: Haworth Press.

Peplau, Letitia, Susan Cochran and Vickie Mays. 1997. "A National Survey of the Intimate Relationships of African-American Lesbians and Gay Men." In *Ethnic and Cultural Diversity Among Lesbians and Gay Men*, edited by Beverly Greene. Thousand Oaks (CA): Sage.

Phelan, Shane. 2001. *Sexual Strangers: Gays, Lesbians, and Dilemmas of Citizenship*. Philadelphia: Temple University Press.

Polikoff, Nancy D. 1993. "We Will Get What We Ask For: Why Legalizing Gay and Lesbian Marriage Will Not 'Dismantle the Legal Structure of Gender in Every Marriage.'" *Virginia Law Review* 79: 1535–1550.

Popenoe, David. 1996. *Life Without Father.* New York: Free Press.

Rauch, Jonathan. 1996. "For Better or Worse?" *The New Republic,* May 6, 18–19.

2004. *Gay Marriage: Why It Is Good for Gays, Good for Straights, and Good for America.* New York: Times Books.

Rimmerman, Craig A. 2002. *From Identity to Politics: The Lesbian and Gay Movements in the United States.* Philadelphia: Temple University Press.

Rochon, Thomas R. 1998. *Culture Moves: Ideas, Activism, and Changing Values.* Princeton: Princeton University Press.

Rosenberg, Gerald N. 1991. *The Hollow Hope: Can Courts Bring About Social Change?* Chicago: University of Chicago Press.

Rothenbuhler, Eric W. 1998. *Ritual Communication: From Everyday Conversation to Mediated Ceremony.* Thousand Oaks (CA): Sage Publications.

Rubenstein, William B. 1997. "Divided We Litigate: Addressing Disputes Among Group Members and Lawyers in Civil Rights Campaigns." *Yale Law Journal* 106: 1623–1681.

Rupp, Leila J., and Verta Taylor. 2003. *Drag Queens at the 801 Cabaret.* Chicago and London: University of Chicago Press.

"Same-Sex Issue Cost $3.1 Million." 1999. *Honolulu Star-Bulletin,* April 24.

Sarat, Austin. 1990. "' . . . The Law Is All Over': Power, Resistance, and the Legal Consciousness of the Welfare Poor." *Yale Journal of Law and the Humanities* 2: 343–379.

Sarat, Austin, and William L. F. Felstiner. 1989. "Lawyers and Legal Consciousness: Law Talk in the Divorce Lawyer's Office." *The Yale Law Journal* 98: 1663–1688.

Sarat, Austin, and Thomas Kearns, eds. 1993. *Law in Everyday Life.* Ann Arbor: University of Michigan Press.

Sarat, Austin, and Jonathan Simon, eds. 2003. *Cultural Analysis, Cultural Studies, and the Law: Moving Beyond Legal Realism.* Durham (NC): Duke University Press.

Sassler, Sharon. 2004. "The Process of Entering into Cohabiting Unions." *Journal of Marriage and Family* 66: 491–505.

Schacter, Jane S. 1994. "The Gay Civil Rights Debate in the States: Decoding the Discourse of Equivalents." *Harvard Civil Rights–Civil Liberties Law Review* 29: 283–317.

Scheingold, Stuart A. 1974. *The Politics of Rights: Lawyers, Public Policy, and Political Change.* New Haven: Yale University Press.

Schneider, David. 1976. "Notes Toward a Theory of Culture." Pp. 197–220 in *Meaning in Anthropology,* edited by Keith H. Basso and Henry A. Selby. Albuquerque: University of New Mexico Press.

Scott, James. 1990. *Domination and the Arts of Resistance.* New Haven: Yale University Press.

Seidman, Steven. 2002. *Beyond the Closet: The Transformation of Gay and Lesbian Life.* New York: Routledge.

Sewell, William H., Jr. 1992. "A Theory of Structure: Duality, Agency, and Transformation." *American Journal of Sociology* 98: 1–29.

1999. "The Concept(s) of Culture." In *Beyond the Cultural Turn: New Directions in the Study of Society and Culture*, edited by Victoria E. Bonnell and Lynn Hunt. Berkeley: University of California Press.

Shanley, Mary Lyndon. 2004. "Just Marriage: On the Public Importance of Private Unions." In *Just Marriage*, edited by Mary Lyndon Shanley. Oxford and New York: Oxford University Press.

Sherrill, Kenneth. n.d. *Same-Sex Marriage, Civil Unions, and the 2004 Presidential Election*. New York: National Gay and Lesbian Task Force Policy Institute.

Sigelman, Lee, and Barbara J. Walkosz. 1992. "Letters to the Editor as a Public Opinion Thermometer: The Martin Luther King Holiday Vote in Arizona." *Social Science Quarterly* 73: 938–946.

Silvestrini, Elaine. 2005. "Rights Groups Say Courts Too 'Hostile.'" *Tampa Tribune*, January 26.

Simmons, Tavia, and Martin O'Connell. 2003. *Married-Couple and Unmarried-Partner Households: 2000. Census 2000 Special Reports*. CENSR-5. Washington, DC: US Census Bureau.

Skolnick, Arlene S. 1991. *Embattled Paradise: The American Family in an Age of Uncertainty*. New York: Basic Books.

Smock, Pamela J. 2000. "Cohabitation in the United States: An Appraisal of Research Themes, Findings, and Implications." *Annual Review of Sociology* 26: 1–20.

Solomon, Alisa. 2004. "State to Church: I Want a Divorce." *Village Voice*, March 3–9.

Solomon, Sondra E., Esther D. Rothblum and Kimberly F. Balsam. 2004. "Pioneers in Partnership: Lesbian and Gay Male Couples in Civil Unions Compared with Those Not in Civil Unions, and Married Heterosexual Siblings." *Journal of Family Psychology* 18: 275–286.

Stacey, Judith. 1996. *In the Name of the Family: Rethinking Family Values in the Postmodern Age*. Boston: Beacon Press.

2004. Untitled contribution to "Can Marriage Be Saved? A Forum." *The Nation*, July 5, 25.

Stiers, Gretchen A. 1999. *From This Day Forward: Commitment, Marriage, and Family in Lesbian and Gay Relationships*. New York: St. Martin's Press.

Stoddard, Thomas B. 1992. "Why Gay People Should Seek the Right to Marry." In *Lesbian and Gay Marriage: Private Commitments, Public Ceremonies*, edited by Suzanne Sherman. Philadelphia: Temple University Press. Reprinted from *OUT/LOOK National Gay and Lesbian Quarterly* 6 (Fall 1989).

Strasser, Mark. 1997. *Legally Wed: Same-Sex Marriage and the Constitution*. Ithaca: Cornell University Press.

Sullivan, Andrew. 1996. *Virtually Normal: An Argument About Homosexuality*. New York: Vintage Books.

Sunstein, Cass R. 1987. "On the Expressive Function of Law." *University of Pennsylvania Law Review* 144: 2,021–2,053.

Swartz, Teresa Toguchi. 2004. "Mothering for the State: Foster Parenting and the Challenges of Government-Contracted Carework." *Gender and Society* 18: 567–587.

Swidler, Ann. 1986. "Culture in Action: Symbols and Strategies." *American Sociological Review* 51: 273–286.

2001. *Talk of Love: How Culture Matters*. Chicago: University of Chicago Press.

Taylor, Verta, Leila J. Rupp and Joshua Gamson. 2004. "Performing Protest: Drag Shows as Tactical Repertoire of the Gay and Lesbian Movement." In *Authority in Contention (Research in Social Movements, Conflicts and Change, volume XXV)*, edited by Daniel J. Myers and Daniel M. Cress. Amsterdam and Oxford: Elsevier JAI.

Taylor, Verta, and Nella Van Dyke. 2004. "'Get Up, Stand Up': Tactical Repertoires of Social Movements." In *The Blackwell Companion to Social Movements*, edited by David A. Snow, Sarah A. Soule and Hanspeter Kriesi. Malden (MA): Blackwell.

Taylor, Verta, and Nancy E. Whittier. 1992. "Collective Identity in Social Movement Communities: Lesbian Feminist Mobilization." Pp. 104–129 in *Frontiers in Social Movement Theory*, edited by Aldon D. Morris and Carol McClurg Mueller. New Haven and London: Yale University Press.

Troiden, Richard. 1998. "A Model of Homosexual Identity Formation." In *Social Perspectives in Lesbian and Gay Studies: A Reader*, edited by Peter M. Nardi and Beth E. Schneider. London and New York: Routledge. Originally published in *Gay and Lesbian Identity: A Sociological Analysis*. New York: General Hall, 1988.

Trubek, David M. 1984. "Where the Action Is: Critical Legal Studies and Empiricism." *Stanford Law Review* 36: 575–622.

US Census Bureau. 2001. *Statistical Abstract of the United States: 2002*. Washington, DC: US Census Bureau.

US Public Law 104–193. 104th Congress, August 22, 1996. *Personal Responsibility and Work Opportunity Reconciliation Act of 1996*.

Vaid, Urvashi. 1995. *Virtual Equality: The Mainstreaming of Gay and Lesbian Liberation*. New York: Anchor Books.

Volgy, Thomas J., Margaret Krigbaum, Mary Kay Langan and Vicky Moshier. 1977. "Some of My Best Friends Are Letter Writers: Eccentrics and Gladiators Revisited." *Social Science Quarterly* 58: 321–327.

"Voters Strongly Oppose Gay Unions." 1997. *Honolulu Star-Bulletin*, February 24.

Waite, Linda J., and Maggie Gallagher. 2000. *The Case for Marriage: Why Married People Are Happier, Healthier, and Better Off Financially*. New York: Doubleday.

Walters, Suzanna Danuta. 2001a. *All the Rage: The Story of Gay Visibility in America*. Chicago: University of Chicago Press.

2001b. "Take My Domestic Partner, Please: Gays and Marriage in the Era of the Visible." In *Queer Families, Queer Politics: Challenging Culture and the State*, edited by Mary Bernstein and Renate Reimann. New York: Columbia University Press.

Warner, Michael. 1999. *The Trouble with Normal: Sex, Politics, and the Ethics of Queer Life*. New York: The Free Press.

Webb, Eugene J., Donald T. Campbell, Richard D. Schwartz and Lee Sechrest. 1966. *Unobtrusive Measures: Non-Reactive Research in the Social Sciences*. Chicago: Rand McNally.

Weeks, Jeffrey, Brian Heaphy and Catherine Donovan. 2001. *Same-Sex Intimacies: Families of Choice and Other Life Experiments*. London: Routledge.

Werum, Regina, and Bill Winders. 2001. "Who's 'In' and Who's 'Out': State Fragmentation and the Struggle over Gay Rights, 1974–1999." *Social Problems* 48: 386–410.

White, Julie A., and Tronto, Joan C. 2004. "Political Practices of Care: Needs and Rights." *Ratio Juris* 17: 425–453.

Whyte, Martin King. 1990. *Dating, Mating, and Marriage.* New York: Aldine de Gruyter.

Willetts, Marion C. 2003. "An Exploratory Investigation of Heterosexual Licensed Domestic Partners." *Journal of Marriage and Family* 65: 939–952.

Wilson, James Q. 2002. *The Marriage Problem: How Our Culture Has Weakened Families.* New York: Harper Collins.

Witt, Stephanie L., and Suzanne McCorkle. 1997. *Anti-Gay Rights: Assessing Voter Initiatives.* Westport (CT) and London: Praeger.

Wittman, Carl. 1972. "Refugees from Amerika: A Gay Manifesto." In *The Homosexual Dialectic,* edited by Joseph A. McCaffrey. Englewood Cliffs (NJ): Prentice-Hall.

Wolfson, Evan. 1994. "Crossing the Threshold: Equal Marriage Rights for Lesbians and Gay Men and the Intra-Community Critique." *New York University Review of Law and Social Change* 21: 567–615.

     2004. *Why Marriage Matters: America, Equality, and Gay People's Right to Marry.* New York: Simon and Schuster.

Yngvesson, Barabara. 1988. "Making Law at the Doorway: The Clerk, the Court, and the Construction of Community in a New England Town." *Law and Society Review* 22: 409–448.

Yuen, Mike. 1998. "Same-Sex Marriage Losing Big." *Honolulu Star-Bulletin,* August 14.

Index